Behold the Stream
A History of
Asian Lutheran Witness

Behold the Stream
A History of
Asian Lutheran Witness

Edmond Yee and Lily R. Wu

Editors

Published by

Association of Asians and Pacific Islanders

Evangelical Lutheran Church in America

To
Pongsak Limthongviratn
A faithful servant in the Lord's vineyard
We
honor your ministry
celebrate your retirement
and
bless you in the names of Truth, Goodness, Beauty and God

Behold the Stream
A History of Asian Lutheran Witness
Editors: Edmond Yee and Lily R. Wu

Association of Asians and Pacific Islanders
Evangelical Lutheran Church in America
8765 W. Higgins Rd., Chicago, IL 60631
www.asianlutherans.com

ISBN 978-0-578-83779-6

Cover design and layout by Sirintip Taveesap

CONTENTS

Preface

There is a river whose streams make glad the city of God....[1]

In Psalm 46, the psalmist describes *a river whose streams make glad the city of God.* This volume tells the story of one of those streams.

This book offers Asian Lutherans in the United States another inspiring contribution to our history. It names many, but not all, of the individuals and the church communities that have been a part of this mighty stream. It will be an invaluable resource to the Evangelical Lutheran Church in America (ELCA) churchwide and synod staff who may not be familiar with the Asian communities in this church. Lastly, *Behold the Stream: A History of Asian Lutheran Witness* will be a boon to future church historians.

Behold the Stream tells of the persistent witness of Asian Lutherans in the United States whose commitment to Jesus Christ compelled us to cross multiple borders, physically, culturally, and spiritually, to share the good news. It depicts our struggles with institutional racism within the church. It illustrates the ebb and flow of Christian ministry, of congregations that flourish and others that thrive for a time. Importantly, it describes the solidarity of Asian Lutherans as we created spaces such as the Asian Lutheran International Conference, a place where diaspora Asians could network with our siblings from Asia.

This work builds upon other histories of Asian Lutherans, most notably *The Soaring Crane: Stories of Asian Lutherans in North America* and *Abundant Harvest: Stories of Asian Lutherans.* What sets this volume apart is the homage it pays to the drops in this mighty stream, the individuals and the Asian congregations and ministries, both named and unnamed, that make up this movement in the US. The thumbnail descriptions and photos of the different churches and ministries and the brief biographies and pictures of Asian leaders emphasize that God works through God's faithful people.

---

[1] Psalm 46. New Revised Standard Version Bible, copyright © 1989 National Council of the Churches of Christ in the United States of America. Used by permission. All rights reserved worldwide.

The stream is at a turning point–where will it flow next? Just as climate change affects the physical world, a kind of cultural climate change impacts the church in North America. Asian Lutherans, then, need to contend with both the unique challenges that come with being diaspora Christian communities and the decline of mainline Christianity in the US. The final chapter of this book, the result of a conversation with Asian Lutheran theologians, offers glimpses of the future turns this stream may take.

In addition to these macro challenges, there are more personal changes in store for our Asian community. *Behold the Stream* is dedicated to the Rev. Dr. Pongsak Limthongviratn. In 1997, he became the ELCA's director for Asian Ministries, (changed to Asian and Pacific Islander ministries later in 1997 and changed again in 2012 to program director for Asian and Pacific Islander ministries). *Acharn*[2] Pongsak has been a point of stability and continuity for ELCA Asian ministries. His anticipated retirement in 2021 will mark the end of an era. The Asian ministry achievements of the past two decades and more are due to his extraordinary intellectual and strategic acumen.

Lastly, I note that *Behold the Stream*, like *The Soaring Crane* and *Abundant Harvest*, is yet another gift from the distinguished scholar Edmond Yee to the Asian Lutheran community in particular and the ELCA at large. Yee has meticulously researched the history of Asian Lutherans in North America. More significantly, Yee played a significant role in many of the events that have shaped Asian ministries in the ELCA. He has been a tireless champion for Asian Lutherans over decades. All of us owe him an enormous debt of gratitude. He has been a professor, a colleague, a mentor, and a friend.

There is a river whose streams make glad the city of God. Let us rejoice and be glad! Behold the stream of Asian Lutherans who faithfully declare the good news of Jesus Christ.

Margrethe Shizuko Chinen Kleiber

---

[2] *Acharn* (origin *Pali)* is a Thai word often translated as elder, pastor or teacher, yet its significance goes beyond the meanings of these English words. To address someone as *acharn* emphasizes relationality. It intimates deeply felt warmth and respect. It compares to the terms guru (*Sanskrit*) or *sensei* (Japanese).

Acknowledgments

Many streams of involvement flowed into one river to create this book. It was only possible because of many people cooperating and taking part. Therefore we say "thank you!" to all contributors and participants as well as their families for having supported them. And we owe a profound gratitude to the four compilers—Kevin Cho, Margrethe S. C. Kleiber, Daniel P. Penumaka and Maria Gracia Sijera-Grant—who contacted pastors and lay leaders for information. Their many hours of steadfast commitment and persistence formed the bedrock of this publication.

We also thank the Resource Management team of the Evangelical Lutheran Church in America (ELCA) for providing a grant for this project. We are deeply grateful to Frederick E. N. Rajan, former executive director, Commission for Multicultural Ministries (CMM), for having established the resource fund, and for his willingness to share his view on the state of the ELCA and the issues faced by the CMM in the 1990s. We salute Albert Starr, present leader of the team, for his good work in getting the grant for us. Their support for Asian ministries has encouraged us.

We wish to thank William E. Wong and Pongsak Limthongviratn for sharing their considerable experience and historical memories with us. Their vantage point in telling the story of Asian Lutheran ministry enables us all to stand on a mountaintop with them, and see how the streams of ministry have flowed.

We are grateful to Sarah Anderson-Rajarigam, Evangeline Anderson-Rajkumar, Surekha Nelavala, Moses Penumaka, J. Paul Rajashekar, Tuhina Rasche, and Teresita C. Valeriano for their insightful comments in helping us to shape our "glimpse" into the future.[1]

To Katie Potempa and Joel Thoreson at the Archives of the ELCA, and to John Hessian at the Lutheran Center, we send heartfelt thanks for unearthing data that we needed for this book. Without their gracious help, this volume would not be as complete as it is.

To David Chen, our appreciation for lending a hand in gathering data from Chinese congregations. We thank him for saying "Yes, I will try."

---

1 Man Hei Yip was also invited, but she was unable to participate at the last minute.

To Margrethe S. C. Kleiber, our deep thanks for being a fresh breeze of unexpected multi-level support. After completing her assignments as a compiler, and having produced project management spreadsheets, she volunteered for more work such as data gathering and proofreading.

We are grateful to have consulted with Thomas Yuen for his freelance portrait and wedding photography experience of 40 years. With his advice, we made final selections of biographical and congregational photos that were received.

And we salute Peter E. Yee for his extraordinary patience in unraveling the mysteries of file transfers and other computer problems. Without him the files could not have been prepared for desktop publishing.

The dedication of graphic designer Taveesap Sirintip made possible the pages that you see here. We thank her for her devotion to this highly detailed task. She brought to life Edmond Yee's concept for the original cover design as well.

To the ever gracious and hospitable Eva Ching-Nakashima, administrative assistant, Multicultural, Ethnic-Specific, Anti-Racism and Justice Team of Domestic Mission, ELCA, we offer a deep bow. We appreciated her efficiency with hotel accommodations, meeting room arrangements, and many other details of support.

Behold the Stream was both our challenge and privilege to produce. Although many individuals took part in this project, the editors assume full responsibility for all errors therein.

The Editors

A Note on Using this Book

This book is divided into six parts, plus two appendixes. Each part and the sub-sections can be read independently.

Part III includes biographies of Asian Lutheran workers under the title "Behold! Thy Servants: Brooks of the Steam." The date that immediately follows the name refers to the year of birth. When the letters "n. d." appear after the name, they mean that 1. for privacy reasons, the person doesn't want the year of her or his birth to be known; or 2. we have no way to find out the date. When "n. i." appears after the name or the dates, this means "no information" was available. And "l. u." stands for "location unknown."

The term "native" indicates the place of birth. When a picture of flowers is placed next to a biography or a congregational profile instead of a photograph, this means 1. for privacy reasons, the individual does not want a photo published; or 2. there is no available picture. Reference, if needed, immediately follows the end of the biography.

An asterisk "*" after a name means that the person is in the process of being rostered in the Evangelical Lutheran Church in America (ELCA). Two "**" indicate that the person is serving an ELCA congregation or ministry but is not in the candidacy process.

The symbol "#NULL!" means that the ELCA Office of the Secretary cannot provide information on when the person's first call started or ended.

For individuals without a "full" (100 words) biography, the name and location of his or her first call congregation are given after the word "Call."

We also remember the saints of the past, some with full biographies and some without, in the "In Memoriam" section.

Chinese personal and place names Romanized in the Wade-Giles or the *pin-yin* or other systems are respected. Likewise, we honor alternate spelling of biblical terms, such as "Imanuel."

"Lo! Thy Servants on the Move: Flowing Far and Wide" shows where some Asian Lutherans made or are still making significant contributions to the church and/or other institutions or organizations. When a person's name first appears, then her or his date of birth immediately follows, in parentheses. The dates in parentheses after that refer to the years they served or are still serving.

Part VI consists of selected appreciations to Pongsak Limthongviratn, to whom this volume is dedicated. The national origins of the contributors are given in parentheses after each person's name.

The list of contributors is in alphabetical order with the person's given name first, followed by the person's surname.

The term US refers to the United States of America. Names of US states are also abbreviated, except when the name of the state is part of a sentence. In some cases, after the name, its abbreviation in parentheses will be used throughout the rest of the article or biography.

The Editors

List of Contributors

Abraham Lu

Adam Sornchai

Albert Lin*

Alfred V. Sagar

Ananda Rao Darla*

Andrew Yee

Asha Mary George-Guiser

Barry Hong

Bea Vue-Benson

Bimen Limbong

C. Lynn Nakamura

Changan (John) Yu

Chiung Hao Wu (Moses)

Chong Im Kim-Chung* (Jenny)

Chulhyuk (Paul) Ko

Clement (Kris) Lee

Corazon Aguilar

Daniel Zhang**

Darcy J. Mittelstaedt

David Chen

Deogracias Olivar

Diakonda Gurning

Dinah Dutta

Doris Ng

Edmond Yee

Eileen Burdick

Emmanuel Joshua Peter Penumaka

Esther Kristiani Sianipar*

Esther Rajashekar

Eunyoung Kim*

Evangeline Anderson-Rajkumar

Evangeline Dai*

Fern Lee Hagedorn

Feronika Rambing**

Frederick E. N. Rajan

Fumi Liang

George Tan

Gladys Chow

Hephzibah Penumaka*

Herbert Shao

Hitoshi Adachi

Hongsun Kim

Hyunho Hong

Isaiah Chow

Israel Daniel Peter Penumaka

J. (Rowena) Wang

J. Paul Rajashekar

Jade Yi

Jae Bum Kim

Jane Shen

Janet M. Corpus

Jayaprakash B. Sabbithi

Jennifer Schultz

Jenny Miu-Ha Wu

Jeremy Shih

Job Ebenezer

John Billa

John Ponnala

Joseph Chu

Joseph H. Li

Joyce Miller

Jua Jay Her*

Julius Miller

Kevin (Sung Yong) Cho

Kristofer Dale Coffman

Kwanza Yu

Kyuzo Miyaishi

Lily R. Wu

Linqing Chu

Lit Inn Wu

Lu Vamlo Vang

Man Hei Yip

Marcos Panahon

Margrethe S. C. Kleiber

Maria Gracia Sijera-Grant

Marian M. Wang

Martin Juan Rafanan

Mary Ling-Hsi Chang

Mary Sagar

Matha Janthapaiboonkajon

Michael Wang

Miho Yasukawa

Mikka McCracken

Monta Limthongviratn

Moses Paul Peter Penumaka

Newman Chiu

Nhiabee Vang

Nirmala Reinschmidt

Nouk Vagh

Omega Varma Sabbithi

Paul Liu*

Paul T. Nakamura

Peter Keomanivong

Peter Shen

Peter Vethanayagamony*

Peter Y. Lai

Peter Y. Wang

Phouthaly Onelangsy

Pongsak Limthongviratn

Rachel San Diego*

Rakesh Peter-Dass

Reginald Mortha

Rita Chirala

Robert Waworuntu

Romeo K. Dabee

Rosalind Moldwin

Ryan Lun

S. Kim Lee-Brown

Saitong Urramporn

Salvaraj Periannan

Samee Singkeovilay

Samuel Silaban

Sang Soo Kim

Sarah Anderson-Rajarigam

Sarah Geddada

Shen Lin

Shongchai Hang

Siew Fong (Andrew) Yong

Simon Lee

Sirintip Taveesap**

Soriya Roeun

Stacy Dee Kitahata

Stephanie Baccam

Sunitha Mortha

Surekha Nelavala

Susan Gaeta

Tasha Genck Morton

Teresita Clemente Valeriano

Thaly Cavanaugh**

Thiem Baccam

Thomas Chen

Timothy Whiteman

Tony Wong

Tuhina Verma Rasche

Uijin Hwang

Vanphone Anlavan**

Victor Thasiah

Violeta Sanders

Wei Zhao**

Wi Jo Kang

William E. Wong

William Siong

Yonsu Kim

Yoshitaka Franklin Ishida

Yutaka Kishino

Introduction
How the Stream Flows

"Take a moment to study this text and painting," said a leader to the group. "Then let's discuss what you see." From "show-and-tell" for children to presentations for adults, people tend to love pictures. You will see many in this book, along with the story-rich essays.

As you read in the Preface, this is the third in a trilogy by and about Asian Lutherans. Before *The Soaring Crane: Stories of Asian Lutherans in North America* appeared, there was "nothing published or systematically written on the subject."[1] *Abundant Harvest: Stories of Asian Lutherans* was next, widening the scope from the US to Asia.[2] Now *Behold the Stream: A History of Asian Lutheran Witness* is our first pictorial, about Asian Lutherans in the Evangelical Lutheran Church in America (ELCA) and its predecessor church bodies. There will be some Canadian information as well, because Canada was a part of the mission territory of The American Lutheran Church and the Lutheran Church in America. Here is what to expect ahead in this book, along with study guide ideas.

First, a word on "Asian" versus "Asian American." "Asian" is a common term in US government and society as a racial and ethnic category. Even in our book's subtitle and contents, and in the ELCA, "Asian ministries" is easily understandable. However, "Asian" is shorthand. (Just as "American" is often shorthand in our context, meaning "North American.") "Asian American" was a term born in the 1960s, when student movement activists banded together for political strength and to assert their own identity. No longer would they be defined by others who used racial terms such as "Orientals" or slurs.

In publishing this book, we also affirm the right of persons to name themselves as they would like. In fact, South Asian, Southeast Asian and Filipino Americans sometimes self-identify as "Brown Asian Americans," to ensure their visibility when "Asian American" might be assumed as East Asian only.[3] It was not until the 1980s that Asian Indian activism in the 1960s

---

[1] Edmond Yee, *The Soaring Crane: Stories of Asian Lutherans in North America* (Minneapolis: Augsburg Fortress, 2002), p. xv.

[2] For details, see Edmond Yee and J. Paul Rajashekar (eds. and comps.), *Abundant Harvest: Stories of Asian Lutherans* (Minneapolis: Lutheran University Press, 2012).

[3] Nadal, Kevin L., "The Brown Asian American Movement: Advocating for South Asian, Southeast Asian, and Filipino American Communities," *Asian American Policy Review, A Harvard Kennedy School Student Publication,* Volume 29 (2018-19), February 2, 2020, p.1. [Hereafter cited as Nadal.]

led to being "identified as a minority group under the Asian umbrella." And not until the year 2000 was the Asian category expanded, with the term "South Asian" popularized for other groups.[4]

In generational diversity, many Asian Americans are "first generation," born in Asia, emigrating to the US. Yet "Asian America" encompasses the 1.5 generation (born in Asia, raised in the US), second, third, and fourth generations as well. Due to longstanding biases and racism, Asian Americans of all generations face tensions and conflict from those who view us as perpetual foreigners who do not belong here. It is important to affirm, therefore, that "Asian America" is not merely a descriptor for Asian people living in the US; it describes Americans of Asian heritage whose home is the US.

It is equally important to affirm that the peoples of "Asian America" are not standing pools or blocks of ice, frozen in time. We are vibrant people in communities of living streams, and people of an eternal river. In Appendix II, "Migration as Metaphor for the Christian Faith," Margrethe S. C. Kleiber provides a theological view on the complexity of our multiple Asian Lutheran American identities.

Part I: The Beginning is about Asian immigration and early Lutheran outreach to Asians in America, and how Asian-led ministries grew. "Generation I," "Generation II" and "Generation III" refer to specific time periods, not to when people came to the US or were born here.

Part II: Congregations and Unique Ministries features our local ministries, alphabetically by ethnic group. These are Asian-led, officially organized, or developing congregations or ministries. You will see what they are doing beyond traditional programs such as worship and Bible studies (though distinctive aspects such as bilingual and multilingual worship may appear). Most are serving immigrant communities, some with vital youth programs, while others have heartfelt hopes and yearnings for relating more fully with younger generations. Note: this is an incomplete picture of our ministry network; it only shows profiles we could gather in 2020. Also, in the "Setting of Congregation/Ministry" sections, the focus is on Asians compared to the total population of a city or town. Sometimes the statistics of other groups are shown, and sometimes they are not.

Part III: Who is Who in Ministry introduces Asian American church workers, ministry leaders; persons in the candidacy process to be rostered in the ELCA; and others whose calling is or was in the wider world. The emphasis is on their professional and educational achievements. (See "A Note on Using This Book," your key to technical details.)

As with Part II, *"Behold Thy Servants: Brooks of the Stream,"* being comprehensive has been an elusive goal. Complete lists of names and information are not available, either from the ELCA or from our research. We offer you (1) 100-word biographies with portraits or a picture of flowers when photographs are not available; (2) a list of pastors by name and first call (provided

---

[4] Nadal, p. 4.

by the ELCA's Office of the Presiding Bishop when information was unavailable from other sources); and (3) "In Memoriam," about deceased saints, as far as we could discover.

"Lo! Thy Servants on the Move: Flowing Far and Wide" is likewise incomplete. However, we can definitely show you a depth and breadth of involvement.

Part IV: Association, Conferences, and Publications tells how our leaders organized an association to strengthen our geographically scattered communities. Next you will see how the Asian Lutheran International Conference was built, a spacious bridge between Asian Lutherans and our counterparts in Asia. Finally, there is an overview of the publications we produced to support our faithful laborers and their ministries.

Part V: Thus So analyzes the Asian ministry past and how societal changes impacted their work. While we anchor this section in history, we also seek a glimpse of the future. To help us with this visioning, we invited eight theologian-leaders to discuss current challenges in the following four areas pertinent to mission and ministry:

- Theologies and theological education.
- Leadership.
- Identities, spiritualities and interfaith relations.
- Community and anti-racist commitments and practices.

Using the concept of migration as a starting point, our theologian-leaders engaged in a broad and rich conversation. We hope that our synopsis will encourage and inspire you and other leaders engaged in strategic planning, as we envision directions that the ELCA Asian ministry stream might take in the future.

Part VI: Words of Appreciation appear in this section from selected leaders in Asia and the US to the Rev. Dr. Pongsak Limthongviratn.

Two theological essays then follow for reflection and discussion.

Appendix I "Perspectives on Reading the Bible in Asian Contexts and Cultures."

Appendix II "Migration as Metaphor for the Christian Faith."

Ideas for Beholding and Sharing the Stream

This gift book will be shared with many partners:

- Asian Lutheran pastors, congregations and ministries.
- Lutheran multicultural and ecumenical partners.
- Bishops and leaders in administration, synodical and evangelical mission work.
- Educational institutions and their students, church historians, researchers.
- International colleagues.

Here are ideas for reflection, journaling, discussions, and action. Take some notes to capture your thoughts, which may be as fleeting as sunlight on the water!

Meditation

Behold the Stream is a gateway for travel: back in time, forward into the present, and toward the time ahead. Let us first reflect on Amos 5:24 on the back cover, the front cover scene, and Psalm 46:4 in the Preface. Do you feel expansive and hopeful in the great outdoors? What elements stand out and why? The scene is both dark and light, as is life; suggesting realism up ahead. And yet this image is warm and spring-like. Sunlight brightens the land, and the tips of the tree leaves. Consider the source: is the stream flowing toward the sky or pouring out from a higher source? Whichever way you interpret it, the water is alive and flowing. What else does your imagination suggest to you?

Engaging with the History

- What stories do you identify with in this book?
- How have societal impacts affected your life and work?
- What have you learned from the past? What would you do differently now?
- What new thoughts have emerged for you about migration, immigration, Asian Americans in ministry? About mission work and program planning?
- Name a barrier that blocks the flow of a ministry stream. With whom might you work to unblock it?
- How do you see God working through this stream of Asian Lutheran witness?

Part I: The Beginning

What impressions do you have of the early denominational attempts at Asian ministry? What were you doing during the eras of Generations I, II, and III?

Generation I: Laying the Foundation

- Which of the issues named still need advocacy today?

Generation II: Building and Expansion

- What lessons learned stand out to you as valuable for Asian ministry today?

Generation III: Reaching for the Horizon

- Which ministry area calls out to you? What step can you next take to help it grow?

Part II: Congregations and Ministries Tour

Enjoy this coast-to-coast tour of local Asian Lutheran ministries in the US. Each one is a part of a flowing stream.

- What unique program ideas attract you the most, and for what groups by age, gender, or location? What more would you like to learn about?
- What step can you take to explore, develop or adapt for your context the idea that beckons most?

Part III: Who is Who in Ministry

Whether studying, working or retired, it is a joy to find our callings in life.

- Are there life paths here that surprise you? Might you surprise yourself by entering into new activities or work? Or encourage someone else's transition?
- What stories uplifted you? Tell others about those persons to inspire them too.
- Organize an intergenerational program or day about finding and celebrating life callings, roles, and career paths. Identify spiritual gifts and how to use them best. Celebrate hidden talents. Affirm God's gifts at work through people.

Part IV: Association, Conferences, and Publications

- Association of Asians and Pacific Islanders (AAPI-ELCA) evolved in direct relationship to the gifts of its active leaders. What directions do you consider the most important to pursue? What written resources (print or online) would boost Asian Lutheran ministries today?
- Share your thoughts with the AAPI–ELCA president through www. asianlutherans. com.
- What aspects of Asian Lutheran International Conference history stood out to you, and why? What do your reflections reveal about possibilities in ministries you are called to?

Part V: Thus So

Reflect on issues and questions raised within the text.

- What wisdom is God revealing to you?
- Where will you share it for the good of the whole community?

Part VI: Appreciations

- Write an appreciation to someone you know and send it to the person!

Appendix I "Perspectives on Reading the Bible in Asian Contexts and Cultures."

- Why do Asian Christians tend to read the Bible literally?
- How might scriptures be like a raft or boat crossing a river?
- What does it mean to reclaim the Bible and re-read it with Asian eyes and ears?

Appendix II "Migration as Metaphor for the Christian Faith."

- Draw on a sheet of paper your family's migration journey.
- Draw on another sheet of paper a depiction of your multiple identities.
- Compare the two side by side. What influences and intersections do you see?
- Organize a church group discussion on Zoom if not in person. Invite all participants to share their drawings. Point out to one another the strengths and gifts you observe. Pray about how to grow in using these gifts, each of us as

brooks of the stream.

The Behold the Stream book project began in January 2020. The goal was to publish it before the next Asian Lutheran International Conference in 2021. Covid-19 complicated this timeline, as it complicated every other area of life and endeavor. Pastors who served as compilers and writers on our team, or who were respondents in the field, were inundated with comforting the sick and dying. Many leaders were unreachable. Some declined, and others did not respond. Seminaries and research facilities were closed or offered limited access. Despite these obstacles, we kept laboring into Winter 2020, doing what we could in the constantly changing situation. We believed that this book contained stories that needed to be told, and would be uniquely encouraging to readers when it arrived.

The stream continues to flow. Let us sit beside the stream together and reflect on its wonders. Then let us walk beside it and see how it speaks to us, individually and in community. The walk will stimulate our creativity and minds as we learn from the past, celebrate our present, and thank God for guidance into the future.

Lily R. Wu

PART I

The Beginning: Asians in USA and Lutheran Witness

I | The Beginning: Asians in the USA and Lutheran Witness

Crossing Many Seas: Asians in the USA

The Chinese discovered America 71 years before Columbus! Gavin Menzies, a British Royal Navy submarine captain, strongly argues this case in his well-documented, though somewhat controversial book *1421: The Year China Discovered America*.[1] In her article "Immigration," Jennifer Snow states that the "Filipino sailors on Spanish galleons escaped from the harsh shipboard life to the shores of California and Louisiana in the 18th century. In Louisiana, 40 years before the United States made the Louisiana Purchase, Filipinos established an isolated *bayou* community that persevered until the great hurricane of 1915."[2] But sizable Asian immigration did not occur until after the California gold rush. The Chinese were the first to arrive. As their numbers grew, the US in 1882 passed a race-based restriction law, the Chinese Exclusion Act. This created a labor shortage, which labor recruiters and missionaries later addressed by recruiting other Asians.

The Japanese were the next group to come, followed by the Koreans, the Indians, and the Filipinos. These early immigrants faced many legal and racist challenges.[3] For example, the entire Japanese population in the contiguous US was sent to internment camps throughout the nation during WWII. However, the "1965 Hart-Celler Act and the Refugee Acts of 1975, 1980, and 1987"[4] cracked the gate wide open for Asian immigration. After Saigon's fall in 1975, America experienced a new wave of immigrants and refugees coming from Southeast Asia.

Today an estimate of more than 22 million Asian Americans live in the US, mostly in urban areas. From the start, Asian immigrants have brought their own way of life to the nation. For example, "at least 80 different schools of Buddhism….virtually the entire main schools of

---

[1] Gavin Menzies, *1421: The Year China Discovered America* (New York: Harper Collins Publishers, 2003).
[2] Jennifer Snow, "Immigration" in Jonathan H. X. Lee, Fumitaka Matsuoka, Edmond Yee and Ronald Y. Nakasone (eds.), *Asian American Religious Cultures* (Santa Barbara: ABC-CLIO, LLC, 2015), p. 54. [Hereafter cited as Snow].
[3] For further reading, see Jennifer Snow, *Protestant Missionaries, Asian Immigrants, and American Ideologies* (New York: Rutledge, 2007).
[4] Snow, p. 61.

Buddhism in Asia are now represented in Los Angeles."[5] Some Asian immigrants were Roman Catholic or Protestant Christian when they arrived. Some became members of churches after they settled here.

In addition Asian cultures, religions, histories, and languages began to flow in the US in various streams other than by Asians themselves:

- Catholic and Protestant missionaries introduced Asian cultures to Europe and the US.
- A good number of US colleges and universities offered Asian subjects in their curricula.
- In the 1970s, Asian American studies became established as an academic discipline, largely in connection with the emerging Asian American movement.[6]

Therefore, Asians from the standpoint of color and texture have undoubtedly enriched the landscape of the nation.

Edmond Yee

---

[5] Kenneth Kenshin Tanaka, *Buddhism on Air: Televised Kaleidoscope of a Growing Religion* (Anaheim: Buddhist Education Center, 2015), p. 5.

[6] Jonathan H. X. Lee, Fumitaka Matsuoka, Edmond Yee, and Ronald Y. Nakasone (eds.), *Asian American Religious Cultures* (Santa Barbara: ABC-CLIO, LLC 2015), pp. xxvi-xxvii.

See! Thy Servants Labor: Asian Lutheran Witness in the USA

Your servants belong to the fastest-growing population in the United States of America. Since the mid-1880s, they have been noticed for various reasons by society, including Lutheran denominations. Here is how the churches initially began their ministries and how they and your servants subsequently formed their partnerships through the Evangelical Lutheran Church in America (ELCA) and its predecessor bodies. However, to paint a complete historical picture, we shall begin our story with the Lutheran Church-Missouri Synod.

The Lutheran Church-Missouri Synod

The Lutheran Church-Missouri Synod (LC-MS) until 1947 was known as The Evangelical Lutheran Synod of Missouri, Ohio, and Other States (TELSMOOS). Compared with other Lutheran denominations in the late 19th and early 20th centuries, it was theologically more conservative than other Lutheran bodies. It was also the first Lutheran body to focus on home missions where Asian ministries were concerned. The earliest Asian Lutheran ministries in North America focused on the Chinese and Japanese.

Chinese Ministry

In 1896 the California-Nevada District of this church "entertained an idea of a ministry with the Chinese in San Francisco, California."[1] While nothing came of this idea, this is the earliest documented discussion about ministry with Asians in America.

In 1936 a group of Chinese Christians in New York City in partnership with the Atlantic District of TELSMOOS organized True Light Lutheran Church, the first Chinese Lutheran congregation in North America. True Light was followed by Prince of Peace Lutheran Church in Vancouver, BC, and Lutheran Church of the Holy Spirit in San Francisco.[2]

Japanese Ministry

The first Japanese Lutheran Church in Los Angeles, CA, grew from the work of Minnesotans Daniel and Ann Schoof, who befriended a group of Japanese men. This group moved to Minnesota when US policy changed, allowing the Japanese detained in US internment camps during WWII to move inland. Later the group moved to Los Angeles, forming a congregation led by Schoof and Toshio Okamoto.[3] This ministry closed its doors in 1998.[4]

---

[1] Edmond Yee, *The Soaring Crane: Stories of Asian Lutherans in North America* (Minneapolis: Augsburg Fortress, 2002), p. 15. [Hereafter cited as Yee].
[2] Yee, pp. 24-18.
[3] Yee, pp. 28-31.
[4] Yee, p. 31.

The United Evangelical Lutheran Church

The United Evangelical Lutheran Church was originally known as the United Danish Evangelical Lutheran Church. When the torch of the missionary movement "was passed to the Americans during the World Missionary Conference at Edinburgh in 1910,"[5] this church sent missionaries to Japan. World War II, however, interrupted their work, and they returned home.

Japanese Ministry

The Board of Foreign Missions (BFM) of this church did not quite know what to do with the returned missionaries since they were still under contract. After much consideration, the board decided that the Rev. and Mrs. Ditlev Gotthard Monrad Bachs should go to Fresno, CA, to initiate a ministry with the *Nisei* (second-generation Japanese Americans). However, internal struggles, including animosity and name-calling between the Bachs and BFM officials, doomed the ministry to failure. BFM discontinued this ministry in 1959.[6]

The United Lutheran Church in America

The United Lutheran Church in America (ULCA) "came into being in 1918 from the merger of the General Synod, the General Council, and the United Synod of the South."[7] It was then the largest Lutheran church in North America.

Japanese Ministry

"Two of its predecessor bodies—the General Council and the General Synod—had mission work in Japan."[8] Still, the ULCA was reluctant to go into Japanese ministry in the US, despite the California Synod's repeated requests. The Japan Evangelical Lutheran Church (JELC) also made appeals. Finally, the Board of American Missions agreed to begin hostel ministry with former internees who had moved inland from the camps. The board also began to reach out to other Japanese in Los Angeles and San Francisco. However, none of these ministries led to an organized congregation.

The American Lutheran Church

The American Lutheran Church (TALC) was formed in 1960 through mergers over time of the Evangelical Lutheran Synod of Iowa and Other States, the Lutheran Synod of Buffalo, and the Evangelical Lutheran Joint Synod of Ohio and Other States. It was initially known as the First American Lutheran Church and then the United Evangelical Lutheran Church before becoming TALC. The South Pacific District of TALC recognized the importance of Asian ministries. A 1979 report to the district's Nineteenth Annual Convention mentioned Joseph Wong as "a consultant of

---

[5] Yee, p. 33.
[6] Yee, pp. 33-39.
[7] Yee, p. 41.
[8] Yee, p. 41.

our Asian-American Ministry." In 1983, the district changed Wong's title to director.[9] The district also organized a Commission for Asian Ministries with a focus on Chinese and Korean ministries. Most of the issues the Lutheran Church in America (LCA) faced in ministry development, as we shall see later, also confronted TALC.

Nevertheless, TALC made progress establishing Asian ministries. Thus when the Evangelical Lutheran Church in America (ELCA) was born in 1988, TALC added ten Asian ministries to the newly organized church.[10]

Chinese Ministry

Donald W. Baron, a Caucasian pastor, initiated TALC's Chinese ministry in Honolulu. It began as a fellowship at Prince of Peace Lutheran Church but gradually evolved to become the Chinese Lutheran Church of Honolulu.[11] TALC also initiated a social ministry in Chinatown, Los Angeles, and a ministry in San Francisco.[12]

Korean Ministry

The South Pacific District also began a Korean ministry in Long Beach, CA, under the leadership of David Kang. He later left TALC, and the ministry was closed.

Missionaries from Japan

The Japan Evangelical Lutheran Church is a missionary-minded institution. In 1965 this church began sending missionaries to other parts of the world. In 1976 the JELC and TALC agreed to welcome the first missionary, Ikuo Takatsuka, to the US. He was assigned to serve in a Caucasian congregation in Iowa. Two others followed in his steps, serving congregations in Florida, and again Iowa. However, this work did not develop into any Japanese congregational ministry in the US.

The Association of Evangelical Lutheran Churches

The Association of Evangelical Lutheran Churches (AELC) was formed in 1976 due to internal struggles within the LC-MS.[13] The AELC was a loosely structured institution of more than four hundred congregations, with limited resources for new mission development.[14]

Chinese Ministry

The Association of Evangelical Lutheran Church's Chinese ministry started in 1983 around Naperville and Warrenville, IL. It was initially financed by Paul Chang, who pastored True Light

---

[9] Yee, pp. 119-121.
[10] Yee, p. 122.
[11] Yee, p. 68.
[12] Yee, pp. 71, 120
[13] Yee, pp. 59-60.
[14] Yee, p. 122.

Lutheran Church in New York City for a while before becoming a real estate businessman. The congregation, Truth Lutheran Church, was led by Far-Dung Tong, who eventually left the ministry. In 1988 this congregation became part of the ELCA.[15]

Korean Ministry

St. Jacobus Evangelical Lutheran Church, Woodside, Queens, NY, was a congregation that broke away from the LC-MS to join the ELCA. It "had a Korean ministry formally related to the congregation."[16] Beginning in 1985, under the leadership of Hun Reo, the AELC and TALC supported this ministry.[17] But this ministry was eventually closed.

The Lutheran Church in America

The Lutheran Church in America came into being in 1962 from the merger of the ULCA and Augustana Synod (AS). Two years before this, the Chinese population in the US stood at 237,292. But as late as the mid-1970s, the LCA was still not ready for the Chinese, refusing Charles Kuo's request to begin the work.[18] Kuo, a one-term president (bishop) of the Evangelical Lutheran Church of Hong Kong (ELCHK), had immigrated to San Francisco and had gathered a group for Bible studies.

However, the LCA changed its mind in 1978 after its Division for Mission in North America (DMNA) appointed Edmond Yee[19] as a half-time resource developer-consultant for Asian ministries and a half-time professor at Pacific Lutheran Theological Seminary (PLTS) in Berkeley, CA. As we shall see, Yee's appointment provided new support for Asian ministries.

Chinese Ministry

Chinese ministry in the LCA was initiated by Mrs. Evodia Swenson and her husband, Victor. They were former AS missionaries to China who were living in Pasadena, CA, in their retirement.[20] They enlisted the help of Wilson Wu,[21] a graduate of the Lutheran Theological Seminary (LTS) in Hong Kong who "had done graduate studies at Ashbury Theological Seminary."[22] At first, the Swensons were this ministry's private sponsors. It was not successful in Pasadena; however, it flourished after Wu moved it to Monterey Park, CA.

Despite Wu's training in Hong Kong and the US, the Pacific Southwest Synod still required him to study another year at PLTS before deeming him qualified for ordination. Wu endured and was ordained in 1965. The group he had gathered formally organized in 1968 as Faith Lutheran

---

[15] Yee, pp. 123-124.

[16] Yee, p. 122.

[17] Yee, p. 122.

[18] Yee, p. 106.

[19] For biography, see Edmond Yee and J. Paul Rajashekar (eds. and comps.), *Abundant Harvest: Stories of Asian Lutherans* (Minneapolis: Lutheran University Press, 2012), pp. 422-426. [Hereafter cited as Yee and Rajashekar.]

[20] Yee, p. 39.

[21] For biography, see Yee and Rajashekar, pp. 413-415.

[22] Yee, p. 55.

Church in Monterey Park.[23]

In 1974, New Life Chinese Lutheran Church in Vancouver, BC, Canada, was established, led by Herman Liu. He was a graduate of the Bible Institute in Hong Kong, LTS, and Lutheran Theological Seminary in Saskatoon, SK., Canada.[24]

Chinese Ministry with the Evangelical Lutheran Church of Hong Kong

In 1981 the Lutheran Church in America and the ELCHK began to explore the possibility of a cooperative Chinese ministry in North America. This discussion led to an agreement that both churches would support a ministry in Toronto, ON, Canada, led by Wing Fai Tsang.[25] The work in Toronto became the first cooperative ministry between the LCA and an Asian Lutheran church body.

Japanese Ministry

The Lutheran Church in America's Japanese ministry in Torrance-Gardena, CA, was started by Paul T. Nakamura,[26] with minimal support from the local synod but with generous gifts from the Yosh Hokama family. This ministry began in 1975 as "Lutheran Oriental Circle" but in 1977 changed its name to Lutheran Oriental Church. It was received in 1979 into the Pacific Southwest Synod as an organized congregation. [27]

Missionaries and Japanese Ministry

Fumio Tani was a theologically trained medical doctor who felt encouraged by the presence of Japanese missionaries in TALC. He decided to come to the US as a self-supporting minister to help with the LCA's outreach to the Japanese. In December 1977, he arrived in Los Angeles to work with the Japanese-speaking community there. "It was his intention to build a church-motel -restaurant complex in Los Angeles for his ministry and to work with Paul T. Nakamura in Torrance."[28] But soon, misunderstandings developed among Tani, DMNA, and the Pacific Southwest Synod. After six months in the US, Tani returned to Japan to resume his medical practice.

Meanwhile, the staff of DMNA felt the need for a Japanese language ministry in Southern California. Yutaka Toda, who had served in Florida under TALC's sponsorship, was called. Toda developed this first Japanese language ministry for the LCA in Garden Grove, CA. After completing his term, he returned to Japan. DMNA called Mikio Noguchi to replace Toda in April 1984. However, the congregants grieving Toda's departure rejected Noguchi, who returned to Japan after one year of service.

---

[23] Yee, pp. 55-56.
[24] Yee, pp. 73-74.
[25] Canada was part of the LCA territory then.
[26] For biography see Yee and Rajashekar, pp. 322-324.
[27] Yee, pp. 74-76.
[28] Yee, p. 113.

At this point, the LCA, TALC, and the JELC felt the need for a three-way consultation, which they held on March 5-7 in Los Angeles. "At the end of the consultation, the group named the cooperative program Japan-America Cooperative Evangelism Program."[29] As a result, the JELC sent Ikuo Takasuka to the US, and the ministry moved to the Lutheran Church of the Resurrection in Huntington Beach. Though the ministry is not an organized congregation, it continues to serve the people in the area today.

Asian Ministry

Generation I: Laying the Foundation (1978-1988)

With Edmond Yee's appointment in 1978, the LCA Asian ministries began to develop slowly. During the ten years he occupied this position, he further developed the LCA's Chinese ministries and began developing new ministries with Southeast Asians.[30] A number of pastors from other- than-Lutheran denominations transferred into the LCA. The LCA, as previously mentioned, also cooperated with the ELCHK.[31] An Asian Caucus, a forerunner of the Association of Asians and Pacific Islanders-Evangelical Lutheran Church in America (AAPI-ELCA), was formed. The Eiichi Matsushita Scholarship Fund for Asian seminary students had been established. However, Asian ministry as a whole was not always smooth sailing, facing the following issues:

- Insufficient resources (financial and educational) along with the lack of trained personnel hampered development.
- Asian ministries, when part of Caucasian congregational expansion programs, often suffered due to questionable motivations on the part of the White congregations, discrimination, racism, and cultural conflicts.
- The older generation of Chinese immigrant pastors distrusted the leadership of the younger generation.
- Memories of historical conflicts between China and Japan disrupted harmony within the community.
- Entry into promising mission fields without competent personnel caused ministries to be abandoned.
- Racism, discrimination, and unequal compensation for Asians (at least initially) within DMNA also affected the morale of Asian pastors.

Nevertheless, by the end of Yee's tenure with DMNA, "19 Asian congregations were added to the LCA and subsequently to the ELCA."[32]

The Evangelical Lutheran Church in America

The Evangelical Lutheran Church in America is the result of the merger of the AELC, TALC, and

---

[29] Yee, p.114.
[30] Yee, pp. 142-144.
[31] Yee, pp. 105-116.
[32] Yee, p. 116.

the LCA.[33] While the Commission for a New Lutheran Church (CNLC) discussed in earnest how to shape the new church, another group deliberated how to impact the yet to be born church. This group, sponsored by the Lutheran Council of the USA, and initially led by African Americans, eventually became the Steering Committee (SC) of the Transcultural Seminars.[34] The SC members came from African, Asian, Latino, Native American, and White communities. Through two Transcultural Seminars in 1981, this group urged the CNLC planners to create a Commission for Women, a Commission for Multicultural Ministries (CMM), and establish a quota system to help the new church become more multicultural and inclusive. The CNLC accepted the recommendations.

When the new institution was born, the ELCA had 31 Asian ministries (New Life Chinese Lutheran Church in Vancouver, BC in 1986 became part of the Evangelical Lutheran Church in Canada. The Toronto ministry did not become a congregation). In this new church, Asian Lutheran ministries and other ethnic ministries were related to CMM. The first director for Asian ministries, William E. Wong,[35] began serving in 1988.

The Shape of the Commission for Multicultural Ministries

With high hopes and expectations, the new church began to move forward. Yet soon the ELCA experienced budget cuts, staff reductions, reconfiguration of different units, low morale, and opposition to the quota system (later called representational principles). Struggling with the forces within and without, Craig Lewis, the first executive director, let "out some anguished cries before he joined the presiding bishop's staff:

> Genuine commitment to justice on part of some in our church has disguised or obscured a strong neoconservative mentality among some members which gravitates away from true justice and equality as we understand it. These neoconservatives claim dedication to equality and justice for all, but are strongly opposed to any specific measures to achieve those objectives. They fail to see that noncooperation with evil is as essential as cooperation with good. Racism and malevolent ethnocentrism are among the principalities and powers with which we must contend. These threats take us by way of the cross, and cause us to ask are we worthy of our calling."[36]

"Then he turned his attention to the ethnic communities. 'The African American, Asian, Hispanic, and Native American membership is called from the periphery of the church to prophesy…but the silence of African American, Asian, Hispanic, and Native American prophecy is deafening!'"[37] Lewis further stated in his report that CMM also had to deal with its "ambiguous, if not ambivalent,"

---

[33] For details of the merger, see Edgar Trexler, *Anatomy of a Merger: People, Dynamics, and Decisions that Shaped the ELCA* (Minneapolis, Fortress Press, 1991).

[34] For details, see Richard J. Perry (ed.), *Catching a Star: Transcultural Reflections on a Church for All People* (Minneapolis: Lutheran University Press, 2004). [The original manuscript of this volume was edited by Lily R. Wu.]

[35] For biography, see Yee and Rajashekar, pp. 406-409.

[36] Yee, p. 158.

[37] Yee, p. 158.

role and function.[38]

During this early era in the ELCA's existence (1988 to 1992), "the challenges CMM faced were not unique" to the commission.[39] The CMM staff was upbeat. However, the Asian community was impacted by xenophobia "unleashed on us, unfortunately, not only from the Whites but also from other ethnic communities."[40]

In 1992 Frederick E. N. Rajan[41] became the executive director of CMM. He set out to strengthen CMM by trying to turn it into a more effective unit. But he faced more challenges than opportunities; some of his plans, though sound, were not popular among various ethnic communities. Meanwhile, Wong found his position shifted again and again by Rajan to meet the staffing needs. These additional responsibilities took time away from Wong's focus on the Asian community. During these transitions Nakamura and Yee each served for a time as interim director of Asian ministries. Yet, due to the caretaker nature of their temporary role, no ministries were started under their tenure.

Asian Ministry

Generation II: Building and Expansion (1988-1996)

As we have seen in Generation I, your faithful servants laid the ground for Asian Lutheran ministries. By the time Wong assumed the directorship in 1988, there were 31 Asian ministries, mostly on the West Coast. At least 90% of the pastors came from overseas, with a good number of them from the Presbyterian tradition. The Lutheran pastors from Taiwan, Hong Kong, and Japan were also unfamiliar with US Lutheranism, its institutional structure, and polities. The LCA and later TALC joined together to provide programs under Yee's direction to "Lutheranize" them, in other words, to familiarize them with the structure, polities, and function of US Lutheran denominations.

Despite Yee's efforts, the pastors continued to adhere to their previous traditions and remained apart from the institution, theologically, liturgically, and functionally. Even if they wanted to be part of the institutions, they were still "like isolated drops of tea flowing in a bucket of milk, unable to penetrate the depth or to spread across the breadth of the bucket."[42]

Nevertheless, Wong was optimistic about the future of Asian ministries because the Constitutions, Bylaws, and Continuing Resolutions (CBCR) of the ELCA mandated the church's emphasis on multicultural ministries. The constitution required a Commission for Multicultural Ministries—the first unit to focus on persons of color and multicultural ministries[43] in the history

---

[38] Yee, p. 158; see also "Report of Executive Director, CMM, Oct. 19-20, 1990." P. 916.

[39] Frederick E. N. Rajan's private email to Edmond Yee, dated August 16, 2020. [Hereafter cited as Rajan.]

[40] Rajan, dated August 16, 2020.

[41] For biography, see Yee and Rajashekar, pp. 347-350; Lee, Matsuoka, Yee, and Nakasone, pp. 731-733.

[42] Yee, p. 205.

[43] Constitutions, Bylaws, and Continuing Resolutions Evangelical Lutheran Church in America (February, 1988), p. 96. [Hereafter cited as CBCR.]

of the US Lutheran denominations. Within the constitution's principles of organization[44] were approaches that supported the work of CMM.

- An interdependence principle that people affected most by a decision were to become the principal party responsible for decision and implementation.[45]
- A representation principle that all staffing, assembly, board, council, and committee positions from the churchwide organization to synod levels were to include representation of 10% persons of color, 40% clergy and 60% lay and 50% women and 50% men.[46]
- A principle that the churchwide organization and synods were to develop and implement plans where 10% of the ELCA membership with in ten years would be persons of color.[47]

For the Asian community, the 10% goal affirmed our place in the ELCA, a 98 percent White denomination. Craig Lewis initially thought that the commission had the potential to be a powerful force for change in the ELCA.

However, newness had its challenges. The CMM Asian ministries program had to be developed from scratch since no previous equivalent program existed in the predecessor Lutheran church bodies. The CMM governance required the formation of an Asian advisory committee and, eventually, the development of an Asian association.[48] Within the ELCA churchwide structure, the concept of a commission that provided "services, advice, and counsel in the area of the commission's specific function"[49] for all the units and expressions of the ELCA was a new and alien concept for Lutherans. Explaining what a commission could and could not do vis-à-vis the larger programmatic units known as divisions proved an ongoing challenge.

Simultaneously, other ELCA churchwide units, synods, congregations, organizations, and staff did not know what to do with this new unit that provided services, advice, and counsel. Wong worked hard to develop relationships, collaborate, and develop partnerships with division staff to access programs and funding streams for Asian ministries.

When Wong assumed the directorship, he was familiar with the Asian Lutheran community. He had met most of the pastors and many lay leaders at ministry gatherings or conferences of the LCA or jointly with TALC. Wong had been part of the Asian delegation to the Transcultural Seminars. And he had begun meeting with Chinese clergy in the San Francisco Bay Area when he was a seminarian at PLTS (1977-1981).

Under these circumstances, how did Wong navigate the uncharted waters of this new church? What was his relationship with the Asian Lutheran community? How did the Asian

---

[44] CBCR, pp. 23-24.
[45] CBCR, p. 23.
[46] CBCR, pp. 23-24.
[47] CBCR, p. 24
[48] CBCR, pp. 96, 59.
[49] CRCR, p. 96.

immigrant pastors understand his role with the commission? Equally important, how did they regard a second generation American-born Chinese who did not speak their languages and commanded limited knowledge of their histories and cultures? What role did racism and xenophobia play in this mix? And what worked for him? The following stories will reveal the challenges facing Asian Lutheran ministry Generation II.

An Asian American "Surrogate Bishop" and His Flock

By the time Wong became the director, the internal conflicts among the Asian pastors known to Yee had subsided. However, the ELCA Asian community continued to struggle with the language barrier, unawareness of how the institution worked, and lack of support from their White colleagues and bishops. Given these realities, Wong became a surrogate bishop to the Asian pastors. He became their connection to this new church body that had no idea how to work with them. They had little or no support synodically or locally for Asian-specific ministries; and a lack of help in negotiating through the system. Incredibly, there was no money for internship sites, especially involving languages other than English.

Yet, three out of four times, the ELCA asked its Asian leaders to start new ethnic-specific ministries, even though mission development may not have been their forte. As an institution, the ELCA was unable to recognize and leverage the strengths and abilities of its Asian leaders.

Despite all the issues, Wong and the leaders worked well together. As an American-born Chinese, he knew how to relate to and work with immigrants while understanding the dynamics of "not being Chinese enough" for the Chinese immigrant pastors. He was respectful to them, listened, and developed relationships. In return, they respected him and were willing to work with him.

"Surrogate Bishop" and Lay Asians

Wong, even more than Yee, served a very diverse and geographically scattered Asian population. At the time of his tenure, an estimated 75% of ELCA Asian members worshiped in English-speaking congregations. American-born Asians and Asian immigrants fluent in English were likely to be among this 75%, especially those second, third, and fourth generation English-speaking Asians whose ancestors had made their homes in the United States since the 19th century.

However, the rest of the ELCA Asian community were immigrants and refugees dealing with first generation survival issues. They needed to cope with the stress of learning a new language and negotiating a new culture. They had to adapt to life in a new context while at the same time needing to remain engaged with their homelands. They were raising children in a new culture with different norms. Many had to learn new occupational skills and deal with financial concerns and economic insecurity. Urban areas drew many in the ELCA Asian community. Former refugees often stayed where Lutheran churches had sponsored them — unless they relocated to reunite with family elsewhere or find more job opportunities. Moreover, they were ill-equipped to deal with American racism, a new experience they did not understand.

Each ethnic group had its own country of origin and varied cultures, languages, and dialects within. As such, their needs differed, depending on where their families had come from, when, and where they settled. Wars and conflicts had also inflicted trauma and fomented factionalism. Noting that the pain of those histories ran deep, Wong recalled, "On top of that, no one talked about historical enmity between the groups in Asia."

As Yee had done, Wong, from time to time, brought key lay leaders and pastors together for spiritual enrichment, fellowship, education, and pastoral care. One focus of the CMM Asian ministries program was to create vital opportunities for fellowship. The leaders needed to see and support one another, speak their first language for in-depth conversations, be nourished by eating familiar foods, and experience being community together.

In-House Consultant and White Colleagues

At the churchwide offices, Wong became the in-house Asian ministry consultant for the entire ELCA. Given the ELCA's ineptness with diversity and his position within the churchwide structure, he carried the burden of providing services, advice, and counsel on all matters Asian, and interpreting Asian ministry, lives, and experiences to the entire church.

As a predominately White denomination, ELCA staff did not naturally reach out to people different from themselves. White coworkers were often oblivious to how racism perpetuates inequalities and injustices; and how racism works for the status quo and the benefit of White persons. Nor did they *have* to know because they were not affected by racism as people of color were. Neither were there consequences for not engaging with people who were racially and ethnically different.

The Division for Outreach, which focused on new ethnic ministry starts, often placed Asian congregations with pre-existing White congregations. Some White congregations were great hosts. However, there was little to no funding available to help new Asian congregations secure their own spaces. Becoming self-supporting was a constant challenge for newly organized Asian congregations.

Asian Advisory Committee

Every CMM ethnic community of the new ELCA had to have an advisory committee made up of representatives from each of the church's nine regions. By design, four members of each advisory committee also served on the CMM board.

In regions with many Asians, there were few problems nominating a representative to fill a regional seat on the Asian Advisory Committee (AAC). In other regions finding representatives was more of a challenge. If last names did not provide enough clues, people would have to self-identify as Asians to become known to the network. Wong turned to the ELCA Office for Research, Planning, and Evaluation to find those persons. It was a constant question for Wong and fellow Asian pastors:

who and where were the Asians spread out across the church? Meeting the newly formed Asian advisory group, Wong knew that there had to be even more people around like this if only he could find them.

The Asian Advisory Committee took its work seriously to help shape the direction of the CMM Asian ministries program with the wisdom of their combined perspectives. Their presence prompted Wong to explain what he was doing and why. They asked hard questions and discussed with him how to improve, offering valuable insights for charting the course.

And though it was not Wong's idea to bring such advisors together, they became a built-in support group. They wanted Asian ministries to succeed. They wanted him to succeed and asked what they could do to be supportive. There were no internal battles, and they worked smoothly together. Some were strong laypersons. Some had minimal experience with church structure, governance, or advisement, other than serving on their congregation councils. "I was fortunate to work with this great group of savvy, articulate folks," Wong recalled. "We had the right chemistry, which made for a great environment."

However, organizing a structure of Asian, Black, Hispanic, and Native American advisory committees for governance was cumbersome, complicated, and costly. The community needed to gather every two years — which required spending for the travel, lodging, and other convening costs — to elect the advisory committee. As Asian ministries expanded beyond Chinese, Japanese, and Korean, they needed to get a varied balance of ethnic representatives to serve. In keeping with the ELCA representation principles, they also sought 40% clergy and 60% lay members for the group, as well as 50% women and 50% men.

Meanwhile, the Asian Lutheran ethnic association was emerging, known as the Association of Asian Lutherans-ELCA. In the face of churchwide budget reductions and the cumbersome nature of the original plan for governance, CMM deemed it more straight forward for this new association to provide advisement. Therefore, CMM disbanded the AAC. "We did feel a sense of loss," Wong said. "We did everything we could to be as successful as we could be, and we did well."

The advisory committee lasted four years until CMM reorganized. The commission's steering committee no longer needed to include four advisory committee members, as the Churchwide Assembly would elect the CMM steering committee. Broad representation would be easier to find, too, from the churchwide level.

Wong remained on staff to serve as the coordinating director for the ELCA multicultural mission strategy — mobilizing people to achieve the ELCA goal that 10% of its membership would be people of color. However, more change was ahead. In less than two years, Wong returned to serving as both the director for Asian ministries and the coordinating director for multicultural mission strategy.

Racism and Xenophobia at Work

Wong noticed that for many White colleagues, their primary need was for a representative of color on their council or committee, not the more expansive vision outlined in the CBCR of the ELCA about becoming a diverse church. At no point did churchwide leadership bring the entire staff together to discuss how to create a church with 10% persons of color. There were no consequences if a churchwide unit failed to engage in achieving the 10% goal. Much was in flux, and many issues were not being addressed, such as equality of mobility, compensation, and church leaders getting to know their Asian pastors.

The Commission for Multicultural Ministries was an afterthought to most churchwide colleagues. The CMM was working in isolation. It was not integral to the life of the ELCA, but on the sidelines without power to make pervasive changes. Wong observed, "Half the battle was getting White colleagues to see that they needed what we could offer." He further noticed that "we weren't winning the hearts and minds of the typical ELCA member." When a unit executive or colleagues *did* invite him to come to a meeting, hope was born anew.

Despite all the racism and xenophobia at work, Asian colleagues made many sacrifices for the sake of the gospel. Most chose to stay in the ELCA and not join denominations that offered more support. Former refugee leaders, in particular, thankful for sponsorship in their time of need, hooked their wagons to the ELCA despite the hardships they faced in it.

Wong was inspired by their commitment, by "the good folks, and the Asian pastors who did their best in the face of great challenges." He tried to provide the same for them as White pastors were getting. Why? "I did it for the call, the people, and the vision of what Asian ministries can be. Through these Asian colleagues and fellow CMM colleagues, I experienced God's Pentecost vision for a multicultural church for all people. There is a place for everyone at God's banqueting table."

Ecumenical Connections and Partners

In 1988 there was a growing concern in the Asian community about an increase in anti-Asian violence and incidents in the US. Wong examined this issue during his first year serving as the director for Asian ministries. He soon learned of the Ecumenical Working Group of Asian Pacific Americans (EWGAPA), a partnership of colleagues working together to study the rise in the violence, to advocate and act against it, including making recommendations to their respective denominations. Wong contacted EWGAPA, and they invited him to participate.

Through the Ecumenical Working Group of Asian Pacific Americans, Wong networked with ecumenical counterparts and partners in other church bodies active in Asian ministries long before the ELCA. Specifically, these were the American Baptist Churches, Episcopal Church USA, Presbyterian Church USA, Reformed Church in America, and United Church of Christ. Wong developed a deeper understanding of the Asian American Christian experience, took part in an informal support group, and conversed with Asian colleagues on a wide range of topics related to Asian ministries, the Asian American experience, and being an Asian minister serving within church institutional structures.

Another outcome for Wong was an invitation to join another Asian ministry alliance, the Pacific Asian American Canadian Education Project (PAACE). This group worked together to develop and produce educational and congregational resources for a pan-Asian English-speaking audience. PAACE opened the door to a different network of Asian ministry counterparts serving in the above-mentioned mainline church bodies and the United Church of Canada. In time, Stacy D. Kitahata,[50] Division for Global Mission, served as an ELCA representative to PAACE, and Wong chaired the PAACE governing board for two years.

These ecumenical relationships offered Wong a broader view of Asian American ministries and provided hope for the possibilities of Asian ministries in the ELCA.

What Worked?

Wong's job was not easy. It was lonely at times. But he found support through CMM executive directors Lewis and Rajan; Asian ministry support staff; all the Asian pastors who were working hard; ELCA Asian colleagues; and Yee, Wong's former professor at PLTS. Yee had extensive experience in LCA churchwide Asian ministry and had chaired the CMM design committee.

To strengthen Asian ministries, Wong teamed up with ELCA staff to brainstorm projects. James Y. K. Moy,[51] Division for Ministry, was skilled at grant-writing. They collaborated on funding for continuing education, translating materials, and convening seminarians of color for support and gaining firsthand information about the ELCA. Kitahata led focus groups with Chinese, Japanese, and Southeast Asian leaders. Her reports provided detailed input for ministry planning, evaluation, and development of the CMM Asian ministries program. With James Capers, Division for Congregational Life, Wong and Capers had access to the Cooperative Parish Projects Committee, bringing together the ELCA and the LC-MS to develop Asian-specific evangelism resources.

Organizing ethnic-specific peer continuing education gatherings was a key strategy. As mentioned in the section about the "surrogate bishop and lay Asians," these meetings were paramount for the health, growth, and well-being of Asian leaders, both lay and clergy. They learned best through networking with peers and discussing what did and didn't work for ministry.

Years later, Wong retrospectively found himself echoing what Lewis maintained. According to Tom Holmes, Wong stated that:

> his job was frustrating; because on the one hand the ELCA from its inception in 1988 stated that one of its primary goals was to increase its minority membership to 10% in ten years, but on the other hand placed much of the responsibility for reaching that goal in a commission that had very

---

[50] For biography, see Yee and Rajashekar, pp. 287-289.
[51] For biography, see Yee and Rajashekar, pp. 311-314.

> low funding. The problem…was that the ELCA presented lofty language about becoming a multicultural church but basically did not put its money where its mouth was. [52]

Despite these barriers, Wong had added 16 Asian ministries to the ELCA by the time he returned to parish ministry in 1996. The ELCA now had 47 Asian congregations and ministries. And instead of dealing with structural matters, the next Asian ministries director could devote his time more fully to Asian ministry growth.

Generation III: Reaching for the Horizon (1997-2020)

On March 1, 1997, Pongsak Limthongviratn[53] succeeded Wong as the director for Asian ministries. Within months, his title was changed to director for Asian and Pacific Islander ministries, signifying the potential expansion into yet another area of ministry. Rajan, former executive director of CMM, commented to Yee that even before Limthongviratn became the director, the ELCA

> realized we were operating on an unrealistic churchwide budget. To meet the budgetary shortfall, we were forced to reposition this churchwide organization. This meant revising our churchwide purpose statements, budget reallocation and budget reduction, eliminating departments or merging departments, and rightsizing the staff. The Commission for Multicultural Ministries was no exception. The CMM responded responsibly. [54]

Wong also observed, "the situation in the ELCA headquarters which Pongsak walked into was basically being handed an underfunded mandate."[55]

Limthongviratn grew up in Southeast Asia, received his initial theological education there, and did graduate work in East Asia and the US. He had "an excellent and deeply visionary concept of the nature and function of ministry in Asian/Asian American settings."[56] But he soon encountered the problems that his predecessor faced, plus a few of his own. According to his biographer, Tom Holmes, Limthongviratn echoed Wong in maintaining that "[T]he problem… was that the mandate given to the Commission on [for] Multicultural Ministries had neither the means nor the leverage to hold the feet [of] the leadership at Higgins Road."[57]

Therefore, tensions soon "arose over how to plan new ethnic congregations in the ELCA. Pongsak came into disagreement with some synodical mission directors regarding the model for starting new congregations."[58]

---

[52] Tom Holmes, *Pongsak: Advocate for Asian Ministries* (Bangkok: Luther Seminary in Thailand, 2015), p. 85. [Hereafter cited as Holmes.]

[53] For biography, see Holmes; Yee and Rajashekar, pp. 296-300.

[54] Rajan, dated August 16, 2020.

[55] Holmes, p. 85.

[56] Holmes, p. 11.

[57] Holmes, p. 95. [The ELCA headquarters is located at Higgins Road.]

[58] Holmes, p. 96.

The model used by the then Division for Outreach (DO) in the early days was to fully fund mission developer pastors and resource them fully at least for the first three years. Each year thereafter funding would decrease in increments until it would dry up entirely in five to eight years, when the new congregation would be expected to be organized. It would still be eligible for partnership support for another three to five years until it becomes self-supporting. The model had worked fairly well with new starts in middle-class white communities. [59]

Limthongviratn insisted that this model was not appropriate for Asians. He argued that Asian pastors and developers should be paid below synodical guidelines and supported for a more extended time because it took much longer for Asian congregations to develop. He further contended that "the national church needs to let them [Asians] design their own process because they understand how their culture and community works, even if it doesn't fit neatly into the white American model."[60]

Ruben Duran, the DO director for new congregations, and Sherman Hicks, director for CMM, agreed with Limthongviratn. Hicks stated, "when you talk about some of the ethnic-specific congregations, they're neither European nor American middle-class. When you use a European model, here's all this money upfront, and you have to be self-supporting in three years. That model does not work in some of the ethnic-specific communities, especially if they're not middle class."[61] But not everyone agreed as Duran highlighted through a Seattle situation as a case in point. While the Chinese pastor agreed to receive a salary packet below synodical guidelines for a more extended support period, a White pastor "went straight to the bishop and protested, thinking that he was working for justice and being an advocate for the Chinese pastor."[62]

Even though Duran supported Limthongviratn's position that "the issue has to be framed in context," he acknowledged "that many in the ELCA and even some in the Asian community are concerned about exploiting Asian church workers by not paying them according to North American standard, and thereby depriving them of an adequate pension when they retire."[63]

Two other issues Limthongviratn faced were the lack of pastors who could speak Asian languages and the absence of resources for ministry. To remedy the situation, "[O]utsmarting the *system* was becoming an important part of Pongsak's job description."[64] How did he outsmart the system? Connections, bypassing, and creativity seem to be the answer, as the following stories reveal.

---

[59] Holmes, p. 96.
[60] Holmes, p. 96.
[61] Holmes, p. 100.
[62] Holmes, p. 98.
[63] Holmes, p. 99.
[64] Holmes, p. 92.

National Strategy Plans for Asians and Pacific Islanders

When Limthongviratn joined the CMM staff, the Native American and Alaskan Indian community was the one with a ministry strategy. He immediately made a connection between that community with his own. Guided by his supervisor, Rajan, Limthongviratn convened a group of Asian pastors and leaders to develop the first draft of strategic plans for the Asian and Pacific Islander communities.

Next, to connect the strategy with the grassroots communities, he solicited feedback from about 100 Asian leaders who gathered for an event in the spring of 2001. After formal approval by the leaders, it was presented to the ELCA Churchwide Assembly later the same year. The Assembly approved the plan.

The plan focused on the practical dimensions of ministry rather than on the theological or the theoretical. It had seven directives: congregational development, membership, leadership development, resource development, social ministry, stewardship, and Asian homeland mission work. It served as a guide for Asian and Pacific Islander ministries until 2016 when the AAPI-ELCA biennial assembly approved an updated strategic plan.

The Asian Lutheran International Conference

The Asian Lutheran International Conference (ALIC) began to take shape in 1997 and had its first biennial conference in Hong Kong four years later.[65] Through the ALIC, Limthongviratn reconnected with many churches and leaders in Asia to expand ministries in the US. For example, he was able to connect the Indonesian missions of the Huria Kristen Batak Protestan Church in the US with the ELCA. He expanded the South Asian and Filipino ministries as well.

Resources for Ministry

Saplings will not grow without being watered and nurtured. Similarly, pastors and ministries need culturally appropriate resources in their Asian languages to help them grow and develop their theologies and ministries. Like his predecessors, Limthongviratn was well aware of the need. But he faced technical and marketing issues with the ELCA's in-house publisher, Augsburg Fortress. The Asian community could easily resolve the technical problems of presenting camera-ready formats for printing. However, the marketing issue was insurmountable. The Asian and Pacific Islander community was too small for Augsburg Fortress; any titles published could become losing propositions.

Limthongviratn, therefore, bypassed the publisher and connected with a printing company that he knew in Thailand to meet the community's need for resources. This move allowed him to stretch his limited budget since the printing costs are lower in Bangkok. He also brought 200 pounds of printed materials back to the US from Thailand every time he traveled there, saving transportation costs.

---

[65] For details, see essay in Part IV in this volume.

Center for Chinese Ministry

When the ELCA's predecessor bodies first began ministry with Asian people, they focused on the Japanese. At best, their success was minimal. The focus started to shift with the arrival in Southern California of Wilson Wu, a Lutheran theologically trained in Hong Kong. Chinese ministry gradually became the largest group. Whether it was Chinese ethnocentrism or the desire for self-determination, the leaders of this group in 1997 asked the DO to assign a Chinese staff member to work with them. The DO could not fulfill their request due to budgetary constraints. Moreover, this request was potentially divisive. Historically, the ELCA had regarded the Chinese as a part of the Asian community.

Limthongviratn was undeterred by the rejection. In consultation with the Chinese leaders, he and Rajan decided to organize the Chinese Ministry Center in 2000. To support the center and compensate the director, Limthongviratn creatively persuaded several units of the ELCA to commit a total of $100,000 over three years.

The first director was David Chen,[66] a well-respected pastor among the Chinese Lutherans. Chen retired in 2004 and returned to Taiwan to pursue other interests. The second director, Thomas Chen,[67] served faithfully for 14 years before retiring.

During Thomas Chen's tenure, the ELCA approved its "Human Sexuality: Gift and Trust" statement, causing great consternation among some Asian members and congregations. They interpreted the scriptures differently and did not share the ELCA's core moral values in this regard. As a result, five Chinese congregations left the church, and five others are no longer in close contact with their synods. Limthongviratn's stance was to remain in sincere friendship with them.

No one wanted to succeed the directorship until, at Limthongviratn's urging, David Chen returned. In Chen's own words, "[W]hen Pongsak Limthongviratn asks, I cannot say no."

Limthongviratn worked hand-in-hand with the directors in nurturing and expanding Chinese ministry. And another aspect of the center's activity was the Annual Chinese Pastors' Gathering. The pastors and lay leaders came together for fellowship, continuing education, and spiritual formation.

Asian Leadership Conference

Limthongviratn, like his predecessors, recognized the importance of cultivating leadership in the community. But the ELCA budget constraints prevented him from bringing Asian leaders together for continuing education, fellowship, and networking. To achieve his goal, he bypassed the ELCA by writing grant proposals to Lutheran Brotherhood (now Thrivent), a fraternal organization. From 1997 to 2005, he successfully raised enough grant money to convene about 100 leaders for an

---

[66] For biography, see Yee and Rajashekar, pp. 242-244.
[67] For biography, see Yee and Rajashekar, pp. 244-245.

annual Asian Leadership Conference. However, beginning in 2006, such funding was no longer available, forcing him to discontinue the annual gathering.

Communications, E-letter, and Website

The Evangelical Lutheran Church in America's Asian leaders during generations I and II recognized the importance of communications as a vital link between the community and themselves. Therefore, in those decades before digital technology was widespread, they distributed printed newsletters.

In 1985, the era of generation I, leaders Rajan, Kwang Ja Yu, and Lily R. Wu[68] produced Asian Lutherans in North America (ALINA). It was a joint newsletter from TALC and LCA caucuses of Asian Lutherans in North America.

From 1995 to 1996, the era of generation II, the CMM Asian ministries program supported the editing and production of a Chinese-language Lutheran newsletter in response to the expressed needs of immigrant Chinese pastors and their ministries.

However, the main churchwide outlets for Asian community news and stories at this time included the CMM "Living Waters" newspaper and the large format "ELCA Today" produced by the Commission for Communication for the ELCA Churchwide Assembly in 1989. The other ethnic communities affiliated with CMM also contributed to these multicultural publications.

Limthongviratn was more fortunate in that he could communicate through digital technology. In collaboration with AAPI-ELCA leadership, his office established an e-letter called "Bridge," issued monthly from 2006 to 2017. Lily R. Wu, Maria Gracia Sijera-Grant, and Andrew Yee served as members of the editorial committee. Since 2018 the monthly publication has been transformed into a quarterly communication link. And a website — AsianLutherans.com — was created to tell about community activity and resources and the biennial ALIC gathering.

Asian Church Planting Team

In addition to his clear theological vision on the nature and function of ministry, Limthongviratn also had a passion for church planting. In his wisdom, involving the Asian community in the planning of new ministries was very important. He organized an Asian Church Planting Team with Korean, Chinese, Japanese, South Asian, and Indonesian members, with himself representing the Lao and Thai communities. The team collaborated with the New Start Team of the ELCA and deployed directors for evangelical mission. He also worked closely with both the Chicago-based staff and deployed directors.

As a result of his efforts, the ELCA identified 80 sites and new missions began to flourish. In his 2008 report to the AAPI-ELCA assembly, he could count 125 Asian congregations and ministries, an increase of 78 since he assumed the directorship. A year later the ELCA

---

[68] For biography, see Yee and Rajashekar, pp. 409-411.

Churchwide Assembly approved the "Human Sexuality: Gift and Trust" statement, causing many Asian congregations to leave the institution. As of 2020, the number of Asian congregations and ministries stood at 86.

Sustainable Ministry and Leadership

As we previously stated, Limthongviratn disagreed with the ELCA model for starting new ministries. He had reservations about clergy salary packets and the lack of long-term support. In his view, sustainable ministry and leadership required a different approach to mission and ministry. As with all ELCA ethnic ministries, self-sustainability was a decisive factor as to a ministry's viability.

In the search for sustainability, Limthongviratn advocated a contextual model for Asian pastors' salary packets while being well aware of synodical guidelines for them. He publicly spoke against the ELCA policy because it was not working. For this, he was both affirmed and criticized. He also advocated bi-vocational ministry, constantly reminding Asian colleagues to be prepared for rainy days when support would no longer be available.

In 2019, he teamed up with a number of West Coast directors for evangelical mission to undergird bi-vocational leadership for ministry. They included Teresita Clemente Valeriano,[69] an assistant to the bishop of the Sierra Pacific Synod, and Moses Penumaka, who directs the Theological Education for Emerging Ministries program at PLTS. The outcome was an Asian Lay Evangelist Project to prepare laypersons to be non-stipendiary evangelists for new starts and existing congregations. Domestic Mission and the five West Coast synods provided funding for this project. After completion of the training, participants will receive a certificate from the seminary and their participating synods. This project began in the fall of 2020. Currently (2020), there are 30 Asian congregations and ministries served by bi-vocational persons.

Leadership: Women, Young Adults and Leaders with Non-Lutheran Backgrounds

In his report to the 1998 AAPI-ELCA assembly, Limthongviratn noted that the ELCA had added about 100 newly-ordained Asian pastors to the clergy roster. However, this leadership increase came with blessings and challenges, as his predecessors also knew. One out of every two new leaders came from either non-ELCA or non-Lutheran backgrounds. Theologically conservative but with great evangelical zeal, they brought excitement to the Asian community. The inevitable challenge was how to connect them to the ELCA tradition, with its progressive core values. There is no evidence showing how Limthongviratn responded to this challenge, other than convening the pastors for continuing education, fellowship, and spiritual formation when funding was available.

Limthongviratn has been proactive on women and young adult leadership issues. As a result, 24% of Asian Lutheran clergy today are women, and young adults are more active in

---

[69] For biography, see Yee and Rajashekar, pp.394-396.

significant community roles as well.

To support leadership development, the AAPI-ELCA executive committee administers two scholarship funds: the longstanding Eiichi Matsushita Scholarship Fund and the newly-established Pongsak and Monta Limthongviratn Scholarship Fund,[70] established by Limthongviratn and his wife, Monta. The latter is designated to assist women seminarians.

Asian Ministry Endowment Fund

It had long been Limthongviratn's cherished desire to establish an endowment fund to support activities such as AAPI-ELCA assemblies and ALIC gatherings. The opportunity arose when the Chinese Christian Church in Chicago disbanded in 2006, sold its building, and donated $15,000 to Asian ministries from the sale. The AAPI-ELCA's leaders recommended the establishment of an Asian Ministry Endowment Fund. Limthongviratn appointed a fundraising committee to expand the endowment, such that the balance of the fund grew to $32,000 by 2020.

Conclusion

This second essay in Part I has told the story of early Lutheran denominational attempts in Asian ministries. We have also described how three generations of Asian leaders and their colleagues partnered with the denominations to lead the work forward. Coming up next: Part II, a pictorial overview on the stream of witness flowing today, through the fruitful labor of congregational and ministry leaders. These selected profiles will show how leaders tailored their ministries to meet needs, plant seeds, and flourish.

Edmond Yee, William E. Wong, Pongsak Limthongviratn, and Lily R. Wu

---

[70] For details, see Yee, 129-131.

PART II

Congregations and Unique Ministries

II | Congregations and Unique Ministries

Part I covered how our ministries began, and what the LCA person responsible for Asian ministries and the ELCA Directors of Asian and Pacific Islander Ministries faced. Let's soar high now to see the depth and breadth of our congregational ministries. You will see how Asian Lutherans sought to touch the lives of others with God's good news of healing and transformation.

Bless! Thy Servants' Fruitful Efforts: Congregational Ministries

Your Servants, in partnership with their denominations, have succeeded in establishing Asian Lutheran ministries in the US. Today there are 86 Asian specific congregations and ministries in the Evangelical Lutheran Church in America. How have these ethnic ministries been helped or hindered by Asian, Asian American cultures, religions, histories and American racism? The responses from the congregations/ministries below may provide some answers to this question.

Cambodian

**Christ Lutheran Church on
Capitol Hill Cambodian Ministry**
105 University Ave. W.
St. Paul, MN 55103
Phone No.: 651-222-3619
Year Started/Organized: 1981
Members/Worshipers: 30
Pastor(s): Thaly Cavanaugh**
       (Lay Minister)

Setting of Congregation/Ministry:

St. Paul, MN is home to 308,096 persons (US Census estimate 2019). The three largest ethnic groups are White (56.7%), Asian (18.4%), and Black (16%). In the Twin Cities (St. Paul and Minneapolis) and the vicinity, about 80,000 of the residents are Hmong, and 25% of the Twin Cities Hmong are Christians. The ministry is located in a diverse section of St. Paul, including 15,000 Cambodians as well as Hmong, Lao and Vietnamese.

Unique Ministries:

    1. Cambodian Language:

        The Khmer language features prominently in worship, including scripture readings and the Lord's Prayer in Khmer.

    2. Cambodian Music:

        A musical ensemble plays traditional instruments and music for worship. We also have a choir that sings in Khmer.

    3. Cambodian Egg Roll Fundraiser:

        A Cambodian egg roll sale is a longtime fundraiser for our summer youth program.

Historical and Religio-cultural Impacts:

The Vietnam War, Cambodian culture and language, refugee resettlement experience in the US.

Kristofer Coffman

Cambodian

United Asian Evangelical Lutheran Church

1753 G Ave.

Dakota City, NE 68731

Phone No.: 402-987-3582

Year Started/Organized: 2008

Members/Worshipers: 30

Pastor(s): Soriya Roeun

Setting of Congregation/Ministry:

Dakota City in northeast Nebraska had 1,919 residents in the 2010 Census. Of this total, 64.41% were White, 20.21% Hispanic, and 1.92% Asian. Estimates in 2019 showed 1,859 residents, a population decrease of 3%. United Asian Lutheran emerged from the Asian ministry of Salem Lutheran Church. It now serves Lao, Cambodian, and Thai families in Dakota City and South Sioux City, NE, and Sioux City, IA.

Unique Ministries:

　1. Multilingual Worship:

　　Worship services are in English and are translated into Lao, Cambodian, and Thai as needed.

　2. "Come, See and Eat" Summer Outreach Event:

　　This unique outreach event includes worship, a potluck meal, and fellowship. We intentionally invite non-Christian community members.

　3. Partnership Projects for Service and Language Training:

　　We partner with Nebraska Synod and Salem Lutheran Church for the annual "Helping Hands" service day to prepare school backpacks, blankets, and quilts for distribution. We also offer English as a Second Language classes with Salem volunteers.

Historical and Religio-cultural Impacts:

Southeast Asian cultures; refugee experiences; intergenerational challenges.

Lily R.Wu

Chinese

Bethel Chinese Lutheran Church

6553 40th Ave. N.E.

Seattle, WA 98115

Phone No.:206-524-7631

Year Started/Organized: 1978

Members/Worshipers: 60

Pastor(s): Isaiah Chow

(Emeritus Pastor)

Wei Zhao**

(Lay Minister)

Setting of Congregation/Ministry:

Seattle is the largest city in the Pacific Northwest and one of the fastest-growing in the US. In 2010, within a total population of 608,660, Asians comprised 13.8%, of whom 4.1% were Chinese. By 2018 Seattle's population grew 22.4% to 774,955. This port city of culture and education attracts many Chinese families. Large industry and technology companies such as Amazon and Microsoft are major employers. Bethel Church is about seven miles north of Downtown Seattle and two miles north of the University of Washington.

Unique Ministries:

1. Catechism and Discipleship Training:

   We have classes on Luther's Small Catechism for our seeker friends. We also have classes for members on evangelism. We aim to develop disciples who will multiply the kingdom.

2. Faith, Hope, and Love Fellowship:

   This group addresses real-world issues so participants can apply God's Word to everyday life.

3. Brothers and Sisters Fellowships:

   We have men's and women's ministries that emphasize prayer and encouragement.

Historical and Religio-cultural Impacts:

Christianity; commitment to provide spiritual and pastoral care.

Wei Zhao

Christ Lutheran Church

417 N. Garfield Ave.

Monterey Park, CA 91754

Phone No.: 626-573-2050

Year Started/Organized: 1981

Members/Worshipers: 110

Pastor(s): Daniel Zhang**

      (Lay Minister)

Setting of Congregation/Ministry:

Monterey Park is a city of immigrants that sits within the greater Los Angeles Area, CA. According to 2019 population estimates, it has 59,669 residents, of whom Asians make up 66.5%. Fifty five percent of its residents are foreign-born. Monterey Park's main characteristics are cultural diversity, a highly mobile population, and varying education levels.

Unique Ministries:

    1. Discipleship Training System:

        In preparation for baptism and Christian life, this four-step training includes sessions on the gospel, catechism, new Christian life, and discipleship.

    2. English as a Second Language (ESL) Class:

        We offer ESL classes to enable Chinese speakers to adapt to American life.

    3. Prayer and Evangelism:

        We gather for prayer and fasting on the first Saturday of every month. We also hold a Gospel Lunch program for newcomers.

Historical and Religio-cultural Impacts:

English Language and Chinese Language; American and Chinese cultures; immigration-related needs.

Daniel Zhang

Chinese

Federal Way Chinese Fellowship
c/o 2415 S. 320th St.
Federal Way, WA 98003
Phone No.: 425-985-8108
Year Started/Organized: 2012
Members/Worshipers: 50
Pastor(s): J. (Rowena) Wang

Setting of Congregation/Ministry:

In King County, WA, Federal Way is part of the burgeoning Seattle metropolitan area. Residents are well-educated, with a median age in the mid-thirties. In 2010, the city had a population of 89,306 (2010 US Census). By 2018, the population jumped to 97,044, an increase of 8.7% (US Census). According to 2010 census data, 14.2% were Asian, mostly Korean and Chinese, with many Chinese-speaking households and, increasingly, young couples with children.

Unique Ministries:

1. Children's Ministry:

> We hold classes on traditional Chinese paper cutting and have a Chinese language school.

2. New Immigrant Service:

> We assist newcomers with information on life in the US and help with daily necessities.

3. Pulpit Exchange and Fellowship.*

> As a clergy couple serving two different ministries, we conduct worship services two Sundays a month at each other's church. Members of the two ministries also share in fellowship exchange.

Historical and Religio-cultural Impacts:

Chinese traditional culture and language; needs of immigrants.

J. (Rowena) Wang

[*J. (Rowena) Wang and her husband, Michael Wang, are mission developers of two ministries belonging to two synods, one in Federal Way and one in South King County—Grace Chinese Lutheran Church of South Lake County, where Rowena also served for a couple of years.]

Glory Lutheran Church

2900 W. Carson St.

Torrance, CA 90503

Phone No.: 310-320-9923

Year Started/Organized: 2009

Members/Worshipers: 120

Pastor(s): Newman Chiu

Setting of Congregation/Ministry:

Torrance is a multicultural, multiracial city in the South Bay region of Los Angeles County. The city has the lowest crime rate in the county and is home to more Japanese Americans than anywhere in the US except Honolulu, HI. The Chinese population (5,951 as of 2015) is small relative to the total population (145,182 as of 2018 est.). However, Glory's specialty is reaching out to Chinese students from mainland China, Hong Kong, and Taiwan who attend major universities and community colleges in the area.

Unique Ministries:

1. Mandarin-speaking Worship and Community:

   Young adults are two-thirds of the congregation's membership.

2. Zion Fellowship (Campus Ministry):

   On the University of Southern California campus, which has 5,800 Chinese students, our fellowship group has shared the gospel with more than 3,500 and baptized 220.

3. Next Generation Evangelist Training:

   This program teaches students to start evangelically oriented gatherings. As a result of these trainings, several parents visiting their children from mainland China have requested baptism.

Historical and Religio-cultural Impacts:

Mandarin Chinese dialect and culture; atheism; being raised in a Communist society.

Newman Chiu

Chinese

**Good Neighbor Chinese
Lutheran Church**
308 W. Squantum St.
Quincy, MA 02171
Phone No.: 617-653-3693
Year Started/Organized: 2012
Members/Worshipers: 15
Pastor (s): Ryan Lun

Setting of Congregation/Ministry:

Quincy is a college town with the
largest Asian population in Metropolitan Boston. Of North Quincy's total population of 94,470 in 2019, an estimated 31.2% are Asian, mostly from different regions and dialects in China. Quincy's median age is just under 40, 44.7% of residents hold BA's or higher degrees, and 32.5% are foreign-born. While there are several Chinese evangelical or megachurches in the area, Good Neighbor is the first Cantonese-speaking ministry in the New England Synod.

Unique Ministries:

1. English as a Second Language Bible Study:

   Native speakers help new Chinese immigrants build vocabulary, practice conversation, and develop their reading ability while we study the Bible.

2. Youth Good Neighbor Program:

   Volunteers serve meals at a homeless shelter and help at a food pantry.

3. Mobile Phone Class for Seniors:

   We offer seniors basic lessons on mobile phones and the internet, enabling them to stay connected to family and the next generation.

Historical and Religio-cultural Impacts:

English language; Chinese dialects, needs of immigrants, youth, and seniors.

Ryan Lun

Grace Chinese Lutheran Church

43-33 91 Pl.

Elmhurst, NY 11373

Phone No.: 718-760-4132

Year Started/Organized: 1993

Members/Worshipers: 120

Pastor(s): Abraham Lu

Chinese

Setting of Congregation/Ministry:

With a population of 88,427, Elmhurst is home to one of New York City's nine Chinatowns. 44% of Elmhurst residents are Asian, 35.7% Hispanic, and 10% Caucasian. 27% of the population lives in poverty. The more than 120 languages and dialects spoken in downtown Elmhurst, where our church sits, reflects the city's diversity.

Unique Ministries:

1. Weekday Inner Life Program:

   We help Chinese immigrants to cope with feelings of uncertainty, frustration, and helplessness by fostering their confidence and spiritual strength in a group setting.

2. Occasional Healing Services:

   We offer worship with prayer and song to root out persistent fears and hurt and seek God's healing power.

Historical and Religio-cultural Impacts:

New and diverse environments; Asian cultures; and the minister's insightful understanding.

Abraham Lu

**Grace Chinese Lutheran Church
of South King County**
1700 Edmonds Ave., N.E.
Renton, WA 90856
Phone No.: 206-409-3389
Year Started/Organized: 2006
Members/Worshipers: 70/40
Pastor(s): Michael Wang

Setting of Congregation/Ministry:

Renton is a fast-growing city in the State of Washington. The population grew from 50,052 in 2000, to 90,927 in 2010, an 81.7% increase. Of the 2010 total, 21.2% were Asian, of whom the majority is Chinese. Renton is also the headquarters of several big companies, with Boeing being the biggest employers. Many congregation members work for these companies, while others are in business, such as restaurants, motels, and markets.

Unique Ministries:

1. Support for Inter-Racial Families:

We provide an arena for inter-racial (Chinese and White) families to celebrate community life, such as the Chinese Spring Festival and the Mid-Autumn Festival, Thanksgiving, and Christmas.

2. Focus on Abundance:

We emphasize God's generosity by providing abundant food and traditional delicacies on festive occasions.

[*Note: Pastor Wang worked at various restaurants before becoming a minister.]

Historical and Religio-cultural Impacts:

Chinese traditional culture; American secular and religious traditions.

Michael Wang

**Heavenly Peace
Lutheran Fellowship**

5415 Powell Blvd.

Portland, OR 97206

Phone No.: 503-860-3388

Year Started/Organized: 2004

Members/Worshipers: 70

Pastor(s): Andrew Yong

Setting of Congregation/Ministry:

Portland is the sixth-largest city on the West Coast, with a population of 583,776 in 2010. Of these persons, 76.1% were White, 9.4% Hispanic, 7.1% Asian, 6.3% Black, and 1.0% Native American. In 2019 the population had grown to an estimated 654,174. During WWII, Portland was an "assembly center" from which the US Government dispatched more than 3,000 people of Japanese ancestry, including US citizens, to different internment camps across the US. In the 1990s, the high-tech industry with companies like Intel began to emerge. After 2000 the growth became significant. Today Portland is one of the cultural centers of the West Coast.

Unique Ministries:

1. Chinese Language School:

   We offer Saturday Chinese language classes for children (K-12).

2. Immigrant Outreach:

   We offer English as a Second Language classes to adult newcomers from mainland China, Hong Kong, and Taiwan.

3. Cultural Activities:

   We are an arena for cultural activities, including Cantonese opera, Chinese folk dance, and Taiji exercise.

Historical and Religio-cultural Impacts:

Chinese culture and language; English language training.

Andrew Yong

Chinese

Joy Fellowship Chinese Outreach
9185 Lexington Ave. N.E.
Circle Pines, MN 55014
Phone No.: 763-784-1971
Year Started/Organized: 2014
Members/Worshipers: 32
Pastor(s): Shen Lin
(Mission Developer)

Setting of Congregation/Ministry:

Circle Pine is a suburb of the Twin Cities, with a population of 4,918 according to the 2010 US Census. 3.4% were Asian. The city is known for its relaxed ambiance. Joy Fellowship is an outreach to Chinese Christians in the northern St. Paul suburbs, where 5,000 Chinese Americans live. It is an outreach of Minnesota Faith Chinese Lutheran Church that meets at Our Savior's Lutheran Church.

Unique Ministries:

1. Evangelical Outreach:

   Each week we share gospel stories with our seeker friends and offer daily bilingual devotions with Christians. We have a 12-member team trained for community outreach. We focus on Jesus as "friend" and encourage the identification and use of spiritual gifts.

2. Food Ministry:

   Table fellowship is central to our ministry. We always have a potluck and share food at our regular gatherings. We prepare more elaborate meals on Chinese Festival occasions.

3. Chinese Choir and Praise Dance Team.

   Our Chinese choir and praise dance team regularly performs at community and Evangelical Lutheran Church in America congregational events.

Historical and Religio-cultural impacts:

Chinese culture; relations between the US and China; stricter immigration policy on educated young professionals; social turmoil in the Twin Cities, and high unemployment rate.

Shen Lin

Kalam Christian Church

140 E. Broadway Ave.

Roslyn, NY 11576

Phone No.: 929-525-2652

Year Started/Organized: 2001

Members/Worshipers: 100

Pastor(s): Chiung Hao Wu* (Moses)

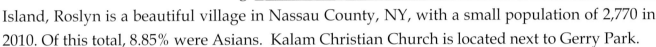

Setting of Congregation/Ministry:

Situated on the North Shore of Long Island, Roslyn is a beautiful village in Nassau County, NY, with a small population of 2,770 in 2010. Of this total, 8.85% were Asians. Kalam Christian Church is located next to Gerry Park.

Unique Ministries:

1. Chinese and English Worship:

   We offer worship services in two Chinese dialects, Mandarin and Min, and provide an English language service for youth.

2. Weekday Prayer and Bible Studies:

   We hold daily prayer meetings. On Wednesdays, Thursdays, and Fridays, we have Bible studies.

3. Art Class:

   On Saturdays (temporarily suspended due to Covid-19).

Historical and Religio-cultural Impacts:

Chinese dialects; immigrant experience in the US; English language and Christianity.

Chiung Hao Wu

Chinese

Ministry to International Students and Scholars
A synodically authorized worshiping community
University of Washington, Seattle, WA
5519 Phinney Ave. N.
Seattle, WA 98103
Phone No.: 206-458-1555
Year Started/Organized: 2009
Participants: 30-50
Pastor(s): Joseph H. Li

Setting of Congregation/Ministry:

Five miles north of downtown Seattle, the University of Washington is the largest in the Northwest, with more than 90,000 students. It is also one of the largest research universities in the US, drawing students and scholars worldwide, including visiting scholars from China. The "Ministry to Chinese Students and Scholars" began in 2009. In 2019, with University Presbyterian Church's (UPC) "Global Friends" program, we expanded to become "Ministry to International Students and Scholars."

Unique Ministries:

1. Hospitality:

   We provide space for weekly gatherings and offer housing assistance and other practical support.

2. Language and Cultural Encouragement:

   We offer English language learning opportunities and provide off-campus excursions so students can experience more of the US.

3. Christian Education:

   Bible studies are opportunities to share the Christian faith.

Historical and Religio-Cultural Impacts:

US culture and society; English language; Christianity and the UPC platform.

Joseph H. Li

Minnesota Faith Chinese Lutheran Church

145 McCarrons Blvd. N.

Roseville, MN 55113

Phone No.: 651-214-8601

Year Started/Organized: 2001

Members/Worshipers: 90

Pastor(s): Vacant

Setting of Congregation/Ministry:

Roseville, MN, a suburb of Minneapolis and St. Paul, boasted 33,660 residents in 2010. By 2019, Roseville's population grew to 36,347, an increase of 8.3%. The majority of Roseville residents are White (81.3% in 2010), with Asians comprising the second largest group (7.3% in 2010). There are currently 18,900 Chinese immigrants, including 7,000 students, visiting scholars, and their families, living in the Twin Cities. Minnesota Faith is the only Lutheran Chinese Church in MN.

Unique Ministries:

1. Outreach Programs:

> We offer retreats, conferences, family gatherings, special celebrations, individualized faith sharing, fellowship meals, visitations, and support for women and senior citizens. Our activities have extended to other US states and even China.

2. Bible Studies:

> We offer daily bilingual chapter-by-chapter Bible study. On Fridays, we have a more comprehensive Bible course.

3. Mission and Music Partnerships:

> We collaborate with other St. Paul Synod congregations as follows: combined services, pulpit exchanges, and community garden work. Our Chinese choir and praise dance team regularly performs at community and Evangelical Lutheran Church in America congregational events.

Historical, Religio-cultural Impacts:

Relations between US and China; US immigration policy; Twin Cities social injustice protests and riots; economic recession with high unemployment rate.

Shen Lin

Chinese

St. Jacobi Evangelical Lutheran Church Chinese Ministry
5406 Fourth Ave.
Brooklyn, NY 11220
Phone No.: 718-439-8978
Year Started/Organized: 2018
Members/Worshipers: 30
Pastor(s): Mary Chang
          (Stated Supply Pastor)

Setting of Congregation/Ministry:

Sunset Park in Brooklyn, NY is an urban area where 152,700 people live. More than one-third are Asian in this borough's first and fastest-growing Chinatown. Cantonese families came in the 1980s, Fuzhou immigrants in the 2000s, and Mandarin-speaking newcomers since 2009. One of every two persons in Sunset Park is immigrant: 42% from China, 23% Central American, and 10% Caribbean. Their average age is 34, and 25% are under age 19. Poverty, affordable housing and school overcrowding are problems. St Jacobi's Chinese outreach focuses on young Mandarin-speaking parents.

Unique Ministries:

    1. Diakonia Studies:

        St. Jacobi offers a two-year program for spiritual formation and theological education.

    2. Youth Program:

        This weekly program includes fellowship and meals together.

    3. Saved-By-Grace Classes and Baptisms:

        This program introduces Lutheran teachings and practices to adults and young persons, and celebrates their baptisms.

Historical and Religio-cultural Impacts:

Chinese immigrant culture; English language; Christian faith and education.

Lily R. Wu

Taiwanese Lutheran Church

10075 Azuaga St.

San Diego, CA 92129

Phone No.: 858-538-8860

Year Started/Organized: 1980

 Members/Worshipers: 200

Pastor(s): Paul Liu*

           Albert Lin*

Setting of Congregation/Ministry:

San Diego, the second-largest city in California, is a diverse urban area 20 miles north of the Mexican border. Its colleges and universities attract students from around the world. Its tourist spots such as San Diego Zoo and Sea World are also popular. Military, aerospace, and biotech industries are important economic drivers.

Unique Ministries:

    1. Outreach to College and University Students:

        New arrivals from Taiwan and China are met at the airport and provided with temporary housing and help navigating US culture.

    2. Intercultural Exchange Summer Program:

        The church hosts young people from Taiwan for a week, then sends young people from the US to Taiwan for their counterpart experience.

Historical and Religio-cultural Impacts:

Internal linguistic realities within the parish; Asian and American cultural diversity.

Paul Liu

Chinese

**Trinity Lutheran Church
Chinese Ministry**

6868 San Gabriel Blvd.

San Gabriel, CA 91775

Phone No.: 425-219-9506

Year Started/Organized: 2019

Members/Worshipers: 80

Pastor(s): Changan (John) Yu

Setting of Congregation/Ministry:

San Gabriel, 10 miles northeast of Los Angeles, is a four-square-mile city of 40,000+ residents, median age 42. Asians are the largest ethnic group (60%), followed by Hispanics (26%) and Caucasians (12%). Trinity Lutheran Church Chinese Ministry began at Bethlehem Lutheran Church, Temple City, CA, in 2017, and moved to Trinity in San Gabriel in 2019. It is in the process of merging with Trinity.

Unique Ministries:

1. Christian Social Service and Community Choir:

> We offer caring group support through community partners for seniors, the disabled, post-disaster counseling, family health education, and leadership development. Members from various churches sing for Sunday worship, senior housing and community events.

2. Table Tennis Ministry and Joy Fellowship:

> Professional *ping-pong* coaches help church and community members to learn and enhance their game. Fellowship circles share interests in cooking, dancing, calligraphy, art, health care, and more, with members of other churches invited to join in.

3. Creative Liturgical Worship:

> Spring Festival celebration using our music compositions and creative ideas to embody and express God's grace in Chinese culture.

Historical and Religio-cultural Impacts:

Liturgical tradition and music; Chinese language and musical culture.

Changan (John) Yu

True Light Lutheran Christian Church

1220 E. Irving Park Rd.

Streamwood, IL 60107

Phone No.: 630-474-6005

Year Started/Organized: 1996

Members/Worshipers: 100

Pastor(s): Lit Inn Wu, Jenny Wu

Setting of Congregation/Ministry:

Streamwood is a northwest suburb of Chicago. With Bartlett and Hanover Park, it is one of three communities in the "tri-village" area. The 2010 census recorded a total of 39,358 residents in Streamwood, the largest racial-ethnic populations being White (37.8%), Hispanic (28.2%), and Asian (15%). Initially a ministry with Mandarin-speaking people, True Light is achieving an intergenerational and multicultural identity.

Unique Ministries:

1. Generational Harmony Ministry:

> We intentionally provide programs and opportunities that encourage listening and foster mutual respect and interaction between the generations. We offer English-speaking ministry for the second generation and joint worship, service activities for seniors and children of single-parent families.

2. Community Service:

> Nursing home visits; Streamwood community events; volunteer work through Habitat for Humanity and Feed My Starving Children for Africa.

3. Evergreen Fellowship:

> A program for elders hosted in younger church members' homes for spiritual learning, games, resource networking, and celebrations.

Historical and Religio-cultural Impacts:

Confucian concepts of harmony and filial piety; Buddhism; communism; atheism; and Chinese popular religions.

Lit Inn Wu

Truth Lutheran Church
503 W. Bauer Rd.
Naperville, IL 60563
Phone No.: 630-416-6476
Year Started/Organized: 1984
Members/Worshipers: 243
Pastor(s): Peter Y. Wang
         Marian M. Wang

Setting of Congregation/Ministry:

Naperville, an affluent suburban city 28 miles west of Chicago, is in DuPage and Will counties. Naperville is predominately White, but its tech companies and excellent school system draw in many Asian families. As of 2016, the Asian population was 14.9%. Two-thirds of Naperville's population of 148,304 (estimated in 2018) are under age 45. People feel an enormous pressure to succeed in career and education, and the intergenerational cultural gap is wide.

Unique Ministries:

1. English Speaking Ministry:

> The English-speaking ministry is intentional outreach to second generation Chinese Americans and Americans from other than Chinese backgrounds. Both English and Chinese services take place at the same time. The two ministries also meet together for a combined service once a month.

2. Small and Fellowship Group Ministry:

> Small groups meet weekly or every other week.

3. Healing Service:

> This ministry began in 2019. We focus on addressing people's grief and pain through an evening of worship, teaching, learning, and prayers for wholeness.

Historical and Religio-Cultural Impacts:

Languages, Chinese and English; cultures, East and West; and secular values.

Peter Y. Wang

Filipino

Eagle Rock Lutheran Church

5032 N. Maywood Ave.

Los Angeles, CA 90041

Phone No.: 323-255-4622

Year Started/Organized: 2004

Members/Worshipers: 47

Pastor(s): Violeta Sanders

Setting of Congregation/Ministry:

Eagle Rock is an ethnically and cul-turally diverse neighborhood of Los Angeles. In 2008, an estimated 34,466 persons lived there, 38.5% of whom were born abroad. Almost one out of every four residents is Asian (24%). While income is relatively high, pockets of poverty also exist. Eagle Rock Lutheran sits in the heart of the city, where one of every five residents (20%) are Filipino or Filipino American.

Unique Ministries:

1. Feeding and Food Distribution:

   We serve food for seniors and homeless people every Saturday from 10-11 am.

2. Outreach Ministry:

   A team visits two convalescent homes every first Sunday of the month.

3. Public Transportation Subsidies:

   In partnership with the Los Angeles County LIFE (Low Income Fare is Easy) program, we provide discounted transportation coupons to seniors, students from low-income families, and the disabled.

Historical and Religio-cultural Impacts:

Local poverty; the biblical sense of care for others.

Violeta Sanders

Filipino

**International Evangelical
Lutheran Church**
7371 Brookhaven Rd.
San Diego, CA 92114
Phone No.: 619-479-1733
Year Started/Organized: 2019
Members/Worshipers: 25
Pastor(s): Deogracias Olivar

Setting of Congregation/Ministry:

San Diego, the second-largest city in California, is a diverse urban area 20 miles north of the Mexican border. Its colleges and universities draw students from around the world and its tourist attractions, such as San Diego Zoo and Sea World, are world-renowned. Military, aerospace, and biotech industries are important economic drivers. The ministry is in a quiet neighborhood where many older adults and retirees live. Most are Mexican, African American, White, and Filipino retirees from the navy and medical professions. Others are students or military personnel. There is also a diversity of religious backgrounds.

Unique Ministries:

1. Ministry to Seniors:

   We provide cultural support to Filipino seniors, who prefer to express themselves in their familiar culture and language.

2. Ministry of Nourishment and Fellowship:

   Our potluck after Sunday worship provides an opportunity for fellowship and the deepening of relationships.

Historical and Religio-cultural Impacts:

Filipino culture, including Semana Santa (Holy Week) traditions and Flores de Mayo parades; language barriers; American racism.

Deogracias Olivar

Saint Matthew's Lutheran Church
Filipino Ministry
1920 W. Glenoaks Blvd.
Glendale, CA 91201
Phone No.: 818-842-3138
Year Started/Organized: 2013
Members/Worshipers: 30
Pastor(s) : Marcos Panahon, Jr.

Filipino

Setting of Congregation/Ministry:

Located 10 miles north of downtown Los Angeles, Glendale is the 23rd largest city in California, with over 200,000 residents as of 2018. Although still predominately White, Glendale is diversifying. Sixteen per cent of its residents are Asian, of whom 7% are Filipino. More than 90% of Glendale's inhabitants reside in single-family homes. After a period of significant development in the 1970s, several large corporations made their headquarters in Glendale.

Unique Ministries:

1. Family and Children's Aid:

We engage in service projects for families and children in need.

2. Filipino Seafarers Program:

In partnership with the Lutheran Maritime Mission, we attend to the spiritual and physical needs of seafarers who pass through Southern California's ports. We share the gospel and offer warm clothes and other necessities.

Historical, Religio-cultural Impacts:

The Filipino culture of familism; religiosity; hospitality.

Marcos Panahon

Hmong

Amazing Grace Ministry

6180 Hwy 65 N.E.

Fridley, MN 55432

Phone No.: 763-571-1500

Year Started/Organized: 2018

Members/Worshipers: 130

Pastor (s): Nhiabee Vang

Setting of Congregation/Ministry:

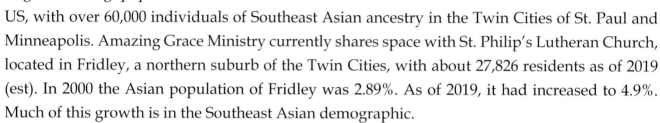

Minnesota is home to the second-largest Hmong population in the US, with over 60,000 individuals of Southeast Asian ancestry in the Twin Cities of St. Paul and Minneapolis. Amazing Grace Ministry currently shares space with St. Philip's Lutheran Church, located in Fridley, a northern suburb of the Twin Cities, with about 27,826 residents as of 2019 (est). In 2000 the Asian population of Fridley was 2.89%. As of 2019, it had increased to 4.9%. Much of this growth is in the Southeast Asian demographic.

Unique Ministries:

1. We are a family-friendly church.

2. We emphasize ministry with children and youth.

3. We share the Lutheran message of grace with the Hmong community.

Historical and Religio-cultural Impacts:

The Hmong clan system.

Nhiabee Vang

Ascension Lutheran Church Hmong Ministry

1236 S. Layton Blvd.

Milwaukee, WI 53215-1653

Phone No.: 414-645-2933

Year Started/Organized: 1983

Members/Worshipers: 343

Pastor(s): Vacant

Setting of Congregation/Ministry:

In 2010, Milwaukee's population was 594,832, breaking down as 40% African American, 37% White, 17.3% Hispanic, and 3.5% Asian. By 2019, the population dropped to 590,157, a 0.8% decrease from 2010. Milwaukee has a reputation for being the most segregated city in the US. Ascension Lutheran Church is in a diverse neighborhood with a large Hispanic population on Milwaukee's south side. This diversity drives Ascension's ministries.

Unique Ministries:

1. Faith and Culture Bridge for Weddings and Funerals:

    Wedding and funeral teams provide both hospitality and guidance to people as they negotiate the norms of traditional wedding and funeral practices in light of their faith.

2. Intergenerational Ministry Transition:

    The Hmong Ministry is currently negotiating the transition from first-generation (primarily Hmong-speaking) to second-generation (mostly English-speaking) leadership.

3. Leadership Development:

    We also participate in leadership trainings such as the Evangelical Lutheran Church in America Hmong Ministry Network conference.

Historical and Religio-Cultural Impacts:

Hmong and American cultures; generational transition.

Margrethe S. C. Kleiber

Hmong

**Good Samaritan
Lutheran Church**
1340 Hazel St. N.
St. Paul, MN 55119
Phone No.: 651-815-7118
Year Started/Organized: 2010
Members/Worshipers: 158
Pastor(s): William T. Siong

Setting of Congregation/Ministry:

By 2000, St. Paul, MN, became home to the second-largest US urban Hmong community. St. Paul had a population of 285,068 (US Census 2010), of whom 15% were Asian. Most were Southeast Asian refugees sponsored to the Twin Cities after the fall of Saigon in 1975. Today many are entrepreneurs with businesses such as charter schools, law firms, medical clinics, and flea markets.

Unique Ministries:

1. Volunteerism:

Congregation members volunteer with Habitat for Humanity, Feed My Starving Children, and the free ice cream and lunch program for children. We have also played music for National Night Out activities.

2. Community Events:

Ministry highlights include our annual Mother's and Father's Day events, New Year celebrations, Christmas and Easter services, picnics, and camping trips. We also participate in leadership trainings such as the Evangelical Lutheran Church in America Hmong Ministry Network conference.

Historical and Religio-cultural Impacts:

The Hmong culture of animism; ancestor worship; the biblical sense of caring; and American culture of volunteerism.

William T. Siong

Hmong

Grace Evangelical Lutheran Church

4836 East Tulare Ave.

Fresno, CA 93727

Phone No.: 559-369-9126

Year Started/Organized: 1987

Members/Worshipers: 400

Pastor(s): Lu V. Vang

Setting of Congregation/Ministry:

Situated in the San Joaquin Valley, Fresno is the largest inland city in California and its fifth-largest city. According to the 2010 census data, it has a population of 484,665. The 2019 estimated figure was 531,576, a 7.5% increase. Of the 2010 total, 12.6% were Asian, with the Hmong being the largest group (3.6%). Fresno is the hub of the surrounding rural agriculture economy. There is religious diversity among the Hmong, including the practice of Shamanism.

Unique Ministries:

1. Hmong Women's Group:

   The women meet regularly for Bible study and singing.

2. Hmong New Year Celebration and Hmong-style Christmas:

   We provide an arena for the Hmong community to gather and celebrate significant events and holidays.

3. Food Distribution:

   Due to COVID-19, we get free food from Small Farm Organization (which buys food from local farmers). Our church then distributes it to those in need.

Historical and Religio-cultural Impacts:

Hmong language and culture; COVID-19 pandemic.

William E. Wong

Hmong

Hmong Central Lutheran Church

301 Fuller Ave. W.

St. Paul, MN 55103

Phone No.: 612-360-9674

Year Started/Organized: 1992

Members/Worshipers: 184

Pastor(s): Nouk Vagh

Setting of Congregation/Ministry:

St. Paul, MN, is home to 308,096 persons (US Census estimate 2019). The three largest ethnic groups are White (56.7%), Asian (18.4%), and Black (16%). In the Twin Cities (St. Paul and Minneapolis) and the vicinity, about 80,000 of the residents are Hmong; and 25% of the Twin Cities Hmong are Christians. The church building is in a neighborhood that was the historic center of Hmong life in the two cities.

Unique Ministries:

1. English Language Worship:

> Our high school and college-age young people lead worship in English once a month. Three Sundays a month, our worship services are in Hmong.

2. Small Groups:

> Sunday mornings before worship, our small groups meet. Our children attend Sunday School while men, women, young couples, college age and youth gather respectively for Bible study and fellowship. Once a month, all the groups gather for the joy of fellowship and Bible study.

3. Healing and Comforting Ministry:

> After Sunday worship, the pastor stays to pray with, counsel, and comfort persons with particular needs.

Historical and Religio-cultural Impacts:

Hmong first and second generation culture gaps in language, culture, food; intergenerational family issues.

Nouk Vagh

Hmong Community Evangelical Lutheran Church

1327 Alleghenyville Rd.
Mohnton, PA 19540
Phone number: 267-975-2773
Year Started/Organized: 1996
Members/Worshipers: 135
Pastor(s): Shongchai Hang

Setting of Congregation/Ministry:

Mohnton in Southeastern PA is a borough of Berks County with 3,043 residents as of Census 2010. White persons comprise 96% of the population, Hispanics of any race 1.69%, African Americans 1.11%, and Asians 0.44%. The congregation shares space with Allegheny Lutheran Church and is specifically dedicated to the Hmong community in three counties: Berks, Philadelphia (Asians 7.8%), and Lancaster (Asians 2.5%).

Unique Ministries:

1. Bilingual Worship in Hmong and English:

   We worship in both languages as a means of celebrating our faith and culture and bringing multiple generations together.

2. Fellowship and Service Activities for Women and Men:

   Our women's group prepares meals once a year for a Lutheran homeless shelter in Reading, PA. We provide two nights of food and shelter for homeless families at church, in partnership with Allegheny Lutheran. The women gather twice a month for in-home Bible study, prayer, and fellowship. The men hold church clean-up days and take fishing trips. We host group picnics. We also have separate women's and men's retreats in the Poconos, followed by a combined post-retreat review gathering.

Historical and Religio-cultural Impacts:

Hmong language and culture; the influence of US life on intergenerational relationships.

Lily R. Wu

Indian and South Asian

**Atlanta Telugu
Mission Church**

A synodically authorized
worshiping community

P. O. Box 400

Decatur, GA 30031

Phone No.: 404-589-1977

Year Started/Organized: 2013

Members/Worshipers: 35-40

Pastor(s): John R. Billa

Setting of Congregation/Ministry:

Peachtree Corners is a suburb of Atlanta, GA, with an estimated 2019 population of 43,905, of whom 9.6% are Asians. It is a multiracial city, with the majority (60.2%) being White. The African American population stands at 23.3%, while 14% are Hispanic of any race. The remaining 2.5% are of two or more races. The population is highly educated, with 52.6% holding a BA and 19% holding MAs or higher degrees. In the past seven years, the Telugu-speaking community in Atlanta and its suburb have changed as more immigrants from southeast India move to the US searching for jobs. Atlanta Telugu Mission Church operates from Christ the King Lutheran Church in Peachtree Corners.

Unique Ministries:

1. Outreach to people of other faiths, primarily Hindu.

2. Monthly fasting intercessory prayers.

3. Lenten Meditations.

4. Counseling for teens and young adults.

5. Celebration of traditional Indian national holidays to reach non-Christians and un-churched Indians.

Historical and Religio-cultural Impacts:

Indian culture; other religious traditions, and Christian practice.

John R. Billa

Indian and South Asian

**Beloved Community
Multicultural Congregation**
A synodically authorized
worshiping community
@ First Evangelical
Lutheran Church
3604 Chatham Rd.
Ellicott City, MD 21042
Phone No.: 301-850-2993
Year Started/Organized: 2018
Members/Worshipers: 20-30
Pastor(s): Surekha Nelavala

Setting of Congregation/Ministry:

Ellicott City has a population of 72,247 (US Census estimate, 2018). The three largest racial groups are White (57.67%), Asian (29.28%), and Black (8.95%). Notably, 68.28% of the city's residents speak English only, while 31.72% speak other languages in their homes. 17.98% speak Asian and Pacific Islander languages. Beloved Community is a mission start of the Delaware-Maryland Synod that grew out of Global Peace Lutheran Fellowship in Frederick, MD.

Unique Ministries:

1. Ministry of Multilingual Worship:

    We use multiple languages in worship, including English, Telugu, Tamil, Sri Lankan, Thai, Chinese, Korean, or Tugaloo.

2. Ministry of Fellowship:

    We build relationships over meals, through cottage prayer meetings, and house gatherings.

3. Ministry of Celebration:

    We celebrate Asian festivals with songs, worship, and food.

Historical and Religio-cultural Impacts:

Local ethnic and cultural diversity; Asian cultures and languages; intergenerational challenges.

Surekha Nelavala

Indian and South Asian

Global Peace Lutheran Fellowship
@ Evangelical Lutheran Church
31 E. Church St.
Frederick, MD 21701
Phone No.: 301-850-2993
Year Started/Organized: 2011
Members/Worshipers: 20-30
Pastor(s): Surekha Nelavala

Setting of Congregation/Ministry:

Frederick, the second-largest city in Maryland, located near Washington, DC, is a college town and a growing bedroom and retirement community of 72,744 residents (2019 est.). Census data from 2010 describes Fredrick's racial and ethnic composition as 55.4% White, 18.4% Black, 16.7% Hispanic, and 6.1% Asian—or 3,800. The city is rich with arts, music, and a diverse workforce. The growing neighborhood near Global Peace Lutheran Fellowship is a predominantly immigrant and migrant community.

Unique Ministries:

1. Cross-cultural Forms of Worship and Community:

We emphasize multicultural and multilingual worship, building an intercultural community with a "salad image" of unity.

2. Outreach Extension into Western Baltimore:

Our outreach includes praise, worship, and other gatherings at churches such as New Hope Lutheran, Columbia, MD, and First Evangelical Lutheran, Ellicott City, MD, and in people's homes.

Historical, Religio-cultural Impacts:

Local ethnic and cultural diversity; largely independent and private cultures; unchurched people seeking new ways to be church.

Lily R. Wu

Good Shepherd South Asian Ministry

A synodically authorized worshiping community
4211 Carol Ave.
Fremont, CA 94538
Phone No.: 510-656-0900
Year Started/Organized: 2005
Members/Worshipers: 40
Pastor(s): Ananda Rao Darla*
      (Lay Minister)

Setting of Congregation/Ministry:

Good Shepherd South Asian Ministry is in the Irvington District of Fremont, CA. Irvington boasts a population of 11,546 within a total city population of 227,934. Irvington is 54.10% Asian, 23.10% White, and 9.14% Black. 50% of the families involved are Telugu speakers from South India; most also understand Hindi.

Unique Ministries:

1. Multilingual Praise and Worship:

   We livestream worship via Zoom and Facebook to the US and other countries.

2. Collaborative Children's Ministry:

   In cooperation with four churches in the Tri-City Fremont area, we offer a children's music program, hold Vacation Bible School, and produce a Christmas pageant.

3. Community Services:

   We hold food and clothing drives, donate to a local food pantry, and participate in programs serving homeless persons.

Historical and Religio-cultural Impacts:

South Asian cultures and languages; immigrant family issues; intercultural relationships with members and children or youth who speak English only.

GSSAM Board

Indian and South Asian

**St. Paul's International
Lutheran Church**
262-22 Union Turnpike
Floral Park, NY 11004
Phone No.: 718-347-5990
Year Started/Organized: 2000
Members/Worshipers: 100
Pastor(s): Israel Daniel Peter Penumaka
        Sarah J. Geddada

Setting of Congregation/Ministry:

Floral Park and Glen Oaks in Queens-Long Island, NY, are suburban neighborhoods where 16,209 persons live. The population breaks down as White (53%), Asian (24%), Hispanic (14%), and African American (7%). St. Paul's International describes itself as a multi-religious community with a diversity of South Asian families.

Unique Ministries:

1. Inter-religious and Multicultural Counseling:

   We offer pre-marital and post-marital counseling for Christian, Hindu, Muslim, Sikh, Jain, Buddhist, and Jewish interfaith couples and specifically Christian counseling for children, youth, and families. We also accompany and guide couples as they prepare for marriage.

2. Interfaith Community Activities and Global Christian Initiative:

   These activities run annually among Catholics, Jews, and Lutherans. These events include a day-long family event with panel presentations, a gospel music concert, summer revival meetings, and a clergy-lay leader prayer breakfast.

3. Telugu (Indian) Christian Ministry:

   We offer a daily one-hour program with songs, scripture readings, homilies, and prayers.

Historical and Religio-cultural Impacts:

Indian culture; Indian Christian pietism; Indian pluralistic backgrounds; inter-religious marriages.

Israel Daniel Peter Penumaka and Sarah Geddada

HKBP California Batak Lutheran Church

401 N. Gibbs St.

Pomona, CA 91767

PO Box 10881,

San Bernardino, CA. 92423

Phone No.: 909-809-8607

Year Started/Organized: 1994

Members/Worshipers: 60

Pastor(s): Feronika Rambing**
        (Leader)

Setting of Congregation/Ministry:

Pomona, CA, sits between the Inland Empire and San Gabriel Valley. Census data from 2010 shows that Asians comprised 8.5% of its 149,058 residents, with Filipinos as the largest group (1.97%), followed by Chinese (1.48%) and other Asians. There is no data on the Indonesian population. Other groups are Hispanic (70.5%), White (12.5%), and Black (7.3%). The church building is in downtown Pomona.

Unique Ministries:

1. Disaster Relief:

    Our congregation has provided relief to earthquake and flood victims in Indonesia and the US

2. Women's, Men's, and Children's Ministry:

    The congregation's women visit the sick and help church neighbors in need. Our men's ministry activities include hiking, fishing, camping, and feeding the homeless. In collaboration with our host congregation, we give Christmas gifts to children whose parents are in prison. At Christmas time, we go caroling at care home facilities.

3. Cultural Ministry:

    We teach Indonesian culture, dance, and music, including folk songs to the children.

Historical and Religio-cultural Impacts:

Indonesian culture; the Christian concept of charity and neighborly love.

Feronika Rambing

Indonesian

Imanuel Indonesian Fellowship

c/o Bethlehem Lutheran Church

3352 Katella Ave.

Los Alamitos, CA 90720

Phone No.: 603-380-1181

Year Started/Organized: 2016

Members/Worshipers: 11

Pastor(s): Robert N. Waworuntu

Setting of Congregation/Ministry:

Los Alamitos is a small city in Orange County, southern California. In 2010 the population was 11,449. The majority is White, followed by Hispanic and Asian (12.8%). The median age is in the late thirties. Although the church building is in Orange County, more Indonesians live in San Bernardino and Los Angeles counties. Therefore, Imanuel also provides Sunday afternoon worship in San Bernardino County at the Cross and Crown Lutheran Church in Rancho Cucamonga.

Unique Ministries:

1. Indonesian Worship Style:

   Worshipers enjoy singing Indonesian hymns, accompanied by native instruments and dance.

2. Immigrant Assistance:

   We offer support to Indonesian immigrants needing legal assistance.

Historical and Religio-cultural impacts:

The Indonesian culture; languages, English and Indonesian; legal needs of immigrants.

Robert N. Waworuntu

Imanuel Indonesian Lutheran Church

c/o Holy Trinity Evangelical Lutheran Church (HTELC)

22 Fox Run Rd.

Newington, NH 03801

Years Started/Organized: 2007

Members/Worshipers: 24

Pastor(s): Vacant

Indonesian

Setting of Congregation/Ministry:

Portsmouth NH, a city of roughly 21,000 people, sits near the mouth of the Piscataqua River, a short, wide river that divides New Hampshire and Maine. The city is also at the hub of a metropolitan region that includes the cities of Rochester and Dover, NH, and many towns: Exeter, Hampton, Greenland, Stratham, Newington, and Rye, NH; Kittery, Eliot, South Berwick and York, Maine; and others.

Unique Ministries:

1. Immigrant outreach:

   We offer English as Second Language with the help of HTELC members.
   We provide income tax preparation, with the help of HTELC members.

2. Cultural Outreach:

   We offer Indonesian Nights events and serve the Indonesian seacoast community in this area.

Historical and Religio-cultural Impacts:

Indonesian culture and language.

Robert Waworuntu

Source of Love Indonesian Lutheran Church
c/o St. Peter's Evangelical Lutheran Church
1000 Taylor Ave.
Scranton, PA 18510
Years Started/Organized: 2007
Members/Worshipers: 10
Pastor(s): Vacant

Setting of Congregation/Ministry:

Scranton is the sixth-largest city in the Commonwealth of Pennsylvania. It is known for Steamtown National Historic Site, with century-old locomotives set on a former rail yard. In a restored 19th-century mill, the Electric City Trolley Museum has interactive exhibits and vintage trolleys. With an estimated population in 2019 of 76,653, it is the largest city in northeastern Pennsylvania and the Scranton-Wilkes-Barre-Hazleton, PA metropolitan statistical area, which has a population of about 570,000.

Unique Ministries:

1. Serving Indonesians in the Scranton-Wilkes-Barre area.

Historical and Religio-cultural Impacts:

Indonesian cultures as they relate to US American life.

Robert Waworuntu

Lutheran Church of the Resurrection Japanese Language Ministry

9812 Hamilton Ave.

Huntington Beach, CA 92646-8014

Phone No.: 714-964-1912

Year Started/Organized: 1988

Members/Worshipers: 30

Pastor(s): Hongsun Kim

Setting of Congregation/Ministry:

Huntington Beach is a seaside town in Orange County, CA. Of the total population of 145,661 (Census 2010), 76.7% were White and 11.1% Asian, with a small percentage of African American and Hispanic residents. The estimated population in 2019 was 199,223, a 4.9% increase since 2010. The neighboring cities of Costa Mesa and Irvine also have a significant Asian presence.

Unique Ministries:

1. Annual Japanese Festival:

   The festival is both a fundraiser and a means of cultural exchange.

2. Mission Trips to Japan:

   Since 2012, mission trips have built meaningful relationships with Ooe Lutheran Church in Kumamoto. We have also facilitated adult learning experiences and youth exchanges with Kyushu Gakuin Lutheran High School.

3. Care Connections Network:

   Serving the needs of Japanese-speaking elders since 2012. Later expanded to include elders of all backgrounds while mindful of Japanese language and culture-specific needs.

Historical and Religio-cultural Impacts:

Japanese culture, language, and the needs of Japanese elders; Japanese expatriate community of business people and students; reticence about religion.

Margrethe S. C. Kleiber

Japanese

Lutheran Oriental Church

2654 W. 164th St.

Torrance, CA 90504

Phone : 310-329-9345

Year Started: 1979

Members/Worshipers: 128

Pastor: Paul T. Nakamura

Setting of Congregation/Ministry:

Torrance is a multicultural and multiracial city in the South Bay region of Los Angeles County. It has the second highest concentration of Japanese Americans in the US, after Honolulu. A number of Japanese companies, including automakers, are located in Torrance. It also has the distinction of having the lowest crime rate in the county.

Unique Ministries:

1. Lutheran Oriental Church members reflect and engage with the racial and cultural realities of our city and nation. For example, the church provides meeting space to support the work of Asian Lutheran and community groups. When the National Coalition of Redress and Reparation was actively seeking redress for the illegal treatment of Japanese Americans, our congregation played a significant role in providing the group a place to meet.

2. We also bring the community together every October through our Annual Bazaar, to share the gospel, to have fun and to raise revenue for our ministry.

Historical and Religio-cultural Impacts:

Injustice of the American legal system on Japanese Americans; multiultural reality of our community.

Paul T. Nakamura

Church of Dream Builders

621 S. Sunkist St.

Anaheim, California 92806

Phone No.: 714-772-2772

Year Started/Organized: 2004

Members/Worshipers: 12-18

Pastor(s): Hyunho Hong

Setting of Congregation/Ministry:

Anaheim is the home of Disneyland Resort with its two theme parks, the Anaheim Convention Center, and many other attractions in a tourism-based economy. Its 351,005 residents (2018 estimates) are mostly White or Hispanic. Asian residents, primarily Vietnamese and Filipino, comprise about 15% of the total population. The city is headquarters to several corporations, with Disneyland Resort and Kaiser Hospital being the biggest employers.

Unique Ministries:

1. Jerry Can Library Ministry for Younger Generations:

   In collaboration with St. Luke's Lutheran in Fullerton, we collect books and gifts for a school in Uganda led by a Korean missionary group. (Jerry Cans are steel containers used in Africa to haul and store water.)

2. Community Education Programs.

   Activities include a book club, basketball, and various classes, including English as a Second Language for adults, fine arts, and free Spanish for kids. Nominal fees for some courses help to pay the teachers.

Historical and Religio-cultural Impacts:

Intercultural barriers in reaching beyond Koreans; bringing in or merging with English as a unifying language.

Hyunho Hong

Light of Grace Lutheran Church

36016 1st Ave. S.

Federal Way, WA 98003

Phone No.: 253-661-9313

Year Started/Organized: 1995

Members/Worshipers: 70

Pastor(s): Sang Soo Kim

Setting of the Congregation/Ministry:

Situated in King County, Federal Way in the Seattle metropolitan area had 89,306 residents in 2010, many of them young and educated. By 2018 estimates, the population grew to 97,044, an 8.7 % increase. Koreans first came to the city in 1885 as laborers. Now, many of the 46,880 Koreans of Washington State live in Federal Way. In the 2010 census, Asians were 14.2% of the city's inhabitants.

Unique Ministries:

  1. *Dasom* (Love) Multicultural School:

    This nonprofit organization offers programs such English class, Taekwondo, and Korean arts. There are also classes to help newcomers to the US Newcomers to adjust to American life.

  2. *Shim-Bang* (Caring):

    The congregation equips members for intentional visitation ministry. They regularly visit those who cannot attend church due to sickness, distance, or time.

  3. Adult Group:

    The focus is on training leaders to improve church and community life through seasonal events. The group also raises funds to buy blankets for homeless people in the area.

Historical and Religio-cultural Impacts:

Korean culture; needs of immigrants and care for members; English language and adjustment to American life; community services.

Sang Soo Kim

Morning Star Fellowship

691 Prospect Ave.

Ridgefield, NJ 07657

Phone No.: 347-975-3896

Year Started/Organized: 2015

Members/Worshipers: 5

Pastor(s): Eunyoung Kim

Setting of Congregation/Ministry:

Ridgefield, NJ is a densely populated borough in northern NJ. Data from the 2010 US Census data show that its 11,032 residents live within a 2.87 square mile area. Ridgefield's racial composition is 61.84% White, 30.04 % Asian, and 3.59% other races. Morning Star is an English-speaking interactive faith and culture ministry in Bergen County. Founded by the Rev. Janet Blair of Zion Lutheran Church, Ridgefield, it serves Korean immigrants and their children.

Unique Ministries:

1. Faith Community for Healing and Support:

   Morning Star Fellowship offers bilingual worship, Bible study, family relationship recovery support, and encouragement to live out our faith in the workplace.

2. Platform for Community Service:

   We strive to be a platform for community service, focusing on neighbors needing help.

3. Korean Language and Culture Program:

   We offer activities for both Asian Americans and Americans of other backgrounds for intercultural learning.

Historical, Religio-cultural Impacts:

Korean language and culture; language barriers in daily life; family stresses; English language; culture and identity in a diverse society.

Eunyoung Kim

**Seattle Covenant
Community Church**
8316 39th Ave. S.W.
Seattle, WA 98136
Phone No.: 253-459-3241
Year Started: 2014
Members/Worshipers: 24
Pastor: Chulhyuk (Paul) Ko

Setting of Congregation/Ministry:

West Seattle, especially for Koreans, is where elderly citizens settle down after retirement. Their children have grown and moved away. Lacking mobility, adaptive skills, and ability to speak English, these elders then have many spiritual and physical problems. They cannot get proper care when they need it. Our congregation is made up of elderly persons and students from Korea.

Unique Ministries:

    1. Daily Visit Service:

        This is mainly for elderly members and relatives who need constant check-ups. These visits provide a way to meet their physical and spiritual needs.

    2. Wednesday Morning Services:
        This service, open to all people, provides opportunities for those who have missed Sunday morning service to hear the Gospel midweek and to understand the love of Christ.

    3. Friday Night Bible Study:

        This program is designed to help students to have a better understanding of the Bible and Lutheranism from a Lutheran perspective.

Historical and Religio-cultural Impacts:

Confucian concept of filial piety; American individualism, and American-born Koreans.

Chulhyuk (Paul) Ko

Seattle Reborn Church

17529 15th Ave. N.E.

Shoreline, WA 98155

Phone No.: 425-330-5276

Year Organized: 2012

Members/Worshipers: 25

Pastor(s): Yonsu Kim

Setting of Congregation/Ministry:

Seattle, the largest city in the Pacific Northwest, is growing rapidly. In 2010, of its 608,660 residents, Asians were 13.8%, including Chinese (4.1%). A 2018 estimate was 774,955 (or a 22.4% increase over eight years). It is a city of culture and education, with an economy driven by industrial, internet, and technology companies. It is also a port of entry for Asians. Immigrant Koreans face financial hardships, cultural adjustments, linguistic struggles, and anxiety about belonging and settling down. Seattle Reborn is in the North City Business District, worshiping at Bethel Lutheran Church facilities.

Unique Ministries:

1. Ministry without Walls:

> We have an active network of small groups meeting at homes, coffee shops, or nearby marts for daily fellowship.

2. Ministry of Helping Hands:

> We offer practical assistance to immigrants through advice, counseling, digital classes, translation of documents, and solving intergenerational issues.

Historical and Religio-Cultural Impacts:

Korean and American cultures; culture of 1.5, second, and third generation Koreans.

Yonsu Kim

Lahu

Christ Lutheran Church
Lahu Ministry
3830 W. Tulare Ave.
Visalia, CA 93277
Phone No.: 559-732-1851
Year Started/Organized: 2006
Members/Worshipers: 200
Pastor(s): Samee Singkeovilay

Setting of Congregation/Ministry:

Visalia is the fifth-largest city in California's San Joaquin Valley, with 124,442 residents predominately White or Hispanic (2010 US Census). 6,768 or 5.4% were Asians. Agriculture drives the economy. The largest US Lahu community lives in Visalia, with 2,600 persons in seven denominations across the city.

Unique Ministries:

1. Culturally Relevant Worship:

   We lead worship mostly in Lahu, with some English parts.

2. Lahu Women's Group:

   Volunteers serve lunch every week at the non-profit Bethlehem Center for persons in need, especially homeless people.

3. Cultural and Caregiving Programs:

   We hold traditional New Year celebrations, in-house prayer for the sick, and Lahu language classes for children and adults.

4. Rebuilding Support Ministry:

   Through the community organization *Samakhom* ("Join Together"), we rebuild houses destroyed by fire in Laos and Thailand and offer financial support for funeral expenses to bereaved families in Southeast Asia and the US.

Historical and Religio-cultural Impacts:

Lahu language and culture; sharing culture with the next generations.

Samee Singkeovilay

Grace Lao Lutheran Ministry

1963 Carlson Blvd.

Richmond, CA 94804

Phone No.: 510-647-8361

Year Organized: 1980

Current Membership: 50

Pastor(s): Vanphone Anlavan**

         (Person-in-charge)

Setting of Congregation/Ministry:

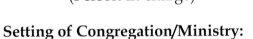

Located on the east side of the San

Francisco Bay, Richmond is a minority-majority city. According to the 2010 US Census, White people comprised 31.4% of Richmond's 103,701 residents, while Asians comprised 13.5%, with 1.6% being Laotian. Educationally, Richmond dwellers compare favorably with the national average, although crime is high. Richmond is home to the Chevron Richmond Refinery, which has been implicated in regional cancer rates and has a history of industrial accidents. The congregation is unique in that almost 99% of the members come from the same tribe in Laos. In the early 1980s, the congregation grew, especially among children. Currently, however, many have relocated in search of better job opportunities.

Unique Ministries:

    1. Children's and Second-Generation Programs:

        Worship is conducted in both Lao and English so that the young will understand the gospel message.

    2. Annual Summer Music Youth Camp:

        Since 2013, fundraisers such as car washes and food sales have supported the music camp.

Historical and Religio-Cultural Impacts:

Bilingual Lao and English community; Christianity; environmental toxins; lack of job opportunities; and next-generation concerns.

Vanphone Anlavan

Laotian

**Lao Evangelical
Lutheran Church**

3978 W. Broadway Ave.

Robbinsdale, MN 55422

Phone No.: 612-396-7217

Year Started/Organized: 1997

Members/Worshipers: 95

Pastor(s): Thiem Baccam

Setting of Congregation/Ministry:

Lao Evangelical Lutheran Church is in the town of Robbinsdale, MN, about five miles from Minneapolis. In 2018 the town's estimated population was 14,500, predominantly White. In the 2010 census, 3.4% were Asian or Pacific Islander, and predominately Southeast Asian. The median age in Robbinsdale is the mid-thirties. The average household size is 3. This city has two elementary schools, a middle school, and a high school.

Unique Ministries:

1. Ministry of Partnership and Service:

We partner with the Lao Association of Churches to provide social and community services to Laotians in the Twin Cities.

2. Ministry of Hospitality and Helping Hands:

We partner with Elim Lutheran Church and Lutheran Social Service to welcome Karen refugee families and resettle them in the US.

3. Ministry to Students Program:

This program focus on the needs of students. We provide backpacks with school supplies to K-12 students and families in need. College-educated volunteers tutor K-12 students. We also implemented a mentor-mentee program that includes physical and team activities, food, and Bible lessons for the youth every month.

Historical and Religio-cultural Impacts:

Buddhism; needs of the community; and the biblical Great Commission.

Thiem Baccam

Reborn Lao Lutheran Church

523 2nd St. N.

Waite Park, MN 56387

Phone No.: 320-774-1140

Year Started/Organized: 2019

Members/Worshipers: 45

Pastor(s): Peter Keomanivong

Setting of Congregation/Ministry:

Waite Park is a small college town in Stearns County, about 70 miles northwest of Minnesota's Twin Cities. The median age in Waite Park is 30 years old. The 2010 US Census reports a population of 6,715, which is 67% White, 20.2% Black, 8.4% Hispanic, and 4.2% Asian. By 2019, the population grew to 7,768. Reborn Lao is a multicultural congregation with Lao and White members ages 7 to 70.

Unique Ministries:

1. Worship and Bible Study Groups:

   Reborn Lao offers worship in Lao and English. Bible studies for adults, young adults, and children meet on Sunday mornings. Additional adult Bible studies meet on the first and third Saturdays of each month.

2. Men's and Women's Groups:

   Small groups meet weekly, with additional check-ins during the week.

3. God's People Group:

   God's People is a group for prayer and fellowship where Reborn Lao members share prayer requests, ask questions, and share news of activities and concerns.

Historical and Religio-cultural Impacts:

Lao and American culture; Lao immigrant needs; intergenerational issues; intercultural Lao and White community.

Lily R. Wu

Laotian

St. Paul Lao Lutheran Church

1200 Walker Ave.

Des Moines, IA 50316

Phone No.: 515-556-5796

Year Started/Organized: 2005

Members/Worshipers: 50

Pastor(s): Phouthaly Onelangsy

Setting of Congregation/Ministry:

Des Moines, the capital of Iowa, is a major center for insurance, finance, and technology. Iowa plays a significant role in US politics as it is the first state to hold a primary during a presidential election year. In the 2010 US Census, Laotians were 0.9% of Des Moines' 203,433 predominantly White population. St. Paul Lao is located in the heart of the city, less than half a mile from the state capitol.

Unique Ministries:

1. Bilingual Lao-English Service Ministry:

> We offer a bilingual service to connect with people beyond the Laotian community.

2. Community Outreach:

> Our cookout parties at church are a way to share the gospel with newcomers. We also help Burmese refugees resettle with food, clothing, and furniture.

3. Young Adult Fellowship in Action:

> Young adults make home visits for prayer and to bring prayer concerns back to the church. We also work at a grassroots nonprofit assisting refugee youth and adults with arithmetic, writing, computer skills, and English.

Historical and Religio-cultural Impacts:

Buddhist roots of Laotian culture; unfamiliarity with Christianity.

Phouthaly Onelangsy

Lutheran Church of the Incarnation

1200 Indian Hills Pkwy. N.E.
Marietta, GA 30068
Phone No.: 770-971-2738
Year Started/Organized: 2016
Members/Worshipers: 40
Pastor(s): Uijin Hwang

Setting of Congregation/Ministry:

Marietta, an affluent suburban city 15 miles northwest of Atlanta, Georgia, is situated in Cobb County. The city's population is predominately White. However, the congregation is multi-racial: 55% Whites, 30% Afro-American, 15% Hispanic and Asian.

Unique Ministries:

1. Wellness Program:

    We offer *Yin* yoga classes. They are open to everyone. The aim is to improve flexibility, mobility, and general health.

2. American Assimilation Helpline Ministry:

    We provide free tutoring for any Marietta students with "refugee" or "immigration" status.

3. Radically Inclusive Outlook/Strategy:

    We are intentional in our efforts to eliminate barriers that exclude people. In 2018 we invited an African-American minister for outreach. We also strive to become an artist-friendly church center, providing space and other support to local artists to acknowledge their contributions to the community.

Historical and Religio-cultural Impacts:

American diversity; Korean culture; health and immigration issues; environmental and ecological concerns.

Uijin Hwang

Pan Asian

Pan-Asian Ministry in Phoenix
A synodically authorized
worshiping community
c/o Mountain View
Lutheran Church
11002 S. 48th St.
Phoenix, AZ 85044
Phone No.: 520-280-6102
Year Started: 2018
Participants: 67
Pastor(s): Corazon Aguilar

Setting of Congregation/Ministry:

In Metropolitan Phoenix, AZ, within a population of 4,192,887 (US Census 2010), the two largest groups racially were White (46.5%) and Hispanic (19.4%). Asians (3.2%) are usually highly educated homeowners in two-income households with children. Most Pan-Asian Ministry attendees are Asian American women with Caucasian spouses. They gather to celebrate their identities as Lutheran-Christian women with their Japanese, Chinese, Pakistani, and Filipina backgrounds. Teenage adoptees from Korea and China, as well as children, also take part.

Unique Programs:

1. Cultural Learning:

Each gathering enjoys a presentation about an aspect of Asian culture.

2. Food and Fellowship:

During a meal, intergenerational sharing of personal experiences builds relationships and strengthens fellowship and discipleship through community support. Participants find a special rapport and comfort.

3. Building Youth Confidence:

Plans are underway to send the teenagers to the Lutheran Multicultural al Youth Leadership Event for empowerment in the broader faith setting.

Historical and Religio-cultural Impacts:

Japanese internmen in the US; Chinese life under Communism; and neighbors of different cultural understandings.

Lily R. Wu

St. Paul Thai Lutheran Church

7416 Dixon St.

Forest Park, IL 60130

Phone: 630-863-8634

Year Started: 1992

Members/Worshipers: 60

Pastor(s): Monta Limthongviratn

      (Lay Minister)

      Pongsak Limthongviratn

      (Interim Pastor)

Thai

Setting of Congregation/Ministry:

Forest Park is a multiracial, multicultural and multi-religious suburban community of Chicago with a population of about 13,000. The number of residents has been declining since 1980. Today they are predominately White or African American, with an average income. Fewer than 10% are Asian and Pacific Islander. It also has a number of homeless persons.

Unique Ministries:

    1. Ministry to the Poor:

> In response to the need of the homeless population, our congregation joined the shelter and meal program of the West Suburb of Chicago. Each summer we provide shelter for about 20 to 25 homeless persons for two weeks. In addition, we deliver enough food for 50 to 60 persons once a month to a church where the homeless have their meals.

    2. Mission Support:

> The congregation provides monetary support to several organizations in Asia. Moreover from 1992 until 2020, the congregation has sent more than one million dollars to several projects there.

    3. Leadership Development:

> Several seminaries in Thailand benefit from the regular financial support given to them by St. Paul Thai. The funds assist faculty members who are pursuing PhD programs. The congregation also brings students from those seminaries to St. Paul Thai Lutheran Church for a six month internship.

Historical and Religio-cultural Impacts:

Buddhism with its concept of karma; Lutheran theologies of grace, peace, and justice.

Pongsak Limthongviratn

Thai

Thai Young Adult Ministry
A synodically authorized
worshiping community
7416 Dixon St.
Forest Park, IL 60130
Phone No.: 224-247-8803
Participants: 20
Pastor(s): Sirintip Taveesap**

(Leader)

Setting of Congregation/Ministry:

The Thai Young Adult Ministry is in multi-racial, multicultural, and multilingual Greater Chicago, where there are many young Buddhist Thais. They prefer to socialize among themselves. The Evangelical Lutheran Church in America, the Metropolitan Chicago Synod, and St. Paul Thai Lutheran Church (SPTLC) sponsor this ministry.

Unique Ministries:

1. Badminton Club:

   The club, using the facility of St. Paul Thai Lutheran Church offers Thai young adults an opportunity to play badminton several evenings a week.

2. Cell Groups:

   This program is for young adults and students living in Chicago.

3. Outreach Trips:

   These trips build relationships between Christians and non-Christians.

Historical and Religio-cultural Impacts:

A fusion of contemporary American-Thai cultures; SPTLC's emphasis on the gospel of love, kindness, and generosity.

Sirintip Taveesap

List of Congregations without Profiles:

Chinese:

Lutheran Church of the Cross: 66 W. Duarte Rd., Arcadia, CA 91007. Pastor: Charles Wang.

Glory Lutheran Church: 580 Hilltop Dr., Chula Vista, CA 91910. Pastor: Vacant.

Faith Lutheran Church: 115 W. Newmark Ave., Monterey Park, CA 91754. Pastor: Vacant

New Light Chinese Christian Church: N. 1700 Rand Rd., Palatine, IL 60074. Pastor: Samuel Scheift**.

Portland Taiwan Lutheran Church: 12405 S. W. Butner Rd., Beaverton, OR 97005. Pastor: Vacant.

First Taiwanese Christian Church: 6875 Synott Rd., Houston, TX 77083. Pastor: Vacant.

Living Truth Chinese Lutheran Church: 10207 N. E. 183rd St., Bothell, WA 98011. Pastor: Vacant.

Grace Chinese Lutheran Church: 538 N. E. 127 St., Seattle, WA 98125. Pastor: Jimmy Hao.

Sammamish Hill Lutheran Chinese Ministry: 22818 S. E. 8th St., Sammanish, WA 98074. Pastor: Wendy Cheung.

Seattle Taiwanese Lutheran Fellowship: 4315 129th Pl. S. E., Bellevue, WA 98006. Pastor: Jeremy Shih.

Indian and South Asian:

Purna Jiwan South Asian Ministry, c/o First Lutheran Church: 3500 W. Fullerton Ave., Chicago, IL 60647. Pastor: Eardley Mendis.

Church of Everlasting Life: 35851 Utica Rd., Clinton Twp, MI 48035. Pastor: John Gill*.

St. John Lutheran Church South Asian Outreach: 23225 Gill Rd., Farming Hills, MI. Pastor: Stella Weller**

Indonesian:

HKBP California: 1609 Hamner Ave., Norco, CA 92860. Leader: Anton Butarbutar**.

HKBP Lutheran Church: 2108 North Euclid Ave., Upland, CA 91784. Leader: Hasudungan Hutajulu**.

HKBP Montclair Lutheran Church: 1401 Poplar St., Denver, CO 80220. Pastor: Vacant.

Japanese:

Fruits of the Spirit: 2706 W. 182nd St., Torrance, CA 90504. Pastor: Hong Sun Kim

Korean:

Advent Lutheran Church: 1416 Vernon St., LaGrange, GA 30240. Pastor: Min Chan Park.

Naperville Yuhllin Church: 2200 Ridge Ave., Aurora IL 60504. Pastor: Vacant.

Abiding Presence Lutheran Church: 10774 Rhode Island Ave., Beltsville, MD 20705. Pastor: Jongkil Na.

Philadelphia Korean Lutheran Church: 211 S. Main St., North Wales, PA 19454. Pastor: Jonathan (Chung Ok) Shin.

Conclusion

Almost all of our ministries are immigrant oriented, as these profiles show. A few are trying to bridge the gap between immigrants and the American born by offering English language worship services. Pastors and leaders are responding to their contexts creatively to meet people's needs and foster their faith and well-being. They are drawing from their socio-cultural, historical and personal resources to serve as best they can.

The profiles also imply that our ministries will continue to be immigrant oriented as long as Asians immigrate to the US. Even so, an ongoing shift is appearing between the immigrant generation and the US born generations. This pattern confirms that our leaders need to look ahead to see how the stream may change course, and to plan for working with that flow for the future.

PART III

Who is Who in Ministry

III | Who is Who in Ministry

Small in number but significant! As of 2018, there were 19,279 Asians and Pacific Islanders in the Evangelical Lutheran Church in America (ELCA), or one percent of the total membership of the church. Yet we have made strong contributions to the ELCA, its predecessor bodies and church-related organizations. Our biography and service lists may be incomplete, due to faded collective memories and the absence of some written records. However, what we do have shows an extensive involvement in many areas of ministry.

Behold! Thy Servants: Brooks of the Stream

Your servants labor faithfully in your vineyard! Here are some of your vessels of living water, past and present. These summaries by or about the leaders are meant to both inform and inspire.

Adachi, Hitoshi Tikhon (1958-), a native of Japan, has served as an Evangelical Lutheran Church in America missionary in Kumamoto, Japan since 2018. He was born into a fourth-generation Russian Orthodox family in Yokohama. Ordained in 2010, he was an assistant to the bishop, Pacifica Synod, and pastor of Resurrection Lutheran Church, Huntington Beach, CA, for eight years. Formerly he was an engineer for Nihon Kohden, a medical device manufacturer in Tokyo, and a business manager for its US subsidiary in California for 25 years.

Education: BE Keio University; MS Massachusetts Institute of Technology; MDiv Luther Seminary.

Aguilar, **Corazon Gutierrez** (1942-), a native of the Philippines, was a scientist before becoming the first Filipina ordained through the Alternate Route Leading to Ordained Service program, Evangelical Lutheran Church in America. She pastored Messiah Lutheran Church, Hayward, CA; developed Maricopa Lutheran Church, Maricopa, AZ; and is currently developing a Pan-Asian ministry in Metropolitan Phoenix, hosted by Mountain View Lutheran in Ahwatukee, Phoenix. She has been a key partner in the Asian Lutheran International Conference, Filipino Lutheran Network, and many other leadership capacities.

Education: BS Adamson University; MS University of the Philippines; MTS Pacific Lutheran Theological Seminary.

[Note: For biographical details, see Edmond Yee and J. Paul Rajashekar (eds. and comps.), *Abundant Harvest: Stories of Asian Lutherans* (Minneapolis: Lutheran University Press, 2012), pp. 231-232.]

Anderson-Rajarigam, **Sarah C**. (1968-), a native of India, is pastor of Grace Evangelical Lutheran Church in Drexel Hill, PA. She was on the faculty at Indian Theological Seminary, Chennai, India before coming to the US. During her doctoral studies, she served as the director of Christian Education at Calvary Lutheran Church in the Bronx, NY.

Education: BSc Jyoti Nivas College; BD The United Theological College; ThM Princeton Theological Seminary; PhD Union Theological Seminary.

Anderson-Rajkumar, **Evangeline** (1963-), a native of India, comes from a three- generation link of Lutheran pastors. Currently she ministers at St. Peter's Lutheran Church and Gethsemane Lutheran Church, Corydon, IN. A prominent scholar and womanist theologian, her writings on body theology are considered primary readings in theology and gender studies. She has served as a professor of theology and women's studies at four seminaries: Serampore College, United Theological College, Columbia Theological Seminary and Lutheran Southern Seminary.

Education: BS Bangalore University; BD, MTh and ThD Serampore University.

Baccam, **Stephanie Sui** (1991-), a native of the US, has served as secretary and member-at-large, Association of Asians and Pacific Islanders-Evangelical Lutheran Church in America. A "pastor's kid" at her home church, Lao Evangelical Lutheran in Robbinsdale, MN, she was a youth group member who led the children's ministry. In college, Baccam became passionate about young adult leadership. She has been a key speaker at various Asian events and an Asian Lutheran International Conference young adult advocate. She continues to be a champion for young leaders today.

Education: BA Bethel University.

Baccam, **Thiem** (1961-), a native of Laos, is pastor of Lao Evangelical Lutheran Church, Robbinsdale, MN. He and his family came to the US as refugees in 1976, leaving Thailand to settle in Decorah, IA. After graduating from seminary, he was called in 1992 to develop a Lao ministry in the Minneapolis area. He was later called to pastor the congregation, which became known for its strong youth leadership programs. Baccam chairs the Lao Caucus of the Association of Asians and Pacific Islanders-Evangelical Lutheran Church in America.

Education: BA Luther College; MDiv Wartburg Theological Seminary.

Billa, **John R.** (1973-), a native of India, has been mission pastor of Atlantic Telugu Mission Church in Atlanta, GA, since 2012. He and his wife are third generation Christians from South India. He taught at two seminaries and pastored in a village before coming to the US in 2005 for further theological training. During doctoral studies at Vanderbilt University, Nashville, TN, he met Bishop Julian Gordy, who invited him to work with Telugu-speaking Indians in Atlanta.

Education: BS Andhra Christian College; BD Union Biblical Seminary; MTh Gurukul Lutheran Theological College; STM Yale Divinity School.

Burdick, Eileen (1962-), a native of the US, is a hospice chaplain at CHI Franciscan Hospice and Palliative Care in Tacoma, WA. After ordination in 2003, Burdick was a parish pastor for 12 years in the Seattle area. Before that, she spent 15 years focused on Japanese business. She was active on the Snohomish County board for health leadership, and facilitated the Respecting Choices Advance Care Planning program. Currently she serves on the Organization Committee of Hope Harbor for end-of-life care in Jefferson County, WA.

Education: BA Whitman College; MDiv Luther Seminary; Board Certification Association of Professional Chaplains.

Chang, Mary Ling-Hsi (1943-), a native of Hong Kong, China, leads an Asian ministry at St. Jacobi Lutheran Church, Brooklyn, NY. Before this, she simultaneously pastored Incarnation Lutheran Church, Cedarhurst, NY while working as a chaplain in New York City. As senior pastor at St. Jacobi (2000-2009), she innovated youth, mothers and bilingual outreach, and organized 59 free concerts for post-9/11 healing through music. Before coming to the US in 1990, she taught music and religious education.

Education: Certificate Northcote College of Education; Diploma Lutheran Bible Institute; MDiv Lutheran Theological Seminary.

Chen, David (1935-), a native of Taiwan, China, is a noted church leader, scholar, and social activist. Pastor of Taiwanese Lutheran Church, San Diego, CA (1979-2000), he was also president of the Association of Asians and Pacific Islanders -Evangelical Lutheran Church in America, and the Association of Taiwanese Christian Churches in North America. In retirement, he has directed the Center for Chinese Ministry (2000-2004 and 2017-present) and teaches theology in Taiwan, China, Thailand, Austria, and Russia.

Education: Diploma Taiwan Lutheran Theological Seminary; MDiv and MSW Waterloo Lutheran University (now Wilfred Laurier University); DMin San Francisco Theological Seminary.

[Note: For biographical details, see Edmond Yee and J. Paul Rajashekar (eds. and comps.), *Abundant Harvest: Stories of Asian Lutherans* (Minneapolis: Lutheran University Press, 2012), pp. [242-244.]

Chen, Thomas, (1942-), a native of Taiwan, China, was the executive director of Taiwan Christian Audio-Visual Association from 1975 to 1986. Afterward he shepherded Li Hsin Presbyterian Church in Taichung before immigrating to the US where he was pastor of Bethlehem Lutheran Church's Chinese ministry in California. Then he became pastor of Grace Taiwanese Lutheran Church (GTLC) in Anaheim, CA. He retired from parish ministry in 2011. While still serving GTLC, he assumed the directorship of Center for Chinese Ministry from 2004-2018.

Education: BCE and MDiv Taiwan Theological College and Seminary; MAR University of Dubuque.

[Note: For biographical details, see Edmond Yee and J. Paul Rajashekar (eds. and comps.), *Abundant Harvest: Stories of Asian Lutherans* (Minneapolis: Lutheran University Press, 2012), pp. 244-245.]

Chirala, Rita W. (1975-), a native of India, is in her first call as pastor of Faith Lutheran Church, Sault Sainte Marie, MI. In India, she held a variety of staff positions: technical support at IBM (2013–2014), technical support at Food Craft Institute (2011-2012), and team coordinator with RPG Paging Services, LTD (1997-2003). In 2014 she immigrated to the US to study theology. She is passionate about strengthening faith communities and securing a vibrant future for the church.

Education: BA University of Delhi; MDiv Lutheran School of Theology at Chicago.

Chiu, Newman (1954-), a native of Taiwan, China, leads Glory Lutheran Church, Torrance, CA, where young adults are two-thirds of the membership. With the Plowing Mission in Taiwan, he evangelized in schools, large companies, factories, and jails, and led a performing troupe that reached thousands through songs, skits, storytelling and gospel messages. With the Evangelical Covenant Church, he planted two congregations in four years and pastored them for 12 years. In the US, he shepherded a 700-member parish in Torrance before becoming an ELCA pastor developer in 2009.

Education: MDiv Chinese Evangelical Seminary; DMin Logos Seminary.

Cho, **Kevin (Sung Yong)** (1970-), a native of South Korea, was the full-time pastor of Prince of Peace Lutheran Church, Denver, CO (2001-2013) and now leads part-time at Mount Calvary Lutheran Church, Colorado Springs. He was active in Rocky Mountain Synod committees for candidacy, cross-cultural ministry, and the Generosity Project. He served widely in Asian Lutheran work as council secretary, Korean Caucus president, discipleship strategist, church planting team secretary.

Education: BA University of Colorado at Boulder; MDiv Iliff School of Theology; CATS Pacific Lutheran Theological Seminary.

Chow, **Gladys** (1945-), a native of China, is known for her longtime lay leadership and hospitality. At Christ Lutheran Church, Monterey Park, CA, she nourished youth by cooking meals at weekly gatherings for a decade. For many years, she managed logistics at all Asian Lutheran Association events hosted by the church. Chow has also chaired the Southwest California Synod Council, Evangelical Lutheran Church in America, and served on the Center for Chinese Ministry executive committee. Before coming to the US in 1974, she worked in Taiwan as a telecommunicator for Singapore-Malaysia Airlines.

Education: BA Christ College, Taiwan.

Chow, **Isaiah** (1930-), a native of China, is pastor emeritus of Bethel Chinese Lutheran Church, Seattle, WA. He was baptized in 1950 in Hong Kong. From 1952-1955 he studied at Evangelical Seminary and the Lutheran Theological Seminary. Chow served as a pastor of the Evangelical Lutheran Church of Hong Kong from 1963 to 1976. Immigrating to the US in 1976, Chow founded Bethel Chinese Lutheran Church two years later. He retired in 1995.

Education: Diploma Lutheran Theological Seminary.

Chu, **Joseph** (1957-), a native of Hong Kong, China, is an associate program director of Lutheran Disaster Response -US, Evangelical Lutheran Church in America (ELCA). He was program director for Asia and the Pacific, Global Mission, ELCA, and director of fundraising and marketing for New Horizons, a social service agency, serving people with developmental disabilities in Los Angeles, CA. He also served parishes in California and Illinois, taught at Redland University, Redlands, CA, and did non-profit administration in the US and Hong Kong.

Education: BA Pacific Lutheran University; MDiv Pacific Lutheran Theological Seminary; MPIA University of California, SD.

Chu, **Linqing*** (1991-), a native of China. After receiving her bachelor's degree in 2014 from Beijing Normal University-Hong Kong Baptist University, she entered Luther Seminary to study theology. She interned at University Lutheran Church of Hope in Minneapolis and did her chaplain residency at M Health Fairview Southdale Hospital in Edina, MN.

Education: BA Beijing Normal University-Hong Kong Baptist University; MDiv Luther Seminary.

Coffman, **Kristofer Dale** (1991-), a native of the US, is an adjunct professor of New Testament Greek and Epistles at Luther Seminary, St. Paul, MN. He is on track to become the first North American Lutheran of Cambodian descent to graduate with a PhD in biblical studies from the University of Minnesota. His mother fled the Cambodian genocide of 1974-1979. His paternal great-grandfather was a missionary in China for the Norwegian-American Lutheran Church. Currently, he is an ordination candidate in the Evangelical Lutheran Church in America.

Education: BA St. Olaf College; MDiv Luther Seminary.

Corpus, Janet M. (1948-), a native of the US, was an assistant to the bishop in the Southeastern Pennsylvania Synod (2001-2006). She taught at the Lutheran Theological Seminary at Philadelphia (1999-2001), chaired the steering committee of the Commission for Women, and served two parishes in Northern California. Her prolific writing for Augsburg Fortress includes adult and Sunday School materials for various ages, summer/camp curricula, and articles for Sunday/Monday Woman.

Education: BA Brandeis University; EdM Harvard; MCP University of California at Berkeley; PhD Massachusetts Institute of Technology; MDiv Andover Newton Theological Seminary; CATS Pacific Lutheran Theological Seminary.

Dabee, Romeo Karamchand (1975-), a native of Guyana, serves as John F. Kennedy Airport community minister and chaplain through the Christ for the World Chapel, a ministry of the Council of Churches of the City of New York. Concurrently he shepherds St. James-St. Matthew's Lutheran Church, South Ozone Park, Metropolitan New York Synod. Ordained in 2005, Dabee served his first call as associate pastor of Our Saviour Lutheran Church, Jamaica, Queens. He is passionate about celebrating the uniqueness and giftedness of all God's children.

Education: DPM and BSc University of Guyana; MDiv and STM Lutheran Theological Seminary at Philadelphia.

Dai, Evangeline* (aka Yu-jen) (1984-), a native of Taiwan, China, studies at Pacific Lutheran Theological Seminary and is an Evangelical Lutheran Church in America Fund for Leaders scholarship awardee. She works as a part-time assistant for the Theological Education for Emerging Ministries office. In 2013 she became a Christian, then moved to the US in 2014, serving at Faith Lutheran Church, Bellaire, TX (2015-2018) as a lay minister, singer, bellringer, and Chinese ministry team member. In 2019 she was an intern chaplain at MD Anderson Cancer Center.

Education: BA National Cheng Chi University.

Darla, Ananda Rao* (n.d.), a native of India, is an intern at New Creation Lutheran Church, San Jose, CA. Raised in the Hindu faith, Darla became a Christian in 1997. After immigrating to the US in 2007, he started attending Good Shepherd South Asian Ministry in Fremont, CA, where he became a Lutheran. Darla is an engineer by training and has worked in Silicon Valley, CA.

Education: BE and MTech Ranchi University, Certificate Pacific Lutheran Theological Seminary.

Dutta, Dinah (1959-), a native of India, is chaplain and spiritual director at Presbyterian Manor in Lawrence, KS. Dutta, a talented scientist and scholar, worked as a cancer researcher in Germany and the US. Her involvement with the church and ministry is extensive: pastor of two congregations, board and committee memberships, and oncology chaplain at the University of Kansas Hospital. She also serves as a behavioral interviewer for mission development, Evangelical Lutheran Church in America.

Education: PhD North-Eastern Hill University; Certificate Pacific Lutheran Theological Seminary; MDiv Wartburg Theological Seminary.

Ebenezer, Job S. (1941-), a native of India, was director of Environmental Stewardship and Hunger Education (1992-2000), Evangelical Lutheran Church in America (ELCA). In 1993 he innovated a rooftop garden at the ELCA, growing vegetables in 40 wading pools. He replicated the model in the US, Africa, Costa Rica, Belize, Ecuador, and India. Now he is president of Technology for the Poor, which he founded in 2006 in Westerville, OH, to promote urban container gardening virtually anywhere.

Education: BSc and MSc University of Madras; MSc Indian Institute of Sciences; PhD Stevens Institute of Technology.

Gaeta, Susan (1972-), a native of South Korea, is a Korean adoptee. She is pastor of Shepherd of the Valley Lutheran Church in Ayer, MA. Previously she worked in specialized ministry with Lutheran Volunteer Corps, Washington, DC. (2009-2016) and served Divine Word Lutheran Church, Milwaukee, WI (2003-2009). A member of the Congregation-based Organizing Team of the Evangelical Lutheran Church in America, she has also been active in anti-racism teams and training. She grew up in the Metropolitan New York area.

Education: BWS Valparaiso University; MDiv Trinity Lutheran Seminary; Certificate Shalem Institute for Spirit Guidance Program.

Geddada, Sarah (1968-), a native of India, has served as an associate pastor at St. Paul's International Lutheran Church, Floral Park, NY since 2014. Before this, she pastored at Redeemer Lutheran Church in Queens, NY. Ordained in 2005, she has supply preached for 40 congregations in the Metropolitan New York Synod, Evangelical Lutheran Church in America and other denominations. She comes from a family that has served for many generations as pastors and evangelists.

Education: BS Andhra University; BEd Nagarjuna University; MS Annamalai University; Certificate+Diploma United Theological College; MDiv Lutheran Theological Seminary; STM Drew University.

Genck Morton, Tasha (1982–), a native of South Korea, adopted and raised in Minnesota's Twin Cities, is associate pastor of Holy Trinity Lutheran Church, Lancaster, PA. Committed to teaching people of all ages about God's grace, she is passionate about the intersection of culture and Law-Gospel theology. Previously she served as associate pastor of St. Andrew Lutheran, Eden Prairie, MN (2008-2013), and as the intern pastor of Christ Lutheran, Charlotte, NC (2006-2007). Genck Morton contributes to Mockingbird Ministries and serves on the Lower Susquehanna Candidacy Committee and Leadership Support Team.

Education: BA Gustavus Adolphus College; MDiv Luther Seminary.

George-Guiser, Asha Mary (1957-) a native of Kuwait, is a trailblazer. First Asian and Indian Lutheran woman ordained (1982). First Asian Lutheran woman to work as a synod staff member, and with the Conference of Bishops and Division for Ministry. And first-ever Asian Lutheran preacher at an Evangelical Lutheran Church in America churchwide assembly. Now in retirement, she is a priest in the Episcopal Diocese of Pennsylvania, and a marriage-family therapist with clergy and laypeople, especially in cross-cultural settings.

Education: BS Neuman College; MDiv Lutheran Theological Seminary at Philadelphia; DMin Eastern Baptist Seminary.

[Note: For biographical details, see Edmond Yee and J. Paul Rajashekar (eds. and comps.), *Abundant Harvest: Stories of Asian Lutherans* (Minneapolis: Lutheran University Press, 2012), pp. 255-257.]

Gurning, Diakonda (1971-), a Batak native of Indonesia, is pastor of Bethel Lutheran Church, Shoreline, WA. Before his ordination in 2019, he led the Indonesian Lutheran Fellowship, a synodically authorized worshiping community of the Northwest Washington Synod, Evangelical Lutheran Church in America (ELCA). He is a social activist for immigration and refugee rights and stands alongside Native Americans to bring justice to their communities. Gurning also co-founded the Indonesian Caucus of the Association of Asians and Pacific Islanders-ELCA.

Education: Certificate Pacific Lutheran Theological Seminary.

Hagedorn, Fern Lee (1953-), a native of the US, is an award-winning filmmaker, multimedia producer, and advocate for gender and racial justice. Director of the Lutheran World Federation/USA's communications office, she also served on the related LWF board. Founder/director of American Bible Society's New Media Translations program, she led team work for fresh visual translations of Bible texts. She served on the Evangelical Lutheran Church in America's Multicultural Ministries and Global Mission boards, and "Faith, Sexism, and Justice" Social Statement Task Force. She currently takes action with the Southeastern Pennsylvania Synod's anti-racism team.

Education: BA Hunter College, University of New York.

[Note: For biographical details, see Edmond Yee and J. Paul Rajashekar (eds. and comps.), *Abundant Harvest: Stories of Asian Lutherans* (Minneapolis: Lutheran University Press, 2012), pp. 257-259.]

Hang, Shongchai (1947-), a native of Laos, has devoted almost 40 years to Southeast Asian newcomer ministry in Philadelphia, PA. Coming to the US in 1979, he became a church leader, family counselor, and president of SEAMAAC (Southeast Asian Mutual Assistance Association Coalition) in Philadelphia. Since 1996 Hang has pastored Hmong Community Evangelical Lutheran Church, Mohnton, PA. Since 2005 he has also been on the staff of SEAMAAC, empowering elders for their educational and wellness needs, health, and safety. In 2017, he won an American Association of Retired Persons Community Hero Award.

Education: BA École Lycée; MDiv Lutheran Theological Seminary at Philadelphia.

[Note: Photo © Jacques-Jean Tiziou/ www.jjtiziou.net]

Her, Jua Jay* (1970-), a native of Laos, is a candidate for ordination in the St. Paul Area Synod. He grew up in a farming family in the Laotian highlands. In 1988, at the age of 18, he came to the US. Since 1991, Her has worked as a machine technician. He is a member of Hmong Central Lutheran Church in St. Paul, MN.

Education: Certificate Wartburg Theological Seminary.

Hong, Barry A. (1947-), a native of the US, is a clinician, professor, and leading advocate for psychology in academic medicine. He was a former member of True Light Lutheran Church, New York City, and was ordained in 1972. Since 1978 he has taught psychiatry and medicine at Washington University School of Medicine, St. Louis, MO. He is also vice-chairman for Clinical Affairs in Psychiatry and chief psychologist at Barnes-Jewish Hospital, St. Louis.

Education: BA Concordia Senior College; MDiv and STM, Concordia Seminary; PhD St. Louis University.

Hong, Hyunho (1971-), a native of South Korea, pastors two California congregations: Dream Builders, Anaheim (since 2009), and St Luke's Lutheran, Fullerton (since 2016). In Korea, he taught English at private academies before embarking on religious and seminary studies. As a fourth-year seminary intern, Hong served as the Church of Dream Builders' solo pastor from mid-2009 until December 2010. In December 2010, he was officially called and ordained in the Evangelical Lutheran Church in America.

Education: BA Methodist Theological University; MTS Lutheran Theological Seminary Saskatoon; MA Seoul National University; MDiv Pacific Lutheran Theological Seminary.

Hwang, Uijin (1971-), a native of South Korea, shepherds the Lutheran Church of the Incarnation (LCI), Marietta, GA. In Korea, he was a student activist in the movement to oust the military government. He also worked in children's ministry for the Presbyterian Church of Korea. After coming to the US in 2001, he served for 12 years as a Methodist pastor in Marietta, Savannah, Edison, and Macon, GA. He joined the Evangelical Lutheran Church in America in 2014, became rostered in 2016, and was installed at LCI in 2017.

Education: ThM Yonsei University; MDiv Candler School of Theology.

Ishida, Yoshitaka Franklin (1959-), a native of Japan, is the director for Asia and the Pacific in the Global Mission (GM) of the Evangelical Lutheran Church in America. Prior to this position, he directed GM's Global Leadership Development Program. He grew up in Japan, the US, and Switzerland, which informs his work in global ministry. Ishida also served parishes in Tinley Park and Elmhurst, IL.

Education: BA St. Olaf College; MA University of Lancaster; MDiv Luther Seminary; DMin Catholic Theological Union.

[Note: For biographical details, see Edmond Yee and J. Paul Rajashekar (eds. and comps.), *Abundant Harvest: Stories of Asian Lutherans* (Minneapolis: Lutheran University Press, 2012), pp.269-271.]

Janthapaiboonkajon, Matha (1965-), a native of Thailand, has been the treasurer for the Association of Asians and Pacific Islanders-Evangelical Lutheran Church in America for eight years. She is a key leader at St. Paul Thai Lutheran Church in Forest Park, IL, where she has served as deacon for sports ministry for the past 25 years. Janthapaiboonkajon also volunteers as a translator (English and Thai) for its bilingual worship service. She worked as a nurse at Cook County Hospital for 30 years and is now retired.

Education: BSN Benedictine University, IL.

Kang, Wi Jo (1930-), a native of South Korea, is the Wilhelm Loehe professor emeritus of world mission at Wartburg Theological Seminary. He was the first Asian to occupy an endowed chair at a Lutheran seminary in North America. Kang had a distinguished academic career, having taught at three US Lutheran seminaries; three US universities (Columbia, Valparaiso, and University of California, LA); a number of theological schools overseas; as well as Yonsei University in Korea. Kang is also deeply concerned about Korean unification and often speaks passionately about the subject.

Education: BA and MDiv Concordia Seminary; MA and PhD University of Chicago.

[Note: For biographical details, see Edmond Yee and J. Paul Rajashekar (eds. and comps.), *Abundant Harvest: Stories of Asian Lutherans* (Minneapolis: Lutheran University Press, 2012), pp. 281-283.]

Keomanivong, Peter (1955–), a native of Laos, is pastor of Reborn Lao Lutheran Church, Waite Park, MN. In 1975 he had just graduated from college when communists took over Laos. He taught accounting and worked for an electrical power company for a few years. But in 1981 he and his family crossed the Mekong River to escape. They spent a year in Thai Philippine refugee camps before the United Methodist Church sponsored them into the US. He worked at the Eaton Corporation for 18 years before becoming a full-time church worker.

Education: Certificate Pacific Lutheran Theological Seminary.

Kim, Eunyoung* (1973-), a native of South Korea, has served at Morning Star Fellowship, Ridgefield, NJ, since 2017. Ordained by the Korean Presbyterian Church, she was assistant pastor at Moak Yang Presbyterian Church, New York City, before assisting the Rev. Janet Blair at Morning Star with Korean ministry from 2015 to 2016. Her education in South Korea and the US has equipped her to minister with immigrants as well as shape a faith community forum for the 1.5 and US born generations.

Education: BA and MDiv Young-nam Theological Seminary; MDiv New York Theological Seminary; ThM Young-nam Theological Seminary.

Kim, Hongsun (1969-), a native of South Korea, raised in Japan, pastors the Japanese Language Ministry at Lutheran Church of the Resurrection, Huntington Beach, CA, and Fruits of the Spirit Lutheran Community, Torrance, CA. Kim is a columnist for a SoCal Japanese language newspaper. He was a panelist for the LGBTQ Allyship Seminar at KQTcon, the first national Korean Queer and Trans Conference, New York City. Also in 2018, he facilitated a workshop for Japanese-speaking LGBTQ at the *Okaeri* ("Welcome Home") Conference, Los Angeles.

Education: BA Kwansei Gakuin University; MS Kentucky Murray State University; Certificate Pacific Lutheran Theological Seminary.

Kim, Jae Bum (1957-), a native of South Korea, works as a hospice chaplain in California. He was the pastor and mission developer of Naperville Yuhllin Church in Naperville, IL, from 2001 to 2013. Before coming to the US in 1977 to study, he worked for Asiana Airlines and SK Telecom and spent the 1996 to 1997 academic year studying at the Lutheran Theological Seminary in Hong Kong.

Education: BA and MPA Chonnam National University; MBA Cheng Chi University; MDiv Luther Seminary; Certificate AMITA Health-Alexian Brothers Medical Center; Board Certification Association of Professional Chaplains.

Kim-Chung, Chong Im* (Jenny) (1968-), a native of South Korea, immigrated to the US with her husband in 1999 and served faithfully as a pastor's spouse. Together they organized in 2005 the Alliance Church, an outreach ministry based out of their home. The group merged with Light of Grace Korean Lutheran Church in 2011. Kim-Chung also founded a non-profit multicultural school. Then, feeling a call to become a pastor, she enrolled and was trained in the Theological Education for Emerging Ministries program at Pacific Lutheran Theological Seminary, Berkeley, CA.

Education: Certificate Pacific Lutheran Theological Seminary.

Kim, Sang Soo (1965-), a native of South Korea, has been serving as the pastor of Light of Grace Korean Ministry, Federal Way, WA, since 2011. He was born into a devout third generation Christian family. After arriving in Federal Way in 1999, he started in 2005 the Alliance Church, which met regularly in his home. In 2011, the group merged with the Light of Grace Korean Lutheran Church in Federal Way. He plays a vital ecumenical role in fellowship programs with Korean churches in the area.

Education: BA Sungkyul University; MDiv Midwest University; Certificate Pacific Lutheran Theological Seminary.

Kim, Yonsu (1969-), a native of South Korea, is the pastor and worship director of Seattle Reborn Church, and a mission developer for the Northwest Washington Synod. An expert in computer crimes/privacy for the Korean government before studying law and Christian ministry, he is a published author in three specialized fields. He preaches in English and Korean at several religious organizations and churches, and is interested in missional multicultural ministry.

Education: LLM University of Washington; MDiv and MTh, Pacific Theological Seminary; BCED Tacoma Bible College.

Kishino, Yutaka (1952-), a native of Japan, was the first Asian Lutheran to be deployed as a mission developer by the Division for Mission in North America, Lutheran Church in America. Kishino also served parishes in Pennsylvania and Texas. From 1989 to 2006 he was the mission director in the Evangelical Lutheran Church in America overseeing new ministry developments in the Pacifica and Southern California West Synods. Following this service, he became an interim pastor serving a number of congregations until his retirement in 2015.

Education: BA St. Paul's Episcopal University; MDiv Lutheran Theological Seminary at Gettysburg.

[Note: For biographical details, see Edmond Yee and J. Paul Rajashekar (eds. and comps.), *Abundant Harvest: Stories of Asian Lutherans* (Minneapolis, Lutheran University Press, 2012), pp. 286-287.]

Kitahata, Stacy Dee (1961-), a native of the US, was elected in 2020 as a co-executive director of Holden Village. Also in the Pacific Northwest, she worked at the Krista Foundation for Global Citizenship; taught intercultural studies at Trinity Lutheran College; and coordinated Region 1 evangelical outreach. In Chicago, she served with the Division for Global Mission, Evangelical Lutheran Church in America, and the Lutheran School of Theology at Chicago. In Southern California, she worked with Lutheran Social Services and The American Lutheran Church Hunger Program.

Education: BA University of California at Los Angeles; MDiv McCormick Theological Seminary.

[Note: For biographical details, see Edmond Yee and J. Paul Rajashekar (eds. and comps.), *Abundant Harvest: Stories of Asian Lutherans* (Minneapolis: Lutheran University Press, 2012), pp. 287-289.]

Kleiber, Margrethe S. C. (1958-), a native of the US, currently serves as an intentional interim pastor for the Metropolitan Washington, D.C. Synod of the Evangelical Lutheran Church in America. In addition to pastoring congregations in California, Virginia, Washington D.C., and London, England, she served as program director for South Asia with the Division for Global Mission from 1998 to 2004. From 1996 to 1998 she was president of the Association of Asians and Pacific Islanders-Evangelical Lutheran Church in America.

Education: BA Yale University; MSW University of Hawaii at Manoa; MDiv Pacific Lutheran Theological Seminary; MSc London School of Economics.

[Note: For biographical details, see Edmond Yee and J. Paul Rajashekar (eds. and comps.), *Abundant Harvest: Stories of Asian Lutherans* (Minneapolis: Lutheran University Press, 2012), pp. 289-292.]

Ko, **Chulyuk (Paul)** (1973-), a native of South Korea, is a highly respected, compassionate, and sincere church leader. He served the church in Korea before coming to the US. He is now the head pastor of Seattle Covenant Community Church in Seattle, WA. He makes an effort to proclaim God's kingdom and glory on earth.

Education: BA and MDiv The Presbyterian General Assembly Theological College and Seminary; MATS Faith Evangelical College and Seminary; Certificate Pacific Lutheran Theological Seminary.

Lai, **Peter Y**. (1947-), a native of Taiwan, China, is an accomplished pianist who became an ordained minister in 1985. First he served as associate pastor at Trinity Lutheran Church, San Gabriel, CA. In 1993, as senior pastor at Christ Lutheran Church, Monterey Park, CA, he transformed the parish into a multicultural congregation. He was Region I coordinator of evangelism and multicultural ministry (1995-2000) and a professor at Trinity Lutheran College. Now retired in Las Vegas, he teaches piano.

Education: Certificate Taiwan Theological College; BA National Cheng Chi University; Certificate University of Minnesota; MDiv Luther Seminary; MTh Fuller Seminary.

Lee, **Clement (Kris)** (1938-), a native of the US, served as head of communication-related departments in the Detroit Council of Churches, American Bible Society, Lutheran Council in the USA, Lutheran Church in America, and the Episcopal Church USA. After the Lutheran/Episcopal Called to Common Mission agreement, he was received as an Episcopal priest, canonically resident in the Diocese of Long Island, NY. Adjunct pastoral NY affiliations included St. Luke's Lutheran Church in Manhattan and the Cathedral of St. John the Divine. He is now retired.

Education: BTh Concordia College, MDiv Concordia Theological Seminary; MA The New School University.

Lee, **Simon** (1947-), a native of Hong Kong, China, has served the Chinese Lutheran Church of Honolulu since 1981. He was one of the founding members of the Center for Chinese Ministry in 2000. Lee supports overseas mission and spearheaded a fundraising project to help an old Lutheran church in Xinyang, Henan, China, to rebuild a new church building in 2006. Chinese Lutheran Church of Honolulu has sent more than 20 members to seminaries.

Education: BTh Lutheran Theological seminary, MA Luther Seminary.

Lee-Brown, **S**. **Kim** (1962-), a native of the US, is pastor of Our Redeemer Lutheran Church, Marion, IL. Previously a pastor at St. John Lutheran, Princeton, IL, and St. John's, Mendota, IL, she has been active with the Northern Illinois Synod in social ministry, professional leadership, and racial justice. She has also been an internship supervisor and a mentor. Nationally, she helped plan for the 1991 Multicultural Youth Leadership Event. Globally, she has participated in two delegations to the Arcot Lutheran Church (India).

Education: BA Barnard College-Columbia University; MDiv Lutheran School of Theology at Chicago.

Li, **Joseph H**. (1967-), a native of China, is a synodically authorized worshiping community pastor at the University of Washington, Seattle. Born into a Catholic family but growing up in China's atheist environment, Li became a believer after meeting some extraordinary Christians. He became an ordained Catholic priest. Later he was drawn to Martin Luther's theology, and became a Lutheran while pursuing his doctorate. From 2010-2015, he pastored a Chinese Lutheran Church in Seattle.

Education: BA Theological and Philosophical Institute of China; MDiv St. Joseph's Seminary; MA Graduate Theological Union; ThD Jesuit School of Theology at Berkeley.

Liang, Fumi (1953-), a native of Japan, is the cultural ministry coordinator at the Lutheran Church of the Resurrection in Huntington Beach, CA, where she manages the daily needs of the Japanese ministry. She is also co-founder and board president of Care Connections Network, an organization providing assistance for older adults to age with safety, comfort, and dignity. Liang received her higher education in Taiwan. After graduation, she married and immigrated to California in 1977, where she raised her family. She is fluent in Japanese, Mandarin Chinese, and English.

Education: BA National Cheng Chi University.

Limbong, Bimen (1969-), a native of Indonesia, is the lead pastor of Christ Lutheran Church in Louisville, KY. Before coming to the US in 1995, he was trained in Indonesia. In the same year St. Mark Lutheran Church in Anchorage, AK invited him to serve as a vicar for two years. While attending Luther Seminary, he served as a lay pastor at Emmanuel Lutheran Church in Minneapolis, MN. After ordination in 2002, he was called to serve the same congregation in Anchorage until 2008. Since then he has served Christ Lutheran as an associate and lead pastor.

Education: STh Batak Protestant Christian Church Theological Seminary; DMin Luther Seminary.

Limthongviratn, Monta** (1958-), a native of Thailand, is the lay pastor at the Thai Community Church of Chicago (aka St. Paul Thai Lutheran Church). Before accompanying her husband Pongsak Limthongviratn to the US in 1989, she served a congregation in Bangkok. She was a graduate student in Biblical studies at the Lutheran School of Theology at Chicago in 2015. She was honored for her ministry at the 13th Assembly of the Association of Asians and Pacific Islanders-Evangelical Lutheran Church in America.

Education: BTh Bangkok Institute of Theology; MA Lutheran School of Theology at Chicago.

Limthongviratn, Pongsak (1955-), a native of Thailand, was the first Thai Protestant to ever earn a PhD in systematic theology. Since 1997 he has directed Asian and Pacific Islander ministries in the Evangelical Lutheran Church in America. Visionary and innovative, he expands ministry capacities with tireless commitment and energy. He is also a professor, regularly teaching intensive theology classes in Thailand. In 2015, he was one of five finalists from North America nominated by the Thai government to receive Thai Royal Decorations.

Education: BTh and MDiv Lutheran Theological Seminary; MTh and PhD Lutheran School of Theology at Chicago.

[Note: For biographical details, see Edmond Yee and J. Paul Rajashekar (eds. and comps.), *Abundant Harvest: Stories of Asian Lutherans* (Minneapolis: Lutheran University Press, 2012), pp. 296-300.]

Lin, Albert* (1962-), a native of Taiwan, China, is pastor of English ministries at Taiwanese Lutheran Church of San Diego. After 26 years in the computer industry, he began seminary studies. After receiving his MDiv degree, he left his management position at Qualcomm to serve in pastoral ministries. He focuses on individual and small-group discipleship, with the emphasis on using Christian life as an example to influence life of others. He started English language ministries in 2016 so that the church can serve immigrant families in Taiwanese, Mandarin Chinese and English.

Education: BA Feng Chia University; MS San Diego State University; MDiv Bethel Seminary.

Lin, Shen (1953-), a native of Taiwan, China, was pastor of Minnesota Faith Chinese Lutheran Church, St. Paul, MN from 2003 to 2020. He was a high school math teacher in Taiwan before coming to the US in 1979. In the US he worked as an IT tech team leader and manager-director at Unisys, Cray Research, Secure Computing for Internet Security (MN), and Morgan Stanley Global Financial Solution (NYC) for 25 years. While working in Minnesota he served as a minister at Evangelical Formosan Church, St. Paul; Taiwanese Fellowship and Como Evangelical Free Church, Minneapolis.

Education: BS Taiwan Normal University; MS Wright State University; MS University of Minnesota; MDiv Bethel Seminary.

Liu, **Paul*** (1963-), a native of Taiwan, China, has served as the senior pastor of Taiwanese Lutheran Church, San Diego, CA, since 2015. After college and seminary in Taiwan, he worked at Cosmic Light, a Christian publishing company, as a pastor in New Zealand, Australia, and Taiwan, and also as a chaplain at Chia-yi Christian Hospital in Taiwan. Liu is a popular Christian TV personality. Since 1999 he has traveled to Taiwan several times a year to record his television show.

Education: MDiv China Evangelical Seminary.

Lu, **Abraham** (1957-), a native of Taiwan, China, is a faithful church leader, missionary, and teacher in the US, Asia, and Europe. He received his undergraduate and seminary education in Taiwan before immigrating to the US in 1985. To prepare himself for Lutheran ministry, he spent one year at Pacific Lutheran Theological Seminary followed by an internship at a congregation in El Cerrito, CA. He is pastor of Grace Chinese Lutheran Church, Elmhurst, NY.

Education: BA Fu-Jen Catholic University; MDiv Taiwan Theological Seminary; CATS Pacific Lutheran Theological Seminary; MA City University of New York; DMin and STM Lutheran Theological Seminary at Philadelphia.

Lun, **Ryan** (1974-), a native of Hong Kong, China, is the first Chinese Lutheran ordained in the New England Synod, Evangelical Lutheran Church in America. His call is to reach out to Chinese communities in the Greater Boston area, and to strengthen ecumenical relationships. In 2012 he founded Good Neighbor Lutheran Church, the first and only Cantonese-speaking congregation in New England Synod, in Quincy, MA. He also serves on the Inter-Church Council of Wollaston and Quincy, and was invited by the Episcopal Diocese of Massachusetts to minister with the St. Paul Cathedral Chinese Congregation.

Education: Dip. in Social Work Hong Kong Polytechnic University; MDiv Wartburg Theological Seminary.

McCracken, Mikka (n.d.), a native of South Korea, was adopted into the McCracken family at the age of six months. She has worked at the Evangelical Lutheran Church in America (ELCA) churchwide organization in various roles, such as director for Strategy and Engagement with ELCA World Hunger, and now as the first executive for Innovation and director of the Innovation Lab. She also serves on the Board of Trustees of Gustavus Adolphus College, and the Vorstand of the ELCA Wittenberg Center in Germany.

Education: BA Gustavus Adolphus College; Certificate University of Illinois; Certificate Harvard Business School Executive Education.

Miller, Joyce A. (1961-), a native of the US, has served in hospital chaplaincy since 1998. Currently she works as a bilingual chaplain at the Nebraska Medical Center. Formerly she was on staff at Alegent Immanuel Medical Center and Bryan LGH Medical Center, both in Nebraska. Besides her chaplaincy work, Miller regularly supply preaches in Evangelical Lutheran Church in America and other mainline churches in Nebraska and Iowa. Before moving to Nebraska, she pastored at Riverton Heights Lutheran, Tukwila, WA, and did chaplaincy for Lutheran Ministries, Seattle, WA.

Education: BA Valparaiso University; MDiv Lutheran School of Theology at Chicago.

Miller, Julius (1957-), a native of India, has pastored Our Redeemer's Lutheran Church, Hancock, MN, since 1999. In India, he worked as an office manager and bookkeeper before serving in Mumbai's slums for several years with a Christian organization. Miller came to the US in 1990. He found work as a hotel front desk clerk in New Jersey before deciding to go to seminary and become a pastor.

Education: BA Bhopal University; MDiv Lutheran Brethren Seminary.

Mittelstaedt, Darcy J. (1972-), a native of South Korea, is a deacon who serves as a bishop's associate in the Southwestern Texas Synod. Previously she was a deacon at Holy Trinity Lutheran Church, Chandler, AZ (2004-2018) and director for Youth and Family Ministry at St. Thomas Lutheran, Omaha, NE while becoming rostered in the Evangelical Lutheran Church in America (ELCA) (1999-2003). Theologically trained at Luther Seminary, her church service includes synodical anti-racism efforts and teamwork for the ELCA Youth Gathering. She is an adoptee raised by a family in Nebraska.

Education: BA Midland University.

Miyaishi, Kyuzo (1929 -), a native of Japan, has devoted 50 years to tentmaking prison ministry. Coming to the US in 1961, he began visiting inmates as a seminarian in 1963, at the Central Correctional Institution (CCI), Columbia, SC. Ordained by the Lutheran Church in America; he worked at CCI as an educator and librarian (1973-2001) known as "Frankie San." Later he helped HIV/AIDS prisoners with end-of-life care. Retired in 2001, he is still volunteering to help, including showing at art galleries 250 works of art created by inmates.

Education: BA Hosei University; MRE Lutheran Theological Southern Seminary.

Moldwin, Rosalind (1938-), a native of the Philippines, was the first chairperson-president, Association of Asians-Evangelical Lutheran Church in America. An inner-city pastor's wife and mother of three in 1960s Detroit, MI, she entered the medical field after observing tremendous needs for health care. From 1976 to 2006, she worked as a PA-C (physician assistant recertified every six years). She trailblazed on Michigan's first licensing board for PAs and as the first PA on Connecticut's medical board.

Education: BA Macalester College; MRE Hartford Seminary; MS Mercy College; Certificate National Commission on the Certification of Physician Assistants.

Mortha, Reginald (1964-), a native of India, was an ordained pastor of the Andhra Evangelical Lutheran Church. He served for 11 years before immigrating to the US where he transferred his membership to the Metropolitan Chicago Synod. He was pastor of Martin Luther Lutheran Church from 2004-2010 and then served as a trauma staff chaplain for Sinai Health Systems for eight years.

Education: BD United Theological College; MA North Park Theological Seminary; MTh Gurukul Theological College and Research Institute.

Mortha, Sunitha (1971-), a native of India, is associate to the bishop as director of Equipping and Resourcing, Metropolitan Chicago Synod. She manages intercultural inventory development also. She was ordained through the Andhra Evangelical Lutheran Church in India. For over 15 years she directed Global Mission Education and Interpretation for the Evangelical Lutheran Church in America. She conceived and launched events on how global and local realities intersect for mission. She developed a 170-member multi-racial, multi-ethnic global musicians community to embody accompaniment in mission.

Education: BA St. Francis College; MA Luther Seminary.

Nakamura, C. Lynn (1956-), a native of the US, is professor emerita of Old Testament and learning technologies, Trinity Lutheran Seminary (TLS) , Columbus, OH, where she taught from 1988 to 2013. She established Mindful Calling, a leadership development and coaching practice in the Columbus area in 2012. From 2017-2018, she served as interim registrar and interim director of graduate studies of TLS at Capital University. And since 2019 she has provided oversight for candidacy and leadership development for the Southern Ohio Synod, Evangelical Lutheran Church in America.

Education: BA Susquehanna University; MDiv Lutheran Theological Seminary at Philadelphia; PhD Princeton Theological Seminary.

Nakamura, Paul T. (1926-), a native of the US, was "the first Asian cleric to provide ministry with Asians in North America and an advocate for multicultural ministries." Born into a Buddhist family, Nakamura eventually became a Christian and then a Lutheran during his seminary studies. A leader in Asian ministry and activism locally and nationally, he organized in Greater Los Angeles the first Japanese church--Lutheran Oriental Church--in the Lutheran Church in America. He has continued to serve there even after his retirement in 1998.

Education: BA Gustavus Adolphus College; BD Augustana Lutheran Seminary

[Notes: For Biographical details and quotation, see Edmond Yee and J. Paul Rajashekar (eds. and comps.), *Abundant Harvest: Stories of Asian Lutherans* (Minneapolis: Lutheran University Press, 2012), pp. 322-324. [Hereafter cited as Yee and Rajashekar.] Yee and Rajashekar, p. 322. See also Part III: Who is Who in Ministries: "Lo! Thy Servants on the Move: Flowing Far and Wide" in this volume.]

Nelavala, Surekha (1970-), a native of India, is an ordained biblical scholar. She has served as adjunct professor at Trinity Lutheran Seminary, United Seminary in Gettysburg, and Pacific Lutheran Theological Seminary while pastoring parishes in Maryland. She is a presenter at international forums, and since 2017 secretary of Asian Lutheran International Conference. Before coming to the US in 2000, she was an executive director of the Women's Desk, United Evangelical Lutheran Churches in India and taught theology at two schools in that country as well.

Education: BSc Sri Venkateswara University; BD and MTh Serampore University; MPhil and PhD Drew University.

Ng, Doris (n. d.), a native of Singapore, was a pastor of Grace Lao Lutheran Church in Richmond, CA (2009-2019). After becoming a Christian in the early 1970s, she attended the Bible Institute of Singapore. She taught at the Assemblies of God Bible School in Thailand, and ministered with the Thai community, mostly with construction workers and maids in Singapore. She came to the US for further education in 1989. Currently she is looking into interim ministry.

Education: Diploma Bible Institute of Singapore; BA North Central University; MDiv and DMin Bethel Theological Seminary.

Olivar, Deogracias (1964-), a native of the Philippines, leads the International Evangelical Lutheran Church (IELC), San Diego, CA. In 2001, he began a Filipino ministry in San Diego, hosted by Hope Lutheran, a White congregation with a declining membership. In 2010 the ministry and congregation merged, with Olivar serving as the solo pastor. In 2018 Hope sold the building, using a portion of the sale to continue Filipino ministry. Thus IELC was born. Olivar, spiritual director of the South Bay Terrace Filipino-American Seniors Association, is also a hospice chaplain.

Education: BS Divine Word College; BD Lutheran Theological Seminary.

Onelangsy, Phouthaly (1967-), a native of Laos, is pastor of St. Paul Lao Lutheran Church, Des Moines, IA. Raised in a devout Buddhist family, he started working at age eight to sustain his family after his father's imprisonment. The family reunited in a refugee camp in Thailand. In 1983 Slate Hill Mennonite Church in Pennsylvania (PA) sponsored them and inspired him to become a Christian and a pastor. He served a Mennonite parish in PA before becoming a Lutheran pastor through the Theological Education for Emerging Ministries program.

Education: Certificate Wartburg Theological Seminary.

Panahon, Marcos Jr. (1973-), a native of the Philippines, was a missionary pastor for 10 years at a Baptist Church in Nueva Ecija before coming to the US in 2008. He then served at Eagle Rock Lutheran Church in Los Angeles. Currently he is a bi-vocational assistant pastor at St. Matthew's Lutheran Church, Glendale, CA for Filipino ministry while also working at EMJ Apparel Group, LLC in Los Angeles.

Education: BTh and BAD Great Shepherd Bible College and Seminary; Certificate Pacific Lutheran Theological Seminary.

Penumaka, Emmanuel Joshua Peter (n.d.), a native of India, is pastor of Trinity Lutheran Church, Lebanon, IN and a PhD candidate in the Lutheran School of Theology at Chicago. Before coming to the US in 2010, he practiced law in the Andhra Pradesh Bar Council. He also served parishes in India and was state program secretary of the Student Christian Movement of India. And for 15 years he served as missionary and pastor of a Chinese church in Hong Kong.

Education: BD United Theological College; MTh Lutheran Theological Seminary.

Penumaka, Hephzibah* (1992–), a native of India, is interning in Washington, DC, while pursuing her MST degree at United Lutheran Seminary. A fifth-generation Lutheran, she lived in Bangalore and Hong Kong before moving to the US with her parents (2000). She has served as vice-president and Queens borough representative of the Lutheran Youth Organization (LYO), Metropolitan New York Synod, and attended the national LYO convention, Mississippi (2009). Penumaka has also been active in national Lutheran Youth Gatherings and in leadership roles at Princeton Theological Seminary.

Education: BA Queen's College, City University of New York; MDiv Princeton Theological Seminary.

Penumaka, Israel Daniel Peter (n.d.), a native of India, has served as pastor developer of St. Paul International Lutheran Church, Floral Park, NY, since coming to the US in 2000 and later became its senior pastor. Ordained in 1989 through Andhra Evangelical Lutheran Church in India, he pastored rural congregations; was program secretary of Student Christian Movement of India; and regional secretary, Asia-Pacific Region, for World Student Christian Federation in Geneva, Switzerland. While pursuing his doctorate in Hong Kong, he served as interim pastor of Kowloon Union Church.

Education: BD, MA and MTh Union Theological College.

Penumaka, **Moses Paul Peter** (1960-), a native of India, is director of the Theological Education for Emerging Ministries program, Pacific Lutheran Theological Seminary. He is a critical thinker regarding dominant theologies, ideologies and technological development. Before coming to the US in 2000, he was pastor of a nine-point rural parish, youth director for 250 parishes of his denomination, and the national general secretary of the Student Christian Movement of India. While studying for his doctoral degree in the US, he developed a South Asian ministry in Fremont, CA.

Education: BD and MTh United Theological College; ThD Graduate Theological Union.

Periannan, **Selvaraj** (1958-), a native of India, is pastor of Hettinger Lutheran Church, Hettinger, ND. Born into a Catholic peasant family in a rural village in Tamilnadu, South India, at age 18, he felt a call to the priesthood. In 1988, he was ordained into the Congregation of Missionary Brothers of St. Francis of Assisi. Later, he became a missionary to Zimbabwe, Burkina Faso (Africa), and the Catholic Dioceses of Bismarck, ND, in 2006. After being a priest for 29 years, he joined the Evangelical Lutheran Church in America.

Education: BA Kamaraj University; BTh St. Paul Seminary.

Peter-Dass, **Rakesh** (n.d.), a native of India, is assistant professor of Religion, Hope College, Holland, MI. He was joint executive secretary for Ecumenical Formation, Gender Justice, and Youth Empowerment for the Christian Conference of Asia. He co-chairs the American Academy of Religion, Theology and Religious Reflection Unit. A prolific author and editor of many books and essays, he also consults for private, public, for-profit, and nonprofit institutions.

Education: BCOM and MCOM Nagpur University; MDBA Indian Institute of Modern Management; MDiv Yale University; DipTh University of London; ThD Harvard University; MBA University of Oxford.

Ponnala, John V. P. R. (1969-), a native of India, is a family advocate coordinator and surgery chaplain at the Johns Hopkins Hospital, Baltimore, MD. He is the area certification chair for Area II of the Association of Professional Chaplains, and serves on the Commission of the Board of Chaplaincy Certification, Inc. His community work empowers people at the margins including the Dalits of India. He is also a board member of the Asian American Community of Frederick, MD.

Education: BD and MA Ecumenical Seminary, The United Theological College; Diploma Bossey Ecumenical Institute of the World Council of Churches.

Rafanan, Martin Juan (1951-), a native of the US, is a political activist pastor. Currently a supply pastor for Pittsburgh Lutheran United Ministries, he previously organized low-wage workers and directed social service and community nonprofits. He was director of the Berkeley Food and Housing Project, the National Conference for Community and Justice, and Gateway Homeless Services. He also served parishes in Berkeley, CA, and St. Louis, MO. The Central States Synod called him to Specialized Ministry from 1994 until he retired in 2017.

Education: BA Simpson University; MDiv Christ Seminary- Seminex; DMin Lutheran School of Theology at Chicago.

Rajan, Frederick E. N. (1949-), a native of India, is a parish pastor, writer, church and healthcare executive, and founding member of numerous social service and interfaith community organizations. From 1992-2006, as executive director for the Commission for Multicultural Ministries in the Evangelical Lutheran Church in America, he advanced interculturalism across the church through boldly innovative programs. He served as vice president for Mission and Spiritual Care at Advocate Health Care, Chicago, from 2006 until his retirement in 2019.

Education: BA and MA Madras University; MDiv and MTh Faith Evangelical Lutheran Seminary.

[Notes: For biographical details, see Edmond Yee and J. Paul Rajashekar (eds. and comps.), *Abundant Harvest: Stories of Asian Lutherans* (Minneapolis: Lutheran University Press, 2012), pp. 347-350. Further see, Part III: Who is Who in Ministries: "Lo! Thy Servants on the Move: Flowing Far and Wide" in this volume.]

Rajashekar, Esther (1948-), a native of India, is a pioneer: the first woman to enter seminary in South India; one the first secretaries for Women in the Church of South India; the first national program secretary for Women, United Evangelical Lutheran Churches; and the first program secretary for the Student Christian Movement of India. She also served churches in India and Geneva, Switzerland before her ordination in 1996. Then she pastored two churches in the US until her retirement in 2015.

Education: BSc Karnataka University; BA United Theological College; MA University of Iowa; STM Lutheran Theological Seminary at Philadelphia.

[Note: for biographical details, see Edmond Yee and J. Paul Rajashekar (eds. and comps.), *Abundant Harvest: Stories of Asian Lutherans* (Minneapolis: Lutheran University Press, 2010), pp. 354-357.]

Rajashekar, J. Paul (1948-), a native of India, is Luther D. Reed professor of systematic theology at United Lutheran Seminary, director of the Asian Theological Summer Institute, and a former academic dean of the seminary. Before coming to the US in 1991, he taught at Gurukul Lutheran Theological College, and United Theological College in India. He served as an executive secretary for dialogue at the Lutheran World Federation. He is a prolific author and editor of many books and essays.

Education: BA St. Philomena's College, University of Mysore; BD United Theological College; STM Concordia Seminary-Seminex; PhD University of Iowa.

[Note: For biographical details, see Edmond Yee and J. Paul Rajashekar (eds. and comps.), *Abundant Harvest: Stories of Asian Lutheran* (Minneapolis: Lutheran University Press, 2012), pp. 357-361.]

Rambing, Feronika**(1962–), a native of Indonesia with roots in Huria Kristen Batak Protestan, leads California Batak Lutheran Church, Pomona, CA. Before parish ministry, she was an assistant director of Admissions and Registrar at Union University of California. With the Evangelical Lutheran Church in America (ELCA), she serves on the Asian Church Planting Team and the Association of Asians and Pacific Islanders-ELCA Executive Committee. She was also an ELCA Churchwide Council member (2011-2014).

Education: MS University of Indonesia; MTh International Theological Seminary; BD Indonesian Christian University; BD Sekolah Tinggi Theologia.

Rasche, **Tuhina Verma** (1979-), a native of the US, is a second generation Indian American ecumenical church leader. A sought-after writer and speaker, she engages at the intersections of faith, identities, and justice. Currently she is the minister of small group at University AME (African Methodist Episcopal) Zion Church in Palo Alto, CA, through a specialized call with the Sierra Pacific Synod, Evangelical Lutheran Church in America. Prior to this, she worked at St. Paul Lutheran Church in Oakland, CA, and Grace Lutheran Church in Palo Alto.

Education: BA Clemson University; MDiv Pacific Lutheran Theological Seminary.

Reinschmidt, **Nirmala** (1958-), a native of India, for the past 20 years has been serving congregations in the Minneapolis/St. Paul area of Minnesota. Currently she is pastor of Christ Lutheran Church, Byron, MN. Before immigrating to the US, she was a senior high school teacher and a member of Arcot Lutheran Church in India. She is married to Paul, an engineer at IBM in Rochester, MN. Together they have one daughter, Hannah, who is a second year student at Baldwin Wallace University, Cleveland, OH.

Education: MDiv and MTh Luther Seminary.

Roeun, **Soriya** (1953-), a native of Cambodia, has pastored United Asian Evangelical Lutheran Church (UAELC), Dakota City, NE, since 2008. In Cambodia, he was a city police officer and then an army sergeant in the Cambodian military during the Vietnam War. He came to the US in 1976 from a refugee camp in Thailand; joined Salem Lutheran Church, Dakota City; and felt the call to ministry in the late 1990s. Trained through the Theological Education for Emerging Ministries program, Roeun was ordained in 2008. He retired in 2019 and serves part-time at UAELC.

Education: Certificate Pacific Lutheran Theological Seminary.

Sabbithi, J.B. (1961–), a native of India, was chaplain at Christian Medical College, Vellore, India, for 15 years, introducing Clinical Pastoral Education there. In Hawaii in 2002, he became the founding chaplain at Kaiser Foundation Hospital, Honolulu, through Pacific Health Ministry. Later he directed counseling services for Hospice Hawaii. In 2019, he accepted a call to Joy of Christ Lutheran Church, Pearl City, HI. He is passionate about how culture influences our end-of-life care decisions.

Education: BA Andhra Christian College; BD United Theological College; DMin Lutheran School of Theology at Chicago; Board Certification Association of Professional Chaplains.

Sabbithi, Omega Varma (1951–), a native of India, is a hospice chaplain at Advocate Aurora Health in the Chicago area. Sabbithi first came to the US in 1991 to study Clinical Pastoral Education (CPE) before returning to India to promote healing ministry with the Christian Medical Association. In 1999, he returned to the US to do his CPE residency. In 2012, to honor his late son Alpha, Sabbithi and his wife founded Team Alpha International, an organization that conducts health camps and gospel meetings in India.

Education: BS Andhra Christian Theological College; BD Serampore University; DMin Chicago Theological Seminary.

Sagar, Alfred V. (1936-), a native of India, retired from Kalamazoo Valley Community College as dean of Learning Resources and dean of Communication Arts. He also taught at two institutions of higher learning. Before coming to the US he was an assistant lecturer at P. R. Government College, and a lieutenant company commander of the National Cadet Corps. He has served the church in a variety of capacities, for leadership development and multicultural ministries.

Education: BA and BA (hons) and MA Andhra University; MSL Western Michigan University.

[Note: For biographical details, see Edmond Yee and J. Paul Rajashekar (eds. and comps.), *Abundant Harvest: Stories of Asian Lutherans* (Minneapolis: Lutheran University Press, 2012), pp. 361-363.]

Sagar, Mary B. (1939-), a native of India, was a professor of mathematics at Anna Aram Satyavathi College before coming to the US in 1967. She managed the Information Center at Kalamazoo Spice Extraction Company while serving the church in a variety of capacities. She was a member of two boards — Women of the Evangelical Lutheran Church in America (ELCA) and the Division for Global Mission — and Treasurer of the Association of Asians-ELCA. Currently she heads the Christian Cancer Center, a family ministry in India.

Education: BA Andhra University; MA Banaras Hindu University; MSL Western Michigan University.

[Note: For biographical details, see Edmond Yee and J. Paul Rajashekar (eds. and comps.), *Abundant Harvest: Stories of Asian Lutherans* (Minneapolis: Lutheran University Press, 2012), pp. 361-363.]

San Diego, Rachel* (1987-), a native of the US, is a student at Pacific Lutheran Theological Seminary. Currently she is interning as a chaplain at the University of California Davis Health. In 2017, she was a prevention coordinator at Advocates for Victims of Violence, AK, leading a coalition to prevent power-based violence. In 2015, she worked as a community health educator at Youth Outreach Waikiki Health, HI. She served youth who were unhoused, incarcerated, and in substance rehabilitation. San Diego was raised in the Christian faith. She became a Lutheran in 2018.

Education: BA University of California, Merced.

Sanders, Violeta (1964-), a native of the Philippines, was ordained in the United Church of Christ in 2008. For the next ten years she served as a pulpit supply pastor. She is now serving the Eagle Rock Lutheran Church, a Filipino ministry, in Los Angeles, CA while concurrently doing chaplaincy work.

Education: BSE Philippine Normal College; MDiv Pacific School of Religion.

Schultz, Jennifer L. (1970-), a native of the US, leads Bethlehem Lutheran Church, Los Alamitos, CA. For twenty years she was a pastor in Washington State. She felt the call to ministry while growing up in Minnesota, especially influenced by her family (her father and two uncles are retired pastors) and her work as a Bible Camp counselor for three summers. She has been active in various leadership positions synodically, and is currently a team leader with the Evangelical Lutheran Church in America Youth Gathering.

Education: BA Gustavus Adolphus College; MDiv Luther Seminary.

Shao, Herbert (1968-), a native of Taiwan, China, is a lieutenant colonel deputy command chaplain at the Headquarters Air Education and Training Command (AETC), Joint Base in San Antonio-Randolph, TX. He assists the command chaplain in directing and maintaining the trained, equipped, and professional AETC Chaplain Corps personnel. He is also responsible for the overall planning, organizing, and implementation of policy for 254 personnel, 42 million dollars in facilities, and an annual budget of over eight million dollars.

Education: BA Trinity Luther College; MDiv Luther Seminary.

Shen, Jane Chen (1941-), a native of China, served as a Southeast Asia regional representative from 2002 to 2005 for the Division for Global Mission, Evangelical Lutheran Church in America. Prior to this call, she pastored a congregation in Washington State. And from 1968 to 1999, Shen worked as an accountant and software developer. After her retirement in 2005, she has volunteered in pastoral ministry at two local assisted living and skilled nursing and rehabilitation facilities.

Education: BS Cheng Gong University; MS Kansas State University; Certificate Pacific Lutheran Theological seminary.

[Note: For biographical details, see Edmond Yee and J. Paul Rajashekar (eds. and comps.), *Abundant Harvest: Stories of Asian Lutherans* (Minneapolis: Lutheran University Press, 2012), pp. 368-370.]

Shen, Peter K. (1938-), a native of China, was a nuclear engineer before completing theological studies in 1996 and pastoring two congregations in Washington State. Then he nurtured relationships and supported witness and service as an Asia-Pacific regional representative for the Evangelical Lutheran Church in America's Division for Global Mission. After retirement in 2005, he has worked as a volunteer in China, coordinating programs for earthquake relief, social ministries, rural community development, health care, church building, and grassroots church leadership development.

Education: BS Taiwan National University; MS University of Minnesota; PhD Kansas State University; Certificate Pacific Lutheran Theological Seminary.

[Note: For biographical details, see Edmond Yee and J. Paul Rajashekar (eds. and comps.), *Abundant Harvest: Stories of Asian Lutherans* (Minneapolis: Lutheran University Press, 2012), pp. 368-370.]

Shih, Jeremy (1957-), a native of Taiwan, China, has led the Seattle Taiwanese Lutheran Fellowship since 2011. Before coming to the US in 1983, he served a parish in Taiwan. In 1986 he was ordained by the Presbyterian Church of the USA. In 1990 he returned to Taiwan where he served two congregations before returning to the US in 2000. He then pastored a congregation in the Reformed Church in America before he was called to serve the First Taiwanese Lutheran Church in Houston, TX (2003-2010).

Education: MDiv Tainan Theological Seminary; DMin San Francisco Theological Seminary.

Sianipar, Esther Kristianti* (1974–), a native of Indonesia, is a third-year student at Luther Seminary. She first came to the US in 1986, returning to Indonesia 18 years later. From 2004 to 2018 she worked there in government, public policy, and non-profit companies focusing on marginalized communities. She has led initiatives for clean and safe water and access to education, technology, health care, and income. She was also active in her church as a Sunday school teacher and coordinator of youth and family ministries.

Education: BA Wittenberg University; MAIA Ohio University.

Sijera-Grant, **Maria Gracia** (1956 -), a native of the Philippines, has been president, Association of Asians and Pacific Islanders–Evangelical Lutheran Church in America (AAPI-ELCA) since 2016. She works with other ELCA ethnic association presidents to advocate and speak in unified ways to model being church together. At First Evangelical Lutheran Church, Ellicott City, MD, she was an associate pastor in 2002, interim senior pastor, and upon retirement in 2019, pastor emeritus. She also served on her Synod Council and Racial Justice Ministry Team and chairs the AAPI Filipino Caucus.

Education: BA Far Eastern University; Certificate Pacific Lutheran Theological Seminary.

Silaban, **Samuel A. K**. (1969-), a native of Indonesia, has served as a chaplain at Lutheran Social Services and Eger Lutheran Homes and Services in New York City since 2017. He was the pastor of Batak Indonesian Lutheran Church in New York City from 2004 to 2013. In 2009 he became a rostered member of the Evangelical Lutheran Church in America. Before coming to the US, he was an ordained pastor of the Huria Kristen Batak Protestan (HKBP) in Indonesia and a professor at the HKBP Bible School for Women.

Education: BD and MTh Huria Kristen Batak Protestan Theological Seminary.

Singkeovilay, **Samee** (1970–), born in Laos of the Lahu tribe, is associate pastor at Christ Lutheran Church in Visalia, CA, responsible for Lahu ministry there. During the Vietnam War, he lived in a refugee camp in Thailand before entering the US in 1991. He worked as a sound technician for Lahu First Assembly of God Church, Visalia. In 2006, he began a new ministry, using Christ Lutheran as a base. Later this group become a part of Christ Lutheran. Singkeovilay was the first Lahu ordained in the Evangelical Lutheran Church in America.

Education: Certificate Pacific Lutheran Theological Seminary.

Siong, William Tue (1973-), a native of Laos, is the pastor/mission developer of Good Samaritan Lutheran Church, St. Paul, MN, reaching out since 2010 to second and third generation Hmong. Previously he pastored Hmong Central Lutheran Church, St. Paul. Siong came to the US in 1988 as a 15 year old refugee, became a Christian in 1991, and was ordained in 2004. He has served on the St. Paul Area Synod Council, and chairs the Hmong Caucus, Association of Asians and Pacific Islanders-Evangelical Lutheran Church in America.

Education: BA Crown College; MDiv and DMin Luther Seminary.

Sornchai, Adam (1982-), a native of the US, is Thai American and pastor of St. John Lutheran Church (Windfall) in Cardington, OH. Since 2014 he has chaired the Northwestern Ohio Synod Worship Committee. Since 2018 he has been an executive board member of the Ohio Council of Churches. He and his wife are foster parents who have adopted four children. He is currently working on a Doctor of Ministry degree at the Methodist Theological School in Ohio in Delaware, OH.

Education: BA and MA St. John's University; MDiv Lutheran Theological Seminary at Gettysburg.

Tan, George (1950-), a native of Hong Kong, China, was an assistant to the bishop for Mission Empowerment (2002-2010) at the Southwest California Synod, and deployed as an Evangelical Lutheran Church in America's Division for Outreach mission director (2006-2010) for congregational new starts/redevelopments. Before this, he built up a Chinese congregation intergenerationally in Berkeley, CA and redeveloped an older adult challenged White parish into a vibrant multiethnic church in Cerritos, CA. He authored *Reconcilable Differences*, a Bible study series on cross-cultural interactions.

Education: B Soc Sc Hong Kong University; MDiv Luther Seminary; MA University of Minnesota; DMin Golden Gate Baptist Seminary.

Taveesap, Sirintip** (1981-), a native of Thailand, has been a missioner to Thai young adults in Greater Chicago since 2018. She was an intern at St. Paul Thai Lutheran Church in 2015. Before coming to the US to serve as a missioner, she was an evangelist in the Hoy Som Suk community in Chiang Mai, Thailand. She was also an editor of a Christian online magazine Voice of Believers and an artist in the Thai Christian Artist group.

Education: BA Rajamangala University of Technology; MDiv McGilvary College of Divinity, Payap University.

Thasiah, Victor (1971-), a native of the US, is an associate professor of Religion and chair of the Religion Department at California Lutheran University. He is an environmental activist and scholar. He is also the founder and executive director of Runners for Public Lands, a 501(c) (3) nonprofit environmental organization that works with runners on climate action, environmental sustainability, the protection and restoration of public lands, and equitable access.

Education: BA UC Santa Cruz; MDiv Princeton Theological Seminary; DPhil University of Oxford.

Urramporn, Saitong (1949-), a native of Thailand, is the longest-serving treasurer of St. Paul Thai Lutheran Church, Forest Park, IL, and the Association of Asians and Pacific Islanders-Evangelical Lutheran Church in America (AAPI -ELCA). She also served on the ELCA Commission for Multicultural Ministries steering committee (2000-2003 and 2005). Raised Buddhist, she first heard about Christianity at schools in Chiang Mai, Thailand. Her pastor calls her "Barnabas" for being a steadfast encourager. For many years she led a traditional Thai dance troupe that performed in worship settings.

Education: Dip McCormick Nursing College; BSc University of St. Francis, IL.

Vagh, Nouk (1964–), a native of Laos, was a Hmong refugee in Thailand before coming to the US in 1982. He converted to Christianity upon arrival, with a passion that drew him to theological studies. With no paid church work available after his graduation in 1988, Vagh became an entrepreneur, starting several small businesses while serving at church in every capacity imaginable. He was ordained in 2019, after completing the Theological Education for Emerging Ministries program. Today he is pastor of Hmong Central Lutheran Church, St. Paul, MN.

Education: BA Crossroads College; Certificate Wartburg Theological Seminary.

Valeriano, Teresita Clemente (1965-), a native of the Philippines, is the director for Evangelical Mission, Sierra Pacific Synod. She was on the Lutheran World Federation staff twice: as secretary of Youth in Church and Society, establishing the first Youth Leadership Formation Program; and later, as regional officer for North America. In California she has worked as a campus pastor, mission developer, and interim associate pastor. She is one of the first openly LGBTQ Asian pastors in the Evangelical Lutheran Church in America.

Education: BSBA University of the East; BCM Asian Institute for Liturgy and Music; MDiv Pacific Lutheran Theological Seminary.

[Note: For biographical details, see Edmond Yee and J. Paul Rajashekar (eds. and comps.), *Abundant Harvest: Stories of Asian Lutherans* (Minneapolis: Lutheran University Press, 2012), pp. 394-396.]

Vang, Lu Vamlo (1962–), a Hmong native of Laos, leads Grace Evangelical Lutheran Church (GELC), Fresno, CA. Vang came to the US as a refugee in 1978 and lived with relatives in Hawai'i and Michigan. By 1984, he worked as a refugee health specialist in Fresno, CA. In 1985, Grace's pastor asked Vang how to encourage regular attendance from the eight Hmong families at GELC. Vang replied, "Worship services in Hmong." Motivated to train for the ministry, Vang became GELC's associate pastor in 1994. Vang now leads the congregation, which worships exclusively in Hmong.

Education: Certificate Pacific Lutheran Theological Seminary.

Vang, Nhiabee (1975-), a native of Laos, came to the US as a refugee in 1987. Since 2018 he has served as a mission developer at Amazing Grace Ministry, a new mission-start in the Minneapolis Area Synod. Prior to his current call, he was a senior pastor at Luther Memorial Lutheran Church, a multicultural congregation on the north side of Minneapolis, MN.

Education: MDiv Luther Seminary.

Vethanayagamony, Peter* (1957–), a native of India, is professor of modern church history and director of the DMin program, Lutheran School of Theology at Chicago (LSTC). He is a prolific author. Before joining LSTC in 2006, Vethanayagamony taught church history in seminaries in India and held administrative positions, including dean of the faculty. He also served over nine years as an outreach minister and missional pastor in Chicago.

Education: BTh Serampore University; BEd and MA Annamalai University; BD and MTh United Theological College; MPhil Osmania University; MTh and PhD Lutheran School of Theology at Chicago.

Vue-Benson, Bea (1967-), a native of Laos, came to the US in 1978 as a refugee, and was ordained in 1994, the first Hmong Lutheran woman pastor in the US. She served two parishes in St. Paul, MN, and on the boards of Lutheran Immigration and Refugee Service and the Commission for Women, Evangelical Lutheran Church in America. Since 2005 she has provided marriage and family therapy after graduate training through a Bush Foundation Fellowship. She is also passionately engaged in restorative justice and nonviolent communication practices.

Education: BA St. Olaf College; MDiv Luther Seminary; MA Adler Graduate School.

Wang, J. (Rowena) (1968-), a native of China, has served as mission developer at Federal Way Chinese Fellowship, Federal Way, WA, since 2010. From 2008-2010 she co-pastored Grace Chinese Lutheran of South King County in Renton, WA. Before coming to the US in 2001, she worked at a subsidiary of the Grain Bureau of Guangdong Province, China. After obtaining her permanent residence in the US, she studied Lutheran theology in Hong Kong. She is also a member of the board of directors, Center for Chinese Ministry.

Education: AA College of Foreign Languages; MDiv Lutheran Theological Seminary.

Wang, Marian M. (1952-), a native of Taiwan, China, was raised in a Buddhist family, but became a Christian in high school. After graduation from Soochow University, she taught elementary school and hosted a gospel radio program. In 1984 in Seattle, she managed senior apartments, and since 2011 has worked for Help at Home, Woodridge, IL. Ordained in 2003 after completing the Theological Education for Emerging Ministries program, she has also since then co-pastored Truth Lutheran Church, Naperville, IL.

Education: BA Soochow University; Certificate Lutheran School of Theology at Chicago.

Wang, Michael (1971-), a native of China, has been a mission developer of Grace Chinese Lutheran Church of South King County (GCLCSKC) since 2008. He immigrated to the US in 1991. After completing high school, he spent seven years working at various Chinese restaurants in the US before becoming a student at the Lutheran Theological Seminary in Hong Kong in 2000. He returned to the US in 2005 and began mission development work in South King County. He was ordained in 2008 and called to GCLCSKC. He is a third generation Christian.

Education: BTh Lutheran Theological Seminary.

Wang, Peter Y. (1951-), a native of Taiwan, China, was reared in a Buddhist family. He became a Christian while attending Soochow University. After graduation, he preached the gospel for seven years through radio stations in Taiwan. In 1984 he moved to Seattle, WA, where he was director of Public Administration for the Overseas Radio and TV, Inc. Seattle office. In 1989, he began studies at Luther Seminary in St. Paul, MN. He has been a pastor at Truth Lutheran Church in Naperville, IL, since 1992.

Education: BA Soochow University; MA National Cheng Chi University; MDiv Luther Seminary.

Waworuntu, Robert (1959-), a native of Indonesia, has served as pastor of Imanuel Indonesian Fellowship since 2015. This is a two-point ministry in Los Alamitos and Rancho Cucamonga, CA. Before coming to California, he led Imanuel Indonesian Lutheran Church in Newington, NH from 2001 to 2014. And before coming to the US to study in 1990, he served parishes in the Christian Evangelical Church in Minahasa, a Protestant denomination in Indonesia.

Education: BTh and BD Jakarta Theological Seminary; MA Louisville Theological Presbyterian Seminary.

Whiteman, Timothy (1955-), a native of the US, is pastor of Central Lutheran Church, Bellingham, WA. Previously he served parishes in North Dakota, California, and Montana. In addition to parish ministry, Whiteman volunteers with community organizations and has served on the board of Lutherwood Camp and Retreat Center in Bellingham, WA. He is a gifted musician, playing a variety of instruments in various local orchestras and musical groups.

Education: BA Seattle Pacific University; MDiv Luther Seminary.

Wong, Tony K. C. (1964-), a native of Hong Kong, China, is the palliative care chaplain at Park Nicollet Methodist Hospital in St. Louis Park, MN. He works closely with his colleagues to provide the best care possible for the body, mind, and spirit. He is also interested in listening to people's spiritual beliefs and in knowing what issues are most important to them in their journey. Before becoming a Lutheran parish pastor, Wong worked in the field of telecommunications.

Education: BS University of Hawaii; MDiv Luther Seminary.

Wong, William E. (1952-), a native of the US, became in 1988 the first director for Asian Ministries in any North American Lutheran denomination. At the Evangelical Lutheran Church in America, he simultaneously filled in as interim executive director for the Commission for Multicultural Ministries, and later served as coordinating director for Multicultural Mission Strategy. Afterwards he was the second Asian to serve as a bishop's assistant in two different synods. He also pastored congregations Arizona and California. In 2012 as an interim pastor, he has served five congregations to date.

Education: BA University of Southern California; MDiv Pacific Lutheran Theological Seminary.

[Notes: For biographical details, see Edmond Yee and J. Paul Rajashekar (eds. and comps.), *Abundant Harvest: Stories of Asian Lutherans* (Minneapolis: Lutheran University Press, 2012), pp. 406-409. For Wong's ministry in the Commission for Multicultural Ministries, Evangelical Lutheran Church in America, see Edmond Yee, *The Soaring Crane: Stories of Asian Lutherans in North America* (Minneapolis: Augsburg Fortress, 2002), pp. 148-154. Further see, Part III: Who is Who in Ministries, "Lo! Thy Servants on the Move: Flowing Far and Wide" in this volume.]

Wu, Jenny Miu-Ha (1962-), a native of Hong Kong, China, serves with her husband at True Light Lutheran Christian Church, Streamwood, IL. Since 1999 she has been responsible for the Chinese-speaking ministry. Previously she assisted the pastor in administration, led small group Bible study and adult Sunday school. Prior to coming to the US she was an evangelist at Hallelujah Lutheran Church in Fanling, Hong Kong and an evangelist/missionary at Ling Liang Chinese Church in Kolkata, India.

Education: BTh Lutheran Theological Seminary; MACS and MAFM Logos Evangelical Seminary.

Wu, **Lily R**. (1952-), a native of the US, is a prolific writer, editor, and speaker. Granddaughter of a Methodist minister and daughter of a deaconess, Wu has since 1981 followed her calling, to build up intercultural society while advocating for Asian concerns. With communications as her skill set, she promoted multicultural, Asian, refugee, women's, racial justice, peace and other ministries in the US. She was also the first Asian American member of the Evangelical Lutheran Church in America's Board of Directors, also known as the Church Council.

Education: BA Pace College; MLS Queens College.

[Notes: For biographical details, see Edmond Yee and J. Paul Rajashekar (eds. and comps.), *Abundant Harvest: Stories of Asian Lutherans* (Minneapolis: Lutheran University Press, 2012), pp. 409-411. Further see, Part III: Who is Who in Ministries: "Lo! Thy Servants on the Move: Flowing Far and Wide" in this volume.]

Wu, **Lit Inn** (1964-), a native of India, is the senior pastor at True Light Lutheran Christian Church, Streamwood, IL. Prior to coming to the US, he ministered with two Chinese congregations in India while also serving as a chaplain at two schools. He began at True Light as a part-time assistant pastor, becoming a full-time minister when the founding pastor retired. He became the senior pastor when English ministry started there, and since 1999 has been shepherding the congregation through various stages of development, changes, challenges and growth.

Education: BTh Lutheran Theological Seminary; MDiv Logos Evangelical Seminary.

Wu, **Chiung Hao* (Moses)** (1970-), a native of Taiwan, China, is pastor of Kalam Christian Church, Roslyn, NY. A fifth-generation Christian, Wu was a rebellious youth who challenged his teachers and left the church. While on military duty, he felt God's call—leading him to fulfill his father's dream that his son become a minister. He served two congregations in Taiwan before coming to the US in 2012 to lead Louisville Taiwanese Presbyterian Church. Later, Wu pastored two parishes in Toronto, Canada, for six years. He joined the Evangelical Church in America in 2020.

Education: MDiv Taiwan Theological Seminary.

Yasukawa, Miho (1973-), a native of Japan, is the pastor of Good Shepherd Lutheran Church in Lena, IL. She encountered Christ through Lutheran missionaries from the US and was baptized at her home congregation, the Japanese Evangelical Lutheran Ooe Church in Kyushu, the southernmost island in Japan. Yasukawa was ordained in 2016. Seeing God's activity in the lives of God's people inspires her ministry.

Education: AA Kyushu Jo Gakuin Junior College; BA Wittenberg University; MA Cornell University; MA and MDiv Lutheran School of Theology at Chicago.

Yee, Andrew (1967-), a native of the US, is an assistant to the bishop, Northwest Washington Synod, Evangelical Lutheran Church in America. He served with Lutheran Volunteer Corps (1991-1992) before working at two parishes: Christ the Servant (1999-2006) and Bethany (2006-2008). He then became director of spiritual care at Josephine Caring Community (2010-2019). Yee often sees God's grace through a social justice lens. He has long been active as an Executive Council leader/advisor with the Association of Asians and Pacific Islanders--Evangelical Lutheran Church in America.

Education: BArch Syracuse University; MDiv Lutheran School of Theology at Chicago.

Yee, Edmond (1938-), a native of China, is professor emeritus of Asian studies, Pacific Lutheran Theological Seminary (PLTS), and a former member of the Core Doctoral Faculty, Graduate Theological Union, of which PLTS is a member school. He is a foundational leader in Asian Lutheran ministry. He is also an author, editor, translator and pursuer of Chinese literature and intellectual history. Selected topics of his many publications include Chinese poetic opera, Chinese culture, Confucianism and Asian American Lutheran church history.

Education: BA Midland College; MDiv Pacific Lutheran Theological Seminary; MA San Francisco State University; CPhil and PhD University of California at Berkeley.

[Notes: For biographical details, see Edmond Yee and J. Paul Rajashekar (eds. and comps.), *Abundant Harvest: Stories of Asian Lutherans* (Minneapolis: Lutheran University Press, 2012), pp. 422-426. Further see, Part III: Who is Who in Ministries: "Lo! Thy Servants on the Move: Flowing Far and Wide" in this volume.]

Yi, Jade (1969-), a native of Taiwan, China, serves as pastor along with her husband, Hector Garfias, at Trinity Lutheran Church in Lynnwood, WA. Before this position, she served three English-speaking congregations in the Metropolitan Chicago area, and was a mission developer at Living Truth Chinese Lutheran Church in Bothell, WA.

Education: BA Dahan Institute of Technology; MDiv Lutheran School of Theological at Chicago; MA Wheaton College.

Yip, Man Hei (1977-), a native of Hong Kong, China, is an assistant professor of systematic theology, Wartburg Theological Seminary. Previously she was a visiting researcher, Boston University School of Theology, connected with the Center for Global Christianity and Mission. Before coming to the US she taught at the Divinity School of Chung Chi College, a constituent college of The Chinese University of Hong Kong. She also worked for the Lutheran World Federation in Geneva, Switzerland and Phnom Penh, Cambodia.

Education: BA and MPhil University of Hong Kong; MA and STM Wartburg Theological Seminary; PhD Lutheran Theological Seminary at Philadelphia.

Yong, Siew Fong (Andrew) (1952-), a native of Malaysia, is mission pastor of Heavenly Peace Lutheran Fellowship, Portland, OR. Before becoming a rostered member of the Evangelical Lutheran Church in America in 2004, he shepherded Lutheran congregations of the Lutheran Church in Malaysia (1980-1982), and in the Evangelical Lutheran Church of Hong Kong (1988-2003). He also served in Christian book publishing ministries: Rock House Publishers (1984-1986) and Taosheng Publishers (1987).

Education: BTh Lutheran Theological Seminary.

Yu, **Changan (John)** (1967-) a native of China, was the executive director of the Christian Social Service Center of Luzhou, China. The center was in partnership with Global Mission, Evangelical Lutheran Church in America (2003-2013). In 2015 he ministered at Christ Lutheran Church in Monterey Park, CA. Since 2017 he has been serving as pastor of Bethlehem Lutheran Church's Chinese ministry.

Education: CM St. John the Baptist Theological College; BS Divinity School of Chung Chi College, The Chinese University of Hong Kong; MTM Asian Institute of Liturgy and Music; BA Trinity Lutheran College; Certificate Pacific Lutheran Theological Seminary.

Yu, **Kwanza** (1946-), a native of China of Korean ancestry, became the first Asian woman ordained in The American Lutheran Church, (a predecessor of the Evangelical Lutheran Church in America, (ELCA). She served Lutheran parishes in Dallas, Chicago, Minneapolis, and Tokyo; directed Ecumenical and Cross-cultural Programming, Women of the ELCA; and governed on the Board of Trustees, Augsburg Fortress (the ELCA's publishing house). Currently, she is a chaplain at the Ebenezer Assisted Living Facility in Edina, MN.

Education: BEd and MEd Ewha Womans University; MA International Christian University; MDiv Luther Seminary; DMin Lutheran School of Theology at Chicago.

Zhang, **Daniel**** (1987-), a native of China, has served as a lay assistant pastor at Christ Lutheran Church in Monterey Park, CA, since 2016. He is responsible for the Chinese ministry of this congregation. He grew up in Shenyang, China, in a Christian family; his father has been a pastor for 30 years. Zhang was a student in mainland China and Hong Kong before coming to the US in 2014 to study for his ThM degree at Logos Evangelical Seminary.

Education: BA Liaoning University; BD Divinity School of Chung Chi College, The Chinese University of Hong Kong.

Zhao, Wei** (1984-), a native of China, is a lay minister of Bethel Chinese Lutheran Church, Seattle, WA. He grew up a firm atheist in China. In 2013 he came to the US to study at the University of Washington. After hearing the gospel, he and his wife began to attend church; they were baptized in 2014 and 2015 respectively. A year later he entered Faith Evangelical Seminary. He assisted Pastor Isaiah Chow at Bethel Church (2016-2019), and after graduation in March 2019, became a full-time minister there.

Education: BE and MA Harbin Institute of Technology; MA and MDiv Faith Evangelical Seminary.

Antonio, Melvin (1941-). Call: St. John Lutheran Church, Bishop, TX.

Bang, Hayley (1982-). Call: Christ Lutheran Church, Paramus, NJ.

Bounma, Bounkeo (1945-). Call: St. Paul Lutheran Church, Des Moines, IA.

Bruning, Jamie Segaran (1970-). Call: Faith Lutheran Church, Sidney, MI.

Butarbutar, Anton. (n. i.).

Chae, Andrew (1932-). Call: Valley Korean Lutheran Church, Chatsworth, CA.

Chan, Ka-Yiu (1960-). Call: Peace Lutheran Church, Lombard, IL.

Chan, Stephen (1959-). Call: Grace Lutheran Church, Chicago, IL.

Chao, David (1930-). Call: Prince of Peace Lutheran Church, Honolulu, HI.

Chao, Timothy (1932-). Call: True Light Lutheran Church, Streamwood, IL.

Chen, Betty (1948-). Call: Glory Lutheran Church, Chula Vista, CA.

Chen, Chi Shih (1939-). Call: New Light Christian Church, Palatine, IL.

Chen, Chu-Wen (1958-). Call: Agape Lutheran Church, San Gabriel, CA.

Chen, Joshua (1961-). Call: Chinese Lutheran Church, Houston, TX.

Chen, Mark (1960-). Call: Grace Taiwanese Lutheran Church, Anaheim, CA.

Cheng, Andrew (1945-). Call: #NULL!

Cheung, Wern Chew (1958-). Call: Grace Chinese Lutheran Church, Seattle, WA.

Chi, Harvey (1944-). Call: First Taiwanese Lutheran Church, Houston, TX.

Chiu, Philip (1948-). Call: Chinese Life Lutheran Church, Alhambra, CA.

Choi, John (1946-). Call: #NULL!

Chong, Daniel (1942-). Call: Chinese Lutheran Church St. Louis, Creve Coeur, MO.

Chookiatsirichai, Sunthi (1945-). Call: Bethlehem Lutheran Church, Minneapolis, MN.

Chung, Young (1957-). Call: Shepherd of the Valley Lutheran Church, Clarissa, MN.

Chutimapongrat, Pongtep (1976-). Call: Thai Christian Fellowship, Whittier, CA.

Clifford, Dara (n. i.). Call: Christ the King Lutheran Church, Combined Locks, WI.

Dostert, Manisha (1969-). Call: St. James Lutheran Church, Fayetteville, NC.

Dovinh, John (1939-). Call: Vietnamese Lutheran Ministry, Seattle, WA.

Erdal, Paul (1966-). Call: American Lutheran Church, Billings, MT.

Erzkus, Benjamin (1987-). Call: St. John's Lutheran Church, Marquette, NE.

Etwaroo, Divendra (1950-). Call: Christ Our Saviour Lutheran Church, Jersey City, NJ.

Fong, Timothy (1954-). Call: Chinese Life Lutheran Church, Alhambra, CA.

Goshi, Joshua (1955-). Call: #NULL!

Ham, Myung (1955). Call: Messiah Lutheran Church, Flushing, NY.

Hamada, Yukio (1939-). Call: Wellington Park Lutheran Church, Milwaukee, WI.

Han, Sung Bae (1971-). Call: Dong Hang Korean Ministry, Lawrenceville, GA.

Han, Youhui (1976-). Call: Chinese Lutheran Church, Houston, TX.

Hao, Jianhua (1960-). Call: Grace Chinese Lutheran Church, Seattle, WA.

Her, Wangkao (1961-). Call: Hmong Central Lutheran Church, St. Paul, MN.

Hostetter, Linda (1953-). Call: Trinity Lutheran Church, Steelton, PA.

Hsieh, Shue-Liang. (n. i.). Call: New Light Christian Church, Palatine, IL.

Huang, Nathan (1928-). Call: Lutheran Church of Honolulu, HI.

Inbarasu, Inba Joshua (1961-). (n. i.).

Jeong, Seokhwan (1971-). Call: Korean Lutheran Church, Colorado Springs, CO.

Jiang, Franklin (1935-). Call: Good Shepherd Lutheran Church, Bloomfield, IA.

Johnson, Vera (1960-). Call: Shepherd of the Hill Lutheran Church, St. Paul, MN.

Kaan, Sze (1955-). Call: Grace Lutheran Church, Chicago, IL.

Kane, Jeffrey (1978-). Call: Messiah Lutheran Church, Schenectady, NY.

Khamvanhthong, Oun (1943-). Call: Grace Lutheran Church, Richmond, CA.

Kim, Chung Woo (1967-). Call: Marin Lutheran Church, Corte Madera, CA.

Kim, Kyoung Ki (1980-): Call: Gloria Dei Lutheran Church, Tacoma, WA.

Kim, Paul (1950-). Call: #NULL!

Kimbauer, Elli (1958-). Call: First Lutheran Church, Los Angeles, CA.

Kim, Sion (1938-). Call: Light of Christ Lutheran Church Korean Ministry, Los Angeles, CA.

Kinnard, Jo (1958-). Call: Holy Redeemer Lutheran Church, Cedar Rapids, IA.

Kung, Emily (1961-).Call: Grace Lutheran Church, Irvine, CA.

Kung, Stephen (1956-). Call: Grace Lutheran Church, Irvine, CA.

Kuo, Ying Chi (1933-). Calls: St. Luke Lutheran Church, Richardson, TX.

Lai, Kam (1930-). Call: St. Jacobi Lutheran church, Brooklyn, NY.

Lai, Tinpo (1953-). Call: Chinese Lutheran Church of Honolulu, Honolulu, HI.

Le, Thuong (1958-). Call: Westminster Vietnamese Lutheran Church, Westminster, CA.

Lee, Chia (1961-). Call: Our Saviour Lutheran Church Hmong Ministry, La Crosse, WI.

Lee, Choong-Quon (1960-). Call: Lutheran Church of Dream Builder, Anaheim, CA.

Lee, James (1949-). Call: Faith Lutheran Church, Stockton, CA.

Lee, Jen-Hao (1962-). Call: Taiwanese Lutheran Church in San Diego, CA.

Lee, Si Bok (1967-). Call: Light of Grace Korean Lutheran Church, Federal Way, WA.

Lee, Suk (1962-). Call: Good Shepherd Lutheran Church, Concord, CA.

Lim, Robert Y. H. (1960-). Call: Grace Lutheran Church, Mathis, TX.

Lin, David* (1954-). Faith Lutheran Church, Monterey Park, CA.

Liu, Zhenchuan (1963-): Call: Living Truth Lutheran Church, Bothell, WA.

Lo, Hansel (1959-). Call: Chinese Lutheran Church, San Francisco, CA.

Lo, Samuel (1951-). Call: Peace Lutheran Church, Lombard, IL.

Louie, William (1956-). Call: Holy Trinity Lutheran Church, West Hatfield, MA.

LoVan, Tom (1963-). Call: Morningside Lutheran Church, Sioux City, IA.

Luong, Nathan (1986-). Call: Trinity Lutheran Church, St. Peter, MN.

Mabugu, Samuel (1958-). Call: Mount Zion Lutheran Church, Tionesta, PA.

Mathai, Philip (1958-). Call: Trinity Lutheran Church, Lanark, IL.

Mendis, Eardley (1945-). Call: Purna Jiwan South Asian Ministry, Chicago, IL.

Moua, Houa (1963-). Call: Agape Hmong Lutheran Ministry, La Crosse, WI.

Mua, Naw-Karl (1959-). Call: Hmong Central Lutheran Church, St. Paul, MN.

Na, Jongkil (1961-). Call: Abiding Presence Lutheran Church, Beltsville, MD.

Nakashima, Glenn (1948-). Call: Grace Lutheran Church, Austin, MN.

Ness, Terje (1900-). Call: #NULL!

Ng, James Kam (1944-). Call: St. Mark's Chinese Lutheran Church, Hacienda Heights, CA.

Park, Min Chan (1961-). Call: Messiah Lutheran Church, Flushing, NY.

Pitcher, Youngshim (1977-). Call: St. Mark Lutheran Church, Washington, IL.

Prashad, Chaitram (1951-). Call: First Lutheran Church, Barron, WI.

Puthiyottil, Cherian (1944-): Call: Central Lutheran Church, Minneapolis, MN.

Qiu, Lin (1961-). Minnesota Faith Chinese Lutheran Church, Roseville, MN.

Rode, Jill (1981-).Call: St. Anthony Park Lutheran Church, St. Paul, MN.

Rumbold, David (1953-). Call: chaplain (l. u.).

Segaran, Gnana (1941-). Call: Salem Lutheran Church, Rosebud, TX.

Shim, Hyuk Tae (1974-): Call: Korean Mission of God, Naperville, IL.

Shimizu, Kohei (1943-). Call: #NULL!

Shin, Jonathan (1959-). Call: Reformation Lutheran Church, Brooklyn, NY.

Singh, Clyde (1949-). Call: Wellington Park Lutheran Church, Milwaukee, WI.

Sisouphanthong, Khamphou (1945-). Call: Zion Lutheran Church, Rockford, IL.

Solon, Rolando (1944-). Call: Holy Trinity, Elkins, WV.

Son, Hang Mo (1962-). Call: Light of Grace Korean Lutheran Church, Federal Way, WA.

Song, Daniel (1952-). Call: interim pastor.

Sunthi, Chookiatsirichai (1945-). Call: Bethlehem Lutheran Church, Minneapolis, MN.

Svaren, Dawna (1953-). Call: Emmanuel Lutheran Church, Moscow, ID.

Ta, Jun-Feng (1966-): Call: Our Savior Lutheran Church, Faulkton, SD.

Tausili, Polaia (1950-). Call: Peace Lutheran Church, Seattle, WA.

Tong, Far-Dung (1946-). Call: Truth Lutheran Church, Naperville, IL.

Torgerson, Jennifer (1984-). Call: St. Andrew's Lutheran Church, Mahtomedi, MN.

Tran, Vanson (1950-).Call: King of Glory Lutheran Church, Fountain Valley, CA.

Tumbuan, Dino (1948-). Call: Emanuel Lutheran Church, Bock, MN.

Vang, Logan (1967-). Call: Ascension Lutheran Church, Milwaukee, WI.

Vannavong, Phetsmone (1955-). Call: St. Paul Lutheran Church, Milwaukee, WI.

Wang, Charlie (1949-). Call: Christ Lutheran Church, Monterey Park, CA.

Wang, Frank (1970-): Call: Bethlehem Lutheran Church, Temple City, CA.

Wang, Peter L. (1940-). Call: Holy Redeemer Lutheran Church, Bellflower, CA.

Wang, Marlon (1935-). Call: First Lutheran Church, Bothell, WA.

Wu, Donald (1941-). Call: St. John's Lutheran Church, Cerritos, CA.

Yu, Agnes (1946-). Call: King of Glory Lutheran Church, Dallas, TX.

Yuen, Shing Chung Royan (1954-). Call: Life Chinese Lutheran Church, Richmond, CA.

Zhou, Le (1969-). Call: Faith Lutheran Church, Monterey Park, CA.

In Memoriam

Chu, **Daniel H. S**. (1928-2013), a native of China, was the first Chinese missionary to Malaya (now Malaysia), sent by the United Lutheran Church in America while he was in Hong Kong. In 1955 he and his family immigrated to the US where he became the first Chinese "to serve as pastor of an all white congregation among all Protestant denominations in North America." In 1981 while serving a white parish in Tacoma, WA, he was asked to develop a Chinese ministry there. He retired in 1983 and the ministry was closed.

Education: BA Wittenberg University; BD Hamma Divinity School.

[Note: For biographical details, see Edmond Yee, *The Soaring Crane: Stories of Asian Lutherans in North America* (Minneapolis: Augsburg Fortress, 2002), p. 78-79.]

Chung-Segré, **Petunia M.** (1944-2017), a native of Jamaica, was a mathematics teacher, parish pastor and community worker. She began seminary studies in 1987, and served as an interim pastor with the Florida-Bahamas Synod, Evangelical Lutheran Church in America. Her first call was in 1991, invigorating Redeemer Lutheran Church in Lauderdale Lakes, FL. From 2006-2010, she worked with the Coalition to End Homelessness. In 2011 she started a community project to reclaim high school youth in Jamaica.

Education: BS and Diploma in Education, University of the West Indies; MDiv Trinity Lutheran Seminary.

Kao, **Samson S**. (1943-2001), Calls: Chonburi Chinese Church, Central, Thailand; Ratchaburi Church and Suriyawaong School, Central Thailand; Emmanuel Baptist Church, Bangkok, Thailand; Sapanluang Chinese Church, Bangkok, Thailand; House of Christ Church, Bangkok, Thailand; Bangkok Institute of Theology and Thailand Full Gospel Theological Seminary, Bangkok, Thailand; Redeemer Taiwanese Lutheran Church, Cupertino, CA.

Kuo, **Charles** (1923-2020), a native of China, was a one-term president of the Evangelical Lutheran Church of Hong Kong and parish pastor there. In the US in the 1970s, he served as a custodian at St. Mark's Lutheran Church, San Francisco, while the Lutheran Church in America (LCA) rejected his efforts to find ministerial work. In 1978 he was rostered with the LCA, and founded the Chinese Lutheran Church (which left the LCA's successor, the Evangelical Lutheran Church in America, after the church passed in 2009 its statement titled "Human Sexuality: Gift and Trust").

Education: Diploma Lutheran Theological Seminary.

Kwok, **Andrew** (1920-2012), a native of China, was pastor of Chinese Life Lutheran Church, Alhambra, CA. Before coming to the US in the early 1970s, he pastored two congregations in Hong Kong. One of them was then the largest Lutheran church there. In the US, Kwok served at Faith Lutheran Church in Monterey Park, CA, hoping to develop a Cantonese-speaking component of that congregation. However, relational issues occurred and the Cantonese-speaking ministry did not materialize. After retirement he started another congregation, non-Evangelical Lutheran Church in America related, in Southern California.

Education: Diploma Lutheran Theological Seminary.

[Note: For details, see Edmond Yee, *The Soaring Crane: Stories of Asian Lutherans in North America* (Minneapolis: Augsburg Fortress, 2002), pp. 106-107.]

Liu, **Herman Tien Chiu** (1929-2017), a native of China, developed the first Canadian Asian ministry of the Lutheran Church in America: New Life Chinese Church, Vancouver (1975-1984). Baptized at 17 in China but homeless at age 20 in Hong Kong, he worked in various ministry roles before a Lutheran World Federation grant enabled him to study toward ordination in Canada. Two years after Liu organized New Life, 97 members and 30 Sunday school students were attending.

Education: Diploma, Lutheran Theological Seminary; Diploma, Chung Chi College; B.A. Hwa Kiu College; STM Lutheran Theological Seminary Saskatoon.

Magalee, **John E**. (1924-2009), a native of Guyana, was the first person of South Asian heritage ordained by a predecessor body of the Evangelical Lutheran Church in America, in 1950. He pastored St. Paul Lutheran Church, New York City (1950-1957) before a career as a US Army chaplain in the US, Vietnam, and Germany. He received many awards, including the Bronze Star Medal. After retiring as a colonel in 1985, he went to Riverside, CA, and served for more than 15 years as pastor of several churches in the area.

Education: BS Gustavus Adolphus; BD Northwestern Theological Seminary.

Matsushita, **Eiichi** (1930-1984), "a native of Japan, was an acknowledged sociologist." He grew up in a samurai-turned-merchant family in Tokyo. He was an intellectual with a complex personality, a keen mind and an appreciation for art, especially Japanese woodblock prints. As a mid-level executive director in early 1980s, he occupied the highest office in North American Lutheranism ever held by an Asian. "The Philadelphia Planning Study was one of the most significant contributions Matsushita made to the Lutheran Church in America."

Education: AB Keio University; AB Gettysburg College; BD Lutheran Theological Seminary at Gettysburg.

[Notes: For biographical details and quotations, see Edmond Yee and J. Paul Rajashekar (eds. and comps.), *Abundant Harvest: Stories of Asian Lutherans* (Minneapolis: Lutheran University Press, 2012), pp. 304-306. [Hereafter cited as Yee and Rajashekar]. Yee and Rajashekar, p. 304. Yee and Rajashekar, p. 305.]

Moy, **James Y. K**. (1934-2020), a native of the US, was an intellectual with a plentiful tool box. The first Asian to serve twice in assistant to the bishop positions, Moy's career spanned the church, society and academia: parish pastor, college dean at two institutions, grant writer for Seattle Opportunity Industrialization Center, director for Lutheran Community Services, and a churchwide staff member for the Division for Social Ministry Organizations and Division for Ministry. He died grieving over the death of his beloved wife, Mabel.

Education: BA Valparaiso University; BD Lutheran Theological Seminary at Gettysburg; MA Columbia University; PhD Ohio University.

[Notes: For biographical details, see Edmond Yee, *The Soaring Crane, Stories of Asian Lutherans in North America* (Minneapolis: Augsburg Fortress, 2002), pp. 165-171; Edmond Yee and J. Paul Rajashekar (eds. and comps.), *Abundant Harvest: Stories of Asian Lutherans* (Minneapolis: Lutheran University Press, 2012), pp. 311-314; Further see, Part III: Who is Who in Ministries: "Lo! Thy Servants on the Move: Flowing Far and Wide" in this volume.]

Ujiie, Shigeru Samuel (1921-2013), a native of the US, was the pastor of Faith Lutheran Church, Long Beach, CA from 1962-1992. His first ministerial aspiration was to be a missionary to Japan, but his dream never came through. During WWII Ujiie served in the Army in Philippines and Japan. After the war he ministered in the San Francisco Bay Area and Los Angeles before becoming the pastor of Faith Lutheran Church. After his retirement, he continued to serve the church without salary until his death.

Education: BA Wittenberg College; BD Hamma School of Theology.

[Note: For biographical details, see Edmond Yee, *The Soaring Crane: Stories of Asian Lutherans in North America* (Minneapolis, Augsburg Fortress, 2002), pp. 51-54.]

Wong, Joseph (1927-2017), a native of US, was a social activist missionary-at-large of The American Lutheran Church in Los Angeles, from 1973 until his retirement. During the Great Depression, his father sent him and the rest of the family to China. Returning to the US after World War II, Wong served in the Air Force before pursuing Christian ministry, shepherding parishes in Oklahoma, Wisconsin, and Minnesota. In Chinatown LA, he worked with various organizations and youth.

Education: BA Phillips University; Diploma Concordia Lutheran Seminary, Springfield; PhD California Graduate School of Theology.

Wu, Wilson (1928-2003), a native of China, was the first Chinese Lutheran pastor to organize a Chinese Lutheran congregation and a Lutheran Chinese language school in North America. He was also the very first Asian Lutheran worker-priest in the 1960s. To support his family in Taiwan, he sold plastic products in the US made by a Lutheran World Federation-owned factory in Hong Kong. As a pioneer, Wu suffered racism in the church, but was influential in his parish and the wider church in developing Asian ministries.

Education: Diploma Lutheran Theological Seminary.

[Note: For biographical details, see Edmond Yee and J. Paul Rajashekar (eds. and comps.), *Abundant Harvest: Stories of Asian Lutherans* (Minneapolis: Lutheran University Press, 2012), pp. 413-415.]

Bowley, **Richard H**. (1948-2015). Call: St. Anthony Lutheran Church, Los Altos, CA.

Cheung, **Paul** (1952-2009). Call: Grace Chinese Lutheran Chapel, Seattle, WA.

Diduangleuth, **Ben** (1941-2020). Call: Laotian Worshiping Community, Olathe, KS.

Her, **Neugyia** (1957-2011). Call: Luther Memorial Lutheran Church, Minneapolis, MN.

Hsieh, **Mao Rung** (1948-2012). Call: Portland Taiwanese Lutheran Church, Beaverton, OR.

Hsu, **Paul** (1923-1999). Call: Chinese Lutheran Church, Houston, TX.

Koo, **Justus** (1937-1997). Call: Ebenezer Lutheran Church, San Francisco, CA.

Lee, **Hong S**. (1947-2017). Call: Korean Lutheran Church, Colorado Spring, CO.

Lin, **John** (1931-2015). Call: Christ Evangelical Lutheran Church, Brooklyn, NY.

Nguyen, **Ha X**. (1938-1998). Call: Vietnamese Lutheran Church, Fountain Valley, CA.

Ong, **Dwight** (1933-1996). Call: Immanuel Lutheran Church, Burns, WY.

Pan, **Cheng Hsi** (1941- 2018). Call: Chinese Lutheran Church, Houston, TX.

Ramnarine, **Roshandeen J.** (1938-2020). Call: Bethel Lutheran Church, Los Angeles, CA.

Reo, **Hun** (1928-2002) Call: St. Jacobus Lutheran Church, Woodside, NY.

Shum, **Benjamin W**. (1949-2000). Call: Good Shepherd Lutheran Church, San Francisco, CA.

Tang, **Paul** (1931-2007). Call: Chinese Christian Lutheran Church, Skokie, IL.

Sundram, **Chandra J**. (1954-2017). Call: Indians for Christ Chapel, Rockville, MD.

Tsui, **Lou** (1932-1998). Call : Bible Lutheran Church, New York, NY.

Vang, **Youa K**. (1960-2010). Call: Ascension Lutheran Church, Milwaukee, WI.

Lo! Thy Servants on the Move: Flowing Far and Wide

Your servants have been called to a variety of ministries. This list shows how saints of past and laborers of the present have flowed in regional, churchwide, academic and international faith-based service.

The Evangelical Lutheran Church in America

Church Council

> Feronika Rambing (1962-), (Member: 2011-2014).
>
> J. Paul Rajashekar (1948-),[1] (Member: 2005-2011).
>
> Lily R. Wu (1952-),[2] (Member: 1997-2003).
>
> Man Hei Yip (1977-), (Member: 2014-2015; 2017-2019).

Office of the Presiding Bishop

> Victor Thasiah (1971-)
>> Director of Social Policy (2010-2011).
>>
>> Editor-in-Chief of Journal of Lutheran Ethics (2010-2011).

Division for Church in Society (now Domestic Mission)

> Job Ebenezer (1941-)[3]
>> Associate Director for World Hunger (1987-1992).
>>
>> Director of Environmental Stewardship and Hunger Education (1992-2000).
>
> Victor Thasiah
>> Assistant Director of Studies (2008-2010).
>>
>> Associate Editor of Journal of Lutheran Ethics (2008-2010).

Division for Congregational Ministry (now Domestic Mission)

Board of Directors

> Peter Y. Wang (1951-), (Member: 2002-2005).

Division for Global Mission (now Global Mission)

> Jane Shen (1941-)[4]
>> Regional Representative—Southeast Asia (2002-2005).

---

[1] For biography, see Edmond Yee, *The Soaring Crane: Stories of Asian Lutherans in North America* (Minneapolis: Augsburg Fortress, 2002), pp.95-96 [Hereafter cited as Yee.]; Edmond Yee and J. Paul Rajashekar (eds. and comps.), *Abundant Harvest: Stories of Asian Lutherans* (Minneapolis: Lutheran University Press, 2012), pp. 357-361.[Hereafter cited as Yee and Rajashekar.]

[2] For biography, see Yee, pp.93-95; Yee and Rajashekar, pp. 409-411.

[3] For biography, see Edmond Yee, pp. 174-176.

[4] For biography, see Yee and Rajashekar, pp. 368-370.

Joseph Chu (1957-)
>   Program Director of Asia and the Pacific (2004-2009).

Margrethe S. C. Kleiber (1958-)[5]
>   Area Program Director for South Asia (1998-2002).
>   Director for Asia and the Pacific (2002-2004).

Mikka McCracken (n.d.)
>   Manager of Events and Resources (2010-2011).

Peter Shen (1938-)[6]
>   Regional Representative—Asia Pacific (2002-2005).

Stacy D. Kitahata (1961-)[7]
>   Associate Director for Global Education (1988-1997).

Yoshitaka Franklin Ishida (1959-)[8]
>   Director for Leadership Development and International Communication
>   (1996-2008).
>   Director for Asia and the Pacific (2008-).

Board of Directors

David Yuan-Pin Chou (1922-2010), (Member: 1998-2003).
Esther Rajashekar (1948-), (Member: 1996-2002)[9].
Esther Rajashekar (Member: 2002-2003).
Sarah J. Geddada (1968-), (Member: 2006-2011).
Vincent Peters (n.d.), (Member: 2003-2008).
Wilson Wu (1928-2003), (Member: 1988-1991).

Division for Ministry (now Domestic Mission)

Asha Mary George-Guiser (1957-)[10]
>   Deployed Staff for Conference of Bishops and Division for Ministry to
>   Regions VII and VIII (1988-1994).

James Y. K. Moy[11]
>   Director for Multicultural Leadership Development (1989-1996).

---

[5] For biography, see Yee and Rajashekar, pp. 289-292.
[6] For biography, see Yee and Rajashekar, pp. 368-370.
[7] For biography, see Yee and Rajashekar, pp. 287-289.
[8] For biography, see Yee and Rajashekar, pp. 269-271.
[9] For biography, see Yee and Rajashekar, pp. 354-357.
[10] For biography, see Yee and Rajashekar, pp. 255-257.
[11] For biography, see Yee, 165-171; Yee and Rajashekar, pp. 311-314.

Board of Directors

>J. Paul Rajashekar (Member: 2000-2004).
>
>Vincent Peters (Member: 1997-2003).
>
>Wi Jo Kang (1930–),[12] (Member: 1988-1991).

Division for Outreach (now Domestic Mission)

>George Tan (1950-)[13]
>>Mission Director, deployed to Southwest California Synod (2005-2010).

>Hitoshi Tikhon Adachi (1958-)
>>Coordinator for Asian Ministry, deployed to Pacifica and Southwest California Synods (2013-2018).

>Joseph Chu
>>Associate Program Director, Lutheran Disaster Response (2012-).

>Mikka McCracken
>>Director, ELCA World Hunger, Strategy and Engagement (2015-2019).[14]

>Teresita Clemente Valeriano (1965-)[15]
>>Director for Evangelical Mission, deployed to Sierra Pacific Synod (2018-) (See also Sierra Pacific Synod and Lutheran World Federation—Youth Desk/North America Region).

>Yutaka Kishino (1952-)[16]
>>Mission Director, deployed to Pacifica and Southwest California Synods (1989-2005).

Board of Directors

>Peter K. Shen (Member: 2002-2002).

Division for Social Ministry Organizations (Now Domestic Mission)

>James Y. K. Moy
>>Director for Program Development (1988-1989).

---

[12] For biography, see Yee and Rajashekar, pp. 281-283.
[13] For biography, see Yee, pp. 101-102.
[14] See also Mission Advancement Unit.
[15] For biography, see Yee and Rajashekar, pp. 394-396.
[16] For biography, see Yee and Rajashekar, pp. 286-287.

Mission Advancement

Mikka McCracken

> Program Director, ELCA World Hunger Constituent Engagement and Interpretation (2011-2015).
>
> Director, ELCA World Hunger, Strategy and Engagement (2015-2019).

Commission for Multicultural Ministries: (Now Domestic Mission)

Edmond Yee (1938-)[17]

> Interim Director for Asian Ministries (Oct. 1996-Feb. 1997).

Frederick E. N. Rajan (1949-)[18]

> Director for Advocacy (1988).
>
> Director of Multicultural Mission Strategy (1989-1991).
>
> Executive Director (1992-2006).

Paul T. Nakamura (1926-)[19]

> Interim Director for Asian Ministries (Apr. 15, 1992–Jan. 31, 1993).

Pongsak Limthongviratn (1955-)[20]

> Director for Asian Ministries (1997).
>
> Director for Asian and Pacific Islander Ministries (1997-2012).
>
> Program Director for Asian and Pacific Islander Ministries (2012-).

William E. Wong (1952-)[21]

> Director of Asian Ministries (1988-Feb. 1, 1992).
>
> Interim Executive Director (Dec. 1991-Jan. 1992).
>
> Director for Multicultural Mission Strategy (Feb. 1, 1992-Feb. 1, 1993).
>
> Director of Asian Ministries and Director for Multicultural Mission Strategy (Feb. 1, 1993-Apr. 1, 1994).
>
> Director for Multicultural Mission Strategy (Apr. 1, 1994-Aug. 9, 1996).
>
> Director of Asian Ministries (Feb. 1995-Aug. 9, 1996).

Board of Directors

Charles Matsumoto (1932-), (Member/Chair: 1988-1992).

Linda A. Hostetter (1953-), (Member: 1900-1991).

---

[17] For biography, see Yee and Rajashekar, pp. 422-426.

[18] For biography, see Yee, pp. 156-157; Yee and Rajashekar, pp. 347-350; Jonathan H. X. Lee, Fumitaka Matsuoka, Edmond Yee and Ronald Y. Nakasone (eds.), *Asian American Religious Cultures* (Santa Barbara: ABC-CLIO, 2015), pp. 731-733. [Hereafter cited as Lee, Matsuoka, Yee and Nakasone.]

[19] For biography, see Yee, pp. 49-51; Yee and Rajashekar, pp. 322-324; Lee, Matsuoka, Yee and Nakasone, pp. 676-677.

[20] For biography, see Yee, pp. 154-156; Yee and Rajashekar, pp. 296-300; Tom Holmes, PONGSAK: Advocate for Asian Ministry (Bangkok: Luther Seminary in Thailand, 2015.)

[21] For biography, see Yee, pp. 148-149; Yee and Rajashekar, pp. 406-409.

Steering Committee

Corazon G. Aguilar (1942-), (Member: 2000-2005).

Edmond Yee (Chair: 1992-1996).

James Y. K. Moy (Member: 2002).

Juliet Yuen Wai-Mun Hsia (1936-2000), (Member: 1991-1995).

Margrethe S. Kleiber (Member: 1994-1999).

Peter K. Shen (Member: 1998-2001).

Peter Y. M. Lai (1947-),[22] (Member: 1992-1993).

Rolando Solon (1944-), (Member: 1988-1989).

Saitong Urramporn (1949-), (Member: 2000-2003; 2005).

Wi Jo Kang (1930-), (Member: 2003-2007).

Yoshitaka Franklin Ishida (Member: 1996).

Commission for Women

Steering Committee

Bea Vue-Benson (1967-), (Member: 1991-1997).

Janet M. Corpus (1948-), (Member/Chair: 1998-2003).

Petunia M. Chung-Segré (1944-2017), (Member: 1994-1997).

Women of the ELCA

Kwanja Yu (1946-)[23]

Director for Ecumenical and Cross-Cultural Programming (1988-1993).

Board of Directors

Dinah F. Dutta (1959-), (Member: 2015-2017).

Mary Sagar (Member: 1993-1996; 1996-1999).

Regional Staff

Region I

Peter Yung-Ming Lai (1947-)

Congregation Ministry Coordinator of Multicultural Ministry and Evangelism (1998-2000).

Stacy D. Kitahata

Coordinator of Evangelism and Multicultural Ministry (2001-2009).

---

[22] For biography, see Yee, p. 179

[23] For biography, see Yee, pp. 179-180.

Regions VII and VIII

Asha Mary George-Guiser (See Division for Ministry).

Synod Staff

Metropolitan Chicago Synod

Peter Y. Wang
Associate to the Bishop for Asian Ministry (2001-2002).

Sunitha Mortha (1969-)
Associate to the Bishop: Director for Equipping and Resourcing (2019-).

Metropolitan New York Synod

Lily R. Wu
Assistant to the Bishop for Asian Immigration Outreach (2003-2009).

North/West Lower Michigan Synod

Jamie Segaran Bruning (1970-)
Assistant to the Bishop for Ministry Through the Next Generation (2001-2007).

Northern Texas-Northern Louisiana Synod

Jamie Segaran Bruning
Youth and Family Ministry Coordinator (2008-2012).

Northwest Washington Synod

Andrew Yee (1967-)
Assistant to the Bishop (2019-).

James Y. K. Moy
Assistant to the Bishop (1996-2001).

Pacifica Synod

Hitoshi Tikhon Adachi
Assistant to the Bishop for Finance and Congregational Ministry (2010-2018).
Coordinator for Asian Ministry (2013-2018).

Sierra Pacific Synod

Teresita Clemente Valeriano (1965-)
Assistant to the Bishop (2018-).

William E. Wong
> Assistant to the Bishop (2003-2008).

Southeastern Pennsylvania Synod

Asha Mary George-Guiser
> Assistant to the Bishop for Candidacy, Mobility and Leadership Development (1995-2000). (See also Division for Ministry and Regions VII and VIII).

Janet M. Corpus (1948-)
> Assistant to the Bishop (2001-2006).

Southern Ohio Synod

C. Lynn Nakamura (1956-)
> Director of Candidacy and Leadership Development (2019-).

William E. Wong
> Assistant to Bishop (2009-2012).

Southwest California Synod

George Tan (1950-)
> Assistant to the Bishop for Mission Empowerment (2002-2010).
> Mission Director deployed to Southwest California Synod (2005-2010).

Hitoshi Tikhon Adachi
> Assistant to the Bishop for Finance and Coordinator for Asian Ministry (2013-2018).

Southwestern Texas Synod

Darcy Mittelstaedt (1972-)
> Bishop's Associate (2018-).

Seminary Faculty

Christ Seminary-Seminex, St. Louis, MO

Wi Jo Kang
> Associate Professor of History of Religion and Mission (1974-1978).

Concordia Seminary, St. Louis, MO

Wi Jo Kang

Associate Professor of History of Religion and Mission (1968-1974).

Luther Seminary, St. Paul, MN

Kristofer Coffman (1991-)

Adjunct Professor of New Testament (2019-).

Lutheran School of Theology at Chicago, IL

Peter Vethanayagamony* (1957-)

Associate Professor of Modern Church History (2006-2020).

Professor of Modern Church History (2020-).

Stacy D. Kitahata

Dean of Community (1997-2001).

Lutheran Theological Seminary at Gettysburg, Gettysburg, PA
(Now United Lutheran Seminary)

Surekha Nelavala (1970-)

Visiting Lecturer (2008-2011).

Adjunct Faculty (2018-).

Board of Directors

Vincent Peters (2005-2008).

Lutheran Theological Seminary at Philadelphia, Philadelphia, PA
(Now United Lutheran Seminary)

J. Paul Rajashekar (1948-)

Associate Professor of Systematic Theology (1991-1993).

Professor of Systematic Theology (1993-1999).

Luther D. Reed Professor of Systematic Theology (1999-).

Academic Dean of the Seminary (2000-2012).

Director of Asian Theological Summer Institute (2007-).

Janet M. Corpus

Adjunct Faculty (1999-2001).

Pacific Lutheran Theological Seminary, Berkeley, CA

Edmond Yee

Adjunct Professor of Asian Studies (1978-1982).

Associate Professor of Multicultural Ministry (1983-1992).

Professor of Multi-Cultural Ministry (1992-1998).

Professor of Asian Studies (1998-2008).

Professor Emeritus of Asian Studies (2009-).

Director of Center for Multicultural Ministry (1980-2001).

Director of Theological Education for Emerging Ministries (1988-2008).

Graduate Theological Union,[24] Berkeley, CA

Member of the Faculty (1979-1986).

Member of the Core Doctoral Faculty (1992-2008).

Moses Penumaka (1960-)

Assistant Professor of Contextual Theology (2008-2013).

Director of Theological Education for Emerging Ministries (2008-).

Trinity Lutheran Seminary, Columbus, OH

C. Lynn Nakamura (1956-)

Professor of Old Testament and Learning Technologies (1988-2011).

Surekha Nelavala

Adjunct Faculty (2020-).

United Lutheran Seminary, Gettysburg – Philadelphia, PA

Surekha Nelavala

Adjunct Faculty (2018).

Wartburg Theological Seminary, Dubuque, IA

Man Hei Yip (1977-)

Assistant Professor of Systematic Theology (2020-).

Wi Jo Kang

The Wilhelm Loehe Professor of World Religions and Mission (1980-1998).

The Wilhelm Loehe Professor Emeritus of World Mission (1998-)

College and University Faculty and Staff

Augsburg University, Minneapolis, MN

Vincent Peters (n.d.)

Assistant Professor of Social Work (1988-1995).

---

[24] Pacific Lutheran Theological Seminary is a member school of the Graduate Theological Union.

Bethel University, Arden, MN

Vincent Peters (n. d.)
Professor and Dean of Off-Campus Program (1995-2019).
Director of Service-Learning and Campus Community-Partnership (1997-1999).
Assistant Provost for Off-Campus Program/International Studies (2000-2019).
Assistant Provost (2019).

California Lutheran University, Thousand Oaks, CA

Victor Thasiah
Associate Professor of Religion and Chair of the Department of Religion (2011-).

Hood College, Frederick, MD

Surekha Nelavala
Adjunct Faculty of Religion, Philosophy and Sociology (2008-2010).

Hope College, Holland, MI

Rakesh Peter-Dass (n. d.)
Assistant Professor of Religion (2016-).

Kalamazoo Valley Community College, Kalamazoo, MI

Alfred V. Sagar (1936-)
Assistant Dean for Learning Resources (1972-1976).
Associate Dean for Learning Resources (1976-1980).
Dean of Learning Resources, and Director of Institutional Planning (1980-1998).
Dean of Learning Resources, Director of Institutional Planning, and Dean of Communication Arts (1998-1999).

Lenoir-Rhyne College, Hickory, ND

David Yuan-Pin Chou
Professor of Chemistry (1956-1988).

Macalester College, St. Paul, MN

James Y. K. Moy
Dean and of Men and Assistant Dean of Students (1963-1966).

Messiah College, Grantham, PA

Job Ebenezer
> Visiting Professor of Mechanical Engineering (2001-2006).

New York Institute of Technology, Old Westbury, NY

Job Ebenezer
> Assistant Professor, Mechanical Engineering (1971-1976).

St. Olaf College, Northfield, MN

Vincent Peters
> Assistant Professor of Social Work (1993-1995).

Trinity Lutheran College, Everett, WA

Peter Yung-Ming Lai (1947-)
> Professor of Multicultural Ministry and Evangelism (1995-2000).

Stacy D. Kitahata
> Chair of Intercultural Studies (2008-2010).

University of New Mexico, Albuquerque, NM

Job Ebenezer
> Assistant Professor, Mechanical Engineering and Director, Energy
> Conservative Design (1976-1978).
> Director, Energy Conservative Design (1978-1980).

University of New Mexico-Valencia Campus, Belen, NM

Job Ebenezer
> Associate Director (1981-1983).

Wartburg College, Waverly, IA

James Y. K. Moy
> Director for Student Affairs (1971-1976).

Washington University School of Medicine

Barry Hong (1947-)
> Lecturer/Professor of Psychiatry and Vice Chair for Clinical Affairs
> (1978-)

Lutheran World Federation

North American Region

Fern Lee Hagedorn
Director of Communication and Interpretation (USA) (1983-1987).

Teresita Clemente Valeriano
Regional Officer (2008-2010).

Commission for Communication
Fern Lee Hagedorn (Member: 1984-1987).

Youth Desk

Teresita Clemente Valeriano

Director (2000-2004). (See also Division for Outreach and Sierra Pacific Synod.)

Lutheran World Relief

Board of Directors

Vincent Peters (Member: 1998-2008).

Service to the Church and Related Organizations

Asian Lutheran International Conference Steering Committee

Edmond Yee (Secretary: 2005-2017).
Frederick E. N. Rajan (Chair: 1998-2017).
J. Paul Rajashekar (Chair: 2017-).
Lily R. Wu (Secretary: 1998–2004).
Surekha Nelavala (Secretary: 2017-).
Pongsak Limthongviratn (Coordinator: 1997-).

Commission for a New Lutheran Church

Joseph Wong (1927-2017), (Member: 1982-1986).
Mary Matsumoto (n.d.), (Member: 1982-1986).

Task Force on Special Ministry
Edmond Yee (Member: 1983–1984).

The Design Committee for the Commission for Multicultural Ministries
Edmond Yee (Chair: 1985).

Consultation on Theological Education for a New Lutheran Church

Edmond Yee (Member: 1982-1985).

Lutheran Immigration and Refugee Service

Lily R. Wu
Assistant for Sponsorship Promotion (1980-1987).
Associate for Communications (1988-1990).
Manager for Promotion and Editorial Services (1991-1999).

Board of Directors

Bea Vue-Benson (1967-), (Member: 1995-1998).

Transcultural Seminar Steering Committee

Edmond Yee (Member: 1979-1983).
Joseph Wong (Member: 1979-1983).

Edmond Yee and Maria Gracia Sijera-Grant

PART IV

Association, Conferences, and Publications

IV | Association, Conferences and Publications

Our association is strong in endurance. After 20 years of evolution, it arrived in 1997 with a permanent name, and a clear identity, and a strong commitment to ministry. And in that same year another dream began to sprout into reality. That's the wonder of the Asian Lutheran International Conference (ALIC). Initially it was just a yearning, a dream shared by a few persons. Since then, like a growing sapling, it has become a mighty banyan tree, taking root wherever it touches the ground. It shelters the faithful under its shade where they sing songs, discuss theologies, and talk about ministries and life. Moreover, the production of resources for our ministries is another dream realized.

Thus! Thy Servants Created the Association of Asians and Pacific Islanders-Evangelical Lutheran Church in America

Your servants, like your day-by-day creation itself, also spent time establishing their ever-evolving association. Since Asian Lutherans are geographically scattered throughout the US, the Association of Asians and Pacific Islanders-Evangelical Lutheran Church in America (AAPI-ELCA — hereafter referred to as AAPI) has become an invaluable arena for pooling our spiritual and intellectual resources.

We channeled our efforts through a multi-faceted strategy developed by a leadership committee. We stayed rooted and relevant through streams such as three broad networks and a dozen ethnic ministry caucuses. At times, the AAPI or its predecessor bodies dealt with contentious issues, resulting in passionate debates. Despite our differences, however, the AAPI remains a unified body, advocating for justice, rightness, ministry, and inclusion within the church. Moreover, the association enhances our spiritual growth through Bible studies and fellowship.

Our presidents also bring Asian issues, strengths, and insights to meetings with other Evangelical Lutheran Church in America (ELCA) ethnic association leaders and sometimes to the Church Council.

Our story began in the fall of 1977 when Lloyd Burke, president (now bishop) of the Pacific Southwest Synod of the Lutheran Church in America (LCA), asked Edmond Yee[1] to convene the Asian pastors in the greater Los Angeles area." This group eventually formed the nucleus of the first caucus meeting that took place on September 19-21, 1978, at Faith Lutheran Church in Monterey Park, California."[2] Such a gathering would appear to have been a straight forward proposition. However, tensions had flared up months earlier due to conflicting ideas about proceeding with Yee's installation as resource developer-consultant for Asian ministries for the LCA's Division for Mission in North America (DMNA) and adjunct professor of Asian Studies at Pacific Lutheran Theological Seminary (PLTS).[3]

On the one hand, William Lesher, president of PLTS in Berkeley, CA, and Yee thought it "might be a good idea to gather the Asian clergy for a conference preceding...the installation."[4] Eiichi Matsushita,[5] an official of the DMNA, LCA, wanted the installation to be an academic affair. On the other hand, Malcolm Minnick, director of the Department for Church Extension, DMNA, who was Yee's boss, opposed the idea of an academic installation, based on what he perceived as Yee's "ignorance of what DMNA...was trying to do with the 'minority' communities within the LCA."[6]

After the dust settled, it was decided that Yee's installation as a DMNA staff member would not be part of the conference and that the September conference would involve only West Coast LCA Asian pastors. But the LCA Asian pastors objected. They wanted to include Joseph Wong, a pastor of The American Lutheran Church (TALC) working in Chinatown, Los Angeles. The DMNA officials overruled the objection based on ecclesiastic boundaries. Years later, Yee wrote that [T]he DMNA officials won the battle but not the war,"[7] for Wong ultimately became a member of the group.

When the Asian pastors finally met, DMNA officials spoke eloquently about the church's ministry and mission and listened to what the pastors had to say. The officials also invited Yee to speak. Yee told of the community's strength and needs and concluded with a story of the ancient Chinese philosopher-scholar Mencius' visit to King Hui of Liang. The King asked Mencius what he had brought with him that might profit his kingdom. Mencius replied, "All that matters is that there should be benevolence (仁) and rightness (义)."[8] Yee used this story implicitly to criticize the

---

[1] For biography, see Edmond Yee and J. Paul Rajashekar (eds. and comps.), *Abundant Harvest: Stories of Asian Lutherans* (Minneapolis: Lutheran University Press, 2012), pp. 422-426. [Hereafter cited as Yee and Rajashekar.]

[2] The first Asian (Chinese) Lutheran congregation in the Lutheran Church in America, a predecessor body of the Evangelical Lutheran Church in America.

[3] Yee was appointed resource developer-consultant for Asian ministries for the Division for Mission in North America, LCA, and an adjunct professor of Asian studies at Pacific Lutheran Theological Seminary in Berkeley, CA.

[4] Edmond Yee, *The Soaring Crane: Stories of Asian Lutherans in North America* (Minneapolis: Augsburg Fortress, 2002), p. 125. [Hereafter cited as Yee].

[5] For biography, see Yee and Rajashekar, pp. 304-306.

[6] Yee, p. 126.

[7] Yee, p. 126.

[8] D. C. Lau (trans.), Mencius, vol. 1, p. 3. The character 仁 has been variously translated into English as love, humanness, humanity agape, benevolence, justice, etc., while the character 义 has often been translated as righteousness, oughtness, and rightness.

church's complicity when it came to the matters of justice, benevolence, and rightness.

Stage I: Asian Lutheran Pastors Conference

A second gathering involving most LCA Asian pastors in North America was held in 1979 in Tacoma, WA. At this meeting, the Asian pastors demanded inclusion in the life of the institution. They elected James Y. K. Moy[9] as the chair and developed a governance structure and bylaws under Moy's leadership. And for the first time, a proper name for the group emerged: Asian Lutheran Pastors Conference (ALPC).

This name was the first in a series that reflected the ever-evolving nature of the organization. In the following year, the ALPC changed its name to Biennial Asian Pastors and Professional Workers Conference.

Stage II: Biennial Asian Pastors and Professional Workers Conference

The 1981 conference was held at Our Redeemer Lutheran Church, Garden Grove, CA. Attendees included national church officials, a local bishop, Asian clergy and laypersons of the LCA and TALC, seminarians, and Charles Matsumoto,[10] a member of the LCA Executive Council. Two controversial issues marked this conference: redress and membership inclusion. The redress issue involved Executive Order 9066, signed on February 19, 1942, by President Franklin D. Roosevelt. Executive Order 9066 authorized the internment of 120,000 US citizens of Japanese ancestry during World War II.[11] In the 1970s the Japanese American community demanded redress for the illegal and racist treatment of its people.

The 1981 Asian Lutheran conference planners had invited a speaker from the National Coalition of Redress and Reparation. But after the presentation, "[T]he discussion angered the older generation of Chinese pastors who remembered the atrocities of Japanese soldiers committed in China and to the Chinese during the war."[12] The conference nevertheless endorsed the National Coalition's position.

In 1983 the LCA Executive Council also approved a memorial from the Pacific Southwest Synod on redress and reparation. The DMNA officials asked Yee for guidance. In the end, the task was entrusted to Fern Lee Hagedorn[13] who, in consultation with Paul T. Nakamura[14] and Yee, "produced a two-page document titled: 'February 19, 1942-February 19, 1984: The 42nd Anniversary of Executive Order 9066: Detention and Relocation of 120,000 West Coast Japanese.'"[15]

The second issue involved conference membership. As written, the bylaws did not permit

---

[9] For biography, see Yee and Rajashekar, pp. 311-314.
[10] For biography, see Yee, pp. 99-100.
[11] See Yee, 134-137.
[12] Yee, p. 127.
[13] For biography, see Yee and Rajashekar, pp. 257-259.
[14] For biography, see Yee and Rajashekar, pp. 322-324; Jonathan H. X. Lee, Fumitaka Matsuoka, Edmond Yee, and Ronald Y. Nakasone (eds.), *Asian American Religious Cultures* (Santa Barbara: ABC-CLIO LLC, 2015), pp. 676-677. [Hereafter cited as Lee, Matsuoka, Yee, and Nakasone.]
[15] Yee, p. 136.

laypersons to be members of the conference. Matsumoto "objected to the exclusive nature of the organization."[16] The group overruled his objection, but Matsumoto persisted at the next meeting and won the battle.

This conference also decided to publish a newsletter with Hagedorn and Yee in charge. "But soon problems occurred...Hagedorn resigned from the LCA central staff, and the Chinese-speaking community expressed a lack of interest in the project."[17] The newsletter was in English! The conference also urged the church to provide bilingual materials to support the ministries. [18]

Shortly after the 1981 conference, a group of Chinese pastors felt that the organization did not serve their interests well. So without informing the organization's officers, they formed the Association of Chinese Lutheran Ministerial Workers in North America on June 22-24, 1982. Due to internal problems and the lack of financial support, this group never met again after the first meeting in San Francisco. Its members all returned to the Asian American Caucus meeting in 1983.

Stage III: Asian American Caucus

After the 1981 conference, the organization changed the name to Asian American Caucus, "in keeping with what other ethnic groups in the church called their organizations."[19] The 1983 gathering also heeded Matsumoto's plea to include lay members.

In 1982 Vincent Chin, a Chinese mistaken for being Japanese, was killed by two White auto workers in Detroit, MI, the night before his wedding. "The judge sentenced the two killers to a three-year probation and $3,000.00 fine each."[20] The Asian community was outraged at the leniency of the ruling. Accordingly, the 1983 conference passed a resolution urging the LCA, TALC, the Association of Evangelical Lutheran Churches (AELC), and the Chinese Rhenish Church, Hong Kong Synod, to inform congregations about violence against Asians. It also reaffirmed an earlier resolution urging the churches to hire "ethnic minority professors in all Lutheran seminaries by the fall of 1985."[21] Neither resolution, however, moved the denominations to take action.

Stage IV: Asian Lutherans in North America

In 1985 the Asian American Caucus voted to rename its organization Asian Lutherans in North America (ALINA) — so that all Asian Lutherans in the LCA, TALC, and the AELC in North America could become members. It decided to have two executive boards, one from the LCA and one from TALC. However, the conferees' most energetic discussions related to the emerging new Lutheran church. Accordingly, attendees passed a motion to authorize the two executive boards "to appoint or recommend names of Asians for the New Lutheran Church."[22]

---

[16] Yee, p. 127.
[17] Yee, p. 127.
[18] For details, see Part IV in this volume.
[19] Yee, p. 128.
[20] Yee, p. 133-134.
[21] Yee, p. 129.
[22] Yee, p. 129.

On April 11, 1985, while driving through Texas, Martin Yonts, a DMNA deployed staff member, and Yee came up with an idea: establish a scholarship to assist Asian seminarians in memory of Eiichi Matsushita, who had died in 1984.[23] When Yee presented this idea to ALINA, the attendees generally agreed — but naming the scholarship after a Japanese caused great consternation among the older Chinese pastors. Some of them walked out of the conference after the proposal passed.

"[I]n the same year, a newsletter…under the leadership of Fred Rajan,[24] Kwang Ja Yu, and Lily Wu"[25] was published.[26]

In 1987, the final ALINA conference was held in San Francisco. Attendees devoted most of the time to new Lutheran church transition issues and nominations to various church positions. With the conclusion of this conference, the first chapter of the ever-evolving association ended. A second chapter would begin in a couple of years after the new church's birth in 1988.

Stage V: Association of Asians-Evangelical Lutheran Church in America

With the advent of a new church, Asian Lutherans renamed their organization: Association of Asians-Evangelical Lutheran Church in America (AA-ELCA). Now the association had "an informal structural relationship with CMM (Commission for Multicultural Ministries)"[27] and received financial support from CMM. The association also developed a new set of bylaws, spelling out "its purpose, membership benefits, structure and function, its relationship with the ELCA, and so forth."[28]

When it began, the association was a small group of local pastors, churchwide staff, laypersons, and seminary professors. Congregational presidents and other lay leaders were not yet involved. Furthermore, the emerging association officials and the director of Asian ministries were just starting to discover Asian Lutherans on governing boards, synod councils, churchwide organization offices and divisions, and others who might want to join. As noted earlier, Asian Lutherans are scattered geographically throughout the US. Given this reality, William E. Wong,[29] director for Asian ministries, intentionally supported Asian Lutheran pastors and leaders on his visits to Asian ministry sites. He would also discover Asian lay leaders while on these visits. Even on his multipurpose travels as a CMM representative doing presentations and providing consultations, he would be on the lookout for Asian Lutheran leaders.

However, many US states or regions had no Asian Lutheran-specific ministries or high numbers of Asian Lutherans. It made sense to invite the leaders from those areas to a regular

---

[23] For details, see Yee, pp. 129-131.

[24] For biography, see Yee and Rajashekar, pp. 347-350; Lee, Matsuoka, Yee, and Nakasone, pp. 731-733.

[25] For biography, see Yee and Rajashekar, pp. 409-411.

[26] Yee, p. 129.

[27] Yee, p. 129.

[28] Yee, p. 129.

[29] For biography, see Yee and Rajashekar, pp. 406-409.

gathering instead of traveling to each congregation or site. The benefits were mutual: the association engaged participants in community building efforts, while the leaders found strength and empowerment with Asian Lutheran colleagues.

And what a diverse and growing group the association was! Chinese immigrant pastors had a longstanding relationship with one another and knew how they liked things done. Everything was new for Southeast Asian pastors: the US, the ELCA, the AA-ELCA, what the institutional structures were, and how they operated. (At that time, there was no South Asian Lutheran ministry.)

Craig Lewis, the first CMM executive director, advocated for gathering all the ethnic ministries to advance the work. The ELCA's governing documents were sometimes ambiguous, which opened up paths for the creative shaping of multicultural ministry. "CMM was like a train making tracks," Wong says, "I hopped on with Craig and Fred." Wong remembers it took about two years to get the AA-ELCA up and running. After that initial state, the group met once every two years. The first assembly took place at the same venue with the other ethnic associations, each meeting separately to elect its advisory committee members. This first meeting devoted time to explaining what an association was and could be, besides developing a mission statement and bylaws.

Rosalind ("Sally") Moldwin, a Filipina and a professional physician's assistant, was elected the first president of the AA-ELCA and served until 1993. Her positive and enthusiastic nature reflected the hopefulness of these efforts to develop unity among the diverse community. Her visibility as a leader and a layperson was a promising sign, too, of the association's vote to support women in leadership. Moldwin considered it both an honor and a challenge to serve and enjoyed working with the Executive Committee and Asian ministry desk. A highlight for her included encouraging Asian seminarians through the AA-ELCA's Eiichi Matsushita Scholarship Fund.

By September 1996, the second chapter of our organization ended with Wong's resignation from the CMM. A third chapter began on March 1, 1997, when Pongsak Limthongviratn succeeded Wong. Limthongviratn,[30] along with the association leadership, built on and expanded Wong's work.

Stage VI: Association of Asians and Pacific Islanders-ELCA

At the 1997 conference, the name of the association changed once again. It became AAPI, signifying a transition from the Wong era to the beginning of chapter three. Shortly after that, Limthongviratn's title also changed from director for Asian ministries to director for Asian and Pacific Islander ministries, conveying the inclusion of yet another group.

1997 Assembly, Los Angeles, CA

---

[30] For biography, see Yee and Rajashekar, pp. 296-300; Tom Holmes, *Pongsak: Advocate for Asian Ministries* (Bangkok: Luther Seminary in Thailand, 2015).

At this assembly, the association made four significant decisions:

1. To change the name of the group from AA-ELCA to AAPI-ELCA. This change accommodated a request from a Pacific Islander person who was a seminarian at that time. However, the primary reason was the US Census Bureau's definition of Asian or Pacific Islander as a person with origin in any culture of East Asia, Southeast Asia, Indian subcontinent, or Pacific Islands. This designation applied to our association members as a whole.

2. To produce resources for ministry. Being a diverse community from several countries and cultures, the association faced many challenges, including the lack of appropriate educational materials. One practical issue was how to produce resources in Asian languages. Augsburg Fortress, the ELCA publishing house, was reluctant to publish resources for Asian and Pacific Islander communities due to a limited market. As a result, the association leadership instructed Limthongviratn to find alternative ways to produce Asian language materials.

Los Angeles Airport Marriott, CA, venue of the 1997 Assembly

3. To charge Limthongviratn to explore the possibility of organizing an Asian Lutheran International Conference ALIC). Association President Margrethe S. C. Kleiber[31] worked with Limthongviratn for several months on this project before accepting a call as the ELCA's area program director for South Asia in 1998. To avoid a conflict of interest,[32] Kleiber resigned and turned the presidency to Vice President David Chen[33] at the beginning of 1998.

4. To amend the process of electing AAPI presidents. Since the association's inception, elections for president and vice president occurred every two years. Few people served successive terms, resulting in a lack of continuity. Kleiber and Limthongviratn proposed a plan that provided for greater stability. They suggested that the vice president serve as a kind of president-in-waiting. The understanding is that the vice president will assume the presidency at the end of the president's term in office. Overall, the plan has been successful.

---

[31] For biography, see Yee and Rajashekar, pp. 289-292.

[32] ELCA Personnel Policy states that ELCA employees shall not hold any position on boards or supervisory committees.

[33] For biography, see Yee and Rajashekar, pp. 242-244.

1999 Assembly, Minneapolis, MN

When Limthongviratn assumed the directorship, one of his first initiatives was to develop a strategic plan for Asian and Pacific Islander ministries. Before the 1999 AAPI assembly in Minneapolis, Limthongviratn prepared a National Strategic Plan. After thoughtful discussion, the assembly affirmed the "Asian and Pacific Islander Ministry Strategy." From there, the AAPI sent it to the 2001 ELCA Churchwide Assembly for approval.

Augsburg College, Minneapolis, MN, venue of the 1999 Assembly

2001 Assembly, Seattle, WA

At the 2001 assembly, the association made three crucial decisions:

1. To honor distinguished and Pacific Islander leaders at subsequent assemblies.

2. To eliminate the association membership fee.

3. To bring the association to everyone, as the director for Asian and Pacific Islander Ministries, Limthongviratn sought ways to strengthen its role and increase its impact on the Asian and Pacific Islander community and the wider church. He realized many immigrant pastors were unaware of or uninterested in working with the association. Instead of asking people to join the AAPI, Limthongviratn

Lutheran Bible Institute, Seattle, WA, venue of the 2001 Assembly

suggested that the Executive Committee bring the association to the people who engaged in immigrant congregations and ministries.

This vision led to the innovative approach of the AAPI structuring itself as caucuses. The new bylaw no longer required Asians and Pacific Islanders to become members of the association to participate in the assembly. It also eliminated the membership fee. Limthongviratn convinced respected leaders of the AAPI to endorse his idea. Also, he brought one of the respected elders, Moy, to serve as president between 2003-2006, smoothing the transition. They worked to ensure that caucus leaders had both voice and vote in the association's decision-making processes, expanding the leadership structure from a five-member Executive Committee to an Executive Council. This new structure affirmed the status and function of the caucus chairs and leaders.

Limthongviratn also drafted model bylaws for all caucuses. While the association continues to hold its biennial assembly, several caucuses meet annually in gatherings organized by their leaders. These meetings allow attendees to share issues, needs, challenges, and, importantly, joyful stories from the communities.

2004 Assembly, Orlando, FL

Asians and Pacific Islanders are among the six ethnic groups recognized by the ELCA through the CMM, which later became part of Domestic Mission. From the beginning, all ethnic associations have held their assemblies at different times and in various locations. It was groundbreaking when all association assemblies held their gatherings together in 2004!

The ELCA's restructuring dominated the agendas of all the associations in 2004. Since the ethnic associations related to the wider church through the CMM, changes to the function, structure, and existence of CMM would significantly impact the associations' work. Accordingly, the associations brought their concerns regarding restructuring to ELCA leadership. Nonetheless, restructuring brought significant changes to the CMM. It was renamed Multicultural Ministries, and while it remained a programmatic unit, it no longer received a program budget. As the smallest program unit, under later reorganizations, Multicultural Ministries became part of Congregational and Synodical Mission, which later evolved into Domestic Mission.

2008 Assembly, Monterey Park, CA

In 2008 in Monterey Park, CA, the AAPI organized its largest gathering to date. It was the year that Yee, a respected elder in the Asian and Pacific Islander community, announced his retirement from PLTS and several capacities in the ELCA. In his honor, Limthongviratn wrote a grant to allow him to bring 180 Asian leaders to this event and composed the following song sung during the banquet:

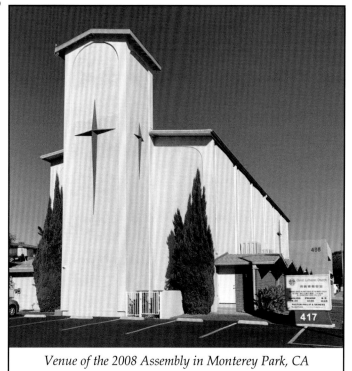

Venue of the 2008 Assembly in Monterey Park, CA

Celebrating Dr. Edmond Yee's Ministry
Lyrics: Pongsak Limthongviratn
Tune: Come, Thou Long-Expected Jesus

1. Edmond Yee is known by many as a man who works for church for decades.
   Love he gives, but his butt got kicked, yet, great role in church he plays.

   Chorus:
   Let us celebrate Ed's ministry in ELCA for decades.
   Though he retired from work he loves, Now he works for Pongsak for free.*

2. Edmond Yee is now ready to get money from Board of Pensions.
   As promised, he will contribute ten percent to Asian fund.

3. We treasure his life and works that God has done in Ed, the man.
   Wishing him and his wife a joyful life as an old, old, old, old man.*

2016 Assembly, Forest Park, IL

The 2016 Assembly met in Forest Park, IL, a suburb of Chicago. This assembly updated the 15-year-old Strategic Plans. The seven core directives of the strategy remained unchanged.

- Congregational Development
- Membership
- Leadership Development
- Resource Development
- Social Ministry
- Stewardship
- Asian Homeland Mission Work

Participants of the 2016 Assembly in Forest Park, IL

The Rev. Winfred Vergara, Missioner for Asiamerica Ministries of The Episcopal Church, joined the assembly and brought greetings from the ECUSA Presiding Bishop Katharine Jefferts Schori.

2018 Assembly, Robbinsdale, MN

In Robbinsdale, MN, a suburb of Minneapolis, the 2018 assembly made history by meeting in conjunction with the European Descent Lutheran Association for Racial Justice. While keeping separate agendas, the two associations joined together in singspiration, prayers, Bible studies, and meals. People left the assembly with fond memories.

In 2018, the AAPI, together with the other ELCA ethnic-specific associations, provided delegates for a task force on diversity. Task Force members developed a report titled "Authentic Diversity" for presentation to the 2019 ELCA Churchwide Assembly in Milwaukee — which received and approved the report by a vote of 844 to 13.[34]

Note: The AAPI Executive Committee postponed the 2020 AAPI assembly, planned for the spring in Seattle, WA, due to Covid-19. The committee has rescheduled the assembly to July 2021, in conjunction with the eleventh ALIC gathering.

Participants of the 2018 Assembly in Robbinsdale, MN

Here is a list of presidents and years served since the birth of the ELCA:

Rosalind Moldwin	1990-1993
Vincent Peters	1993-1995
Margrethe S. C. Kleiber	1995-1998
David Chen	1998-2001
Peter Wang	2001-2003
James Y. K. Moy	2003-2006
Chi Shih Chen	2006-2010
Edmond Yee	2010-2014
Yutaka Kishino[35]	2014-2016
Maria Gracia Sijera-Grant	2016-2018
Maria Gracia Sijera-Grant	2018-2022

Edmond Yee, William E. Wong, Pongsak Limthongviratn, and Lily R. Wu

---

[34] ELCA, *How Strategic and Authentic is Our Diversity; A Call for Confession, Reflection and Healing Action,* fifteenth triennial Churchwide Assembly, Milwaukee, WI, 2019.

[35] For biography, see Yee, 176-177; Yee and Rajashekar, 286-287.

Rejoice! Thy Servants are One:
Asian Lutheran International Conference

Your servants, deeply aware of their rootedness in both shores, East and West, have established a conference to explore the richness of their own cultures and theologies. The theme — Asian Lutheranism, Which Way? — of the first conference developed this premise. Curious? Read on!

The Asian Lutheran International Conference (ALIC) began to take shape in 1996. After William (Bill) E. Wong's[1] resignation from the Commission for Multicultural Ministries (CMM) in Chicago, he sent surplus funds from the Asian ministries budget to Edmond Yee[2] to be used at his discretion. Yee decided to use it to bring seminary faculty and students to the April 1997 Association of Asians-Evangelical Lutheran Church in America (AA-ELCA) assembly in Los Angeles, CA, to explore the idea of an international conference.

Meanwhile, CMM Executive Director Frederick E. N. Rajan[3] and Pongsak Limthongviratn,[4] CMM's director for Asian ministries, discussed this concept in Chicago. They presented the idea of an international gathering to the AA-ELCA Executive Committee, which endorsed it and instructed Limthongviratn to explore its possibility and feasibility.[5]

Initially, ALIC was a loosely structured forum bringing together Asian Lutherans in the US and Lutherans in Asia for theological conversation. But as time went on, the people involved began to realize the significance of this US and Asian connection and its impacts on participants. They articulated a purpose statement for ALIC and set up a governance structure. (We will say more later about funding issues, as well as how ALIC enhanced ministries and inspired people on both sides of the Pacific Rim. The Steering Committee also added a youth and young adults' component to the gatherings, starting with the seventh conference in Chiang Mai, Thailand.)

Purpose

The purpose of the Asian Lutheran International Conference, broad and encompassing, has evolved as follows:

> 1. To address common concerns faced by Asian Lutherans in the Evangelical Lutheran Church in America (ELCA) and Lutherans in Asia through dialogues and networking.

---

[1] For biography, see Edmond Yee, *The Soaring Crane: Stories of Asian Lutherans in North America* (Minneapolis: Augsburg Fortress, 2002), pp. 148-149. [Hereafter cited as Yee]; Edmond Yee and J. Paul Rajashekar (eds. and comps.), *Abundant Harvest: Stories of Asian Lutherans* (Minneapolis: Lutheran University Press, 2012), pp.406-409. [Hereafter cited as Yee and Rajashekar].

[2] For biography, see Yee and Rajashekar, pp. 422-426.

[3] For biography, see Yee and Rajashekar, pp. 347-350; Jonathan H. X. Lee, Fumitaka Matsuoka, Edmond Yee and Ronald Y. Nakasone (eds.), *Asian American Religious Cultures* (Santa Barbara: ABC-CLIO, LLC, 2015), pp. 731-733.

[4] For biography, see Yee, pp. 154-156; Yee and Rajashekar, pp. 296-300; and Tom Holmes, *Pongsak: Advocate for Asian Ministries.* Bangkok: Luther Seminary in Thailand, 2015.

[5] For further information, see Yee, pp. 188-190.

2. To support theological reflection among ELCA Asian Lutherans and Lutherans in Asia about specific cultural issues and develop worship and Christian education resources for ELCA Asian Lutherans and Lutherans in Asia.

3. To address leadership development issues for ministries and theological education for ELCA Asian Lutherans and Lutherans in Asia through interaction with leaders and theologians of Asian background.

Governance

A Steering Committee, composed of members from the US and Asia, governs the conference. The committee functions as the planning team, meeting once a year to outline the next conference. In between meetings, Limthongviratn serves as the coordinator.

On the Move

After approval from the AA-ELCA assembly, Limthongviratn was ready to move. He did so in September 1997 during an (AAPI-ELCA) Southeast Asian Leadership Gathering at Luther Seminary, St. Paul, MN. He and J. Paul Rajashekar, professor at Lutheran Theological Seminary at Philadelphia, sent a proposal to Thomas Batong, Asia secretary, Department for Mission Development, Lutheran World Federation (LWF). In January 1998, the LWF approved their request for $30,000. Batong also proposed three persons from Asia for membership on the first ALIC Steering Committee. They were Naohiro Kiyoshige, president of Lutheran Theological College and Seminary, Japan, Lam Tak Ho, president of Lutheran Theological Seminary (LTS), Hong Kong, and Harlen Simangunsong, ephorus (bishop), Huria Kristen Batak Protestan (HKBP), Indonesia.

The first conference took place in January 1999 at the LTS, Hong Kong, with the theme "Asian Lutheranism — Which Way?" This theme explored the questions of identity. Conference participants articulated the search for a complementary bi-identity: Lutheran and Asian- Asian and Lutheran, with our Asianness firmly connected to both shores. The issues that emerged from this conference, such as "Asian theology and Asian hermeneutic; relationships between North American and Asian churches ...the dynamics of cultures and traditions within the Asian and

Hong Kong Lutheran Theological Seminary, venue of the 1st ALIC

Asian American contexts...."[6] indeed affirm this connectedness.

---

[6] Yee, p. 189.

This first ALIC generated excitement in the Lutheran world. The LWF's Asia Desk, the Advisory Committee for Theological Education in Asia, and the Asian Church Leadership Conference, endorsed the proposal for the second conference. The LWF Asia secretary, Ginda Harahap, pledged funding. Sadly, the funding never materialized.

Since 1999, the ALIC Steering Committee has convened ten more biennial conferences in Asia, with participants from the US, Canada, Asia, Australia, and Europe.

- North America: AAPI-ELCA Executive Committee members, Asian pastors, lay leaders, theologians, and seminarians. ELCA synodical bishops and staff, as well as ELCA churchwide staff, are among the attendees. Conference planners give intentional thought to the representation of women and young adults from the ELCA Asian community.
- Asia: bishops of several churches, pastors, theological educators, staff, laity, seminarians, women, and youth.
- LWF: staff attended the first and the sixth conferences.
- The Lutheran Church in Australia: an Asian staff member attended the seventh to tenth conference.

Making Connections: for Personnel

The ALIC has not only had a significant impact on ministry developments in the ELCA; it has also contributed to leadership development and recruitment.

South Asians in New York City

Before the first ALIC in Hong Kong, Stephen Bouman, bishop of the Metropolitan New York Synod, had noted the growing numbers of South Asians in his jurisdiction but could not find a suitable person to lead a South Asian ministry. At the 1999 conference, he met Israel Daniel Peter Penumaka, a South Asian student at LTS, working on his doctoral degree.

St. Paul's International Lutheran Church, Floral Park, NY

Later Limthongviratn recommended Penumaka to Bouman. Subsequently, Bouman recruited Penumaka, who developed St. Paul's International Lutheran Church in Floral Park, NY.

Filipinos in California

By 2001 both Limthongviratn and Murray Finck, bishop of the Pacifica Synod, ELCA, had become aware of the sizeable Filipino population in San Diego. At ALIC in 2001, Limthongviratn introduced Benjamin Lasegan, head of the Lutheran Church in the Philippines (LCP), to Bishop

Finck. Their meeting led to a cooperative LCP and ELCA Filipino ministry in San Diego, with Lasegan sending Pastor Deogracias Olivar to start outreach into the community.

Indonesians in the US

At ALIC 2004, Ephorus Jubil Raplan Hutauruk of the HKBP, informed Limthongviratn that the HKBP had three ministries located in Seattle, Denver, and New York. After returning to the Lutheran Center in Chicago, Limthongviratn wrote a grant underwriting a consultation on Indonesian ministry in the ELCA. Hutauruk, and the general secretary of HKBP, and the leaders of these three ministries attended this consultation in 2005. The ELCA representatives included staff from

HKBP Lutheran Church in Denver, CO

the Division for Outreach, the Division for Global Mission, and Limthongviratn. As a result, all three HKBP ministries joined the ELCA.

Making Connections: for ALIC-related Students in the US

Through the 1999 ALIC, the Northwest Washington Synod sponsored two Korean students at LTS — Judy Kim and Jae Bum Kim — to come to the US for training. The purpose was to increase Korean personnel in the church. Judy Kim returned to Korea after one year in the US, but Jae Bum Kim stayed. After graduation in 2004, he joined the Metropolitan Chicago Synod, where he organized a ministry.

Similarly, Samuel Chim Pich, a Cambodian student at LTS, was brought over to pursue an MA degree at Luther Seminary. Upon graduation, he became the director of Asian outreach ministry at Morningside Lutheran Church, Sioux City, Iowa. He returned to Cambodia after the congregation left the ELCA in 2006.

Making Connections: Congregations

In the ELCA, 90% of Asian ministries are immigrant ministries. Therefore most pastors or lay leaders are well connected with their homelands. An estimated 20 congregations or ministries, either through ALIC or other channels, are involved in small to large scale mission projects through their ethnic networking. Here are a few examples.

1. Chinese Lutheran Church of Honolulu, HI

Before the Chinese Lutheran Church of Honolulu (CLCH) left the ELCA in 2010-early spring 2011, it had provided significant mission support to Chinese churches for decades, particularly in Henan Province, China. CLCH helped rebuild a church in the provincial City of Xinyang, which, before the formation of the People's Republic of China in 1949, had been a stronghold of Lutheran mission. CLCH's pastor, Simon Lee, also led short-term mission trips to Asia and Europe.

2. St. Paul Thai Lutheran Church, Forest Park, IL

This congregation has focused on its relationships with people in Thailand

St. Paul Thai Lutheran Church, Forest Park, IL

to develop leaders for the church. From 2001 to 2018, the church brought 18 Thai seminarians or college students to Chicago for volunteer service visits. It provided partial scholarships to seven students pursuing PhD studies at US seminaries. Because of this support, there are now five PhD educators teaching in Thailand, one in administrative work, and one retired. St. Paul Thai is currently contributing partial support to two additional PhD students who will return to Thailand in 2021.

3. Lao Evangelical Lutheran Church, Robbinsdale, MN

Pastor Khamdeng Kunthapanya is vice president of the Lao Evangelical Church (LEC). While a student in the Twin Cities, he joined the Lao Lutheran Church in Robbinsdale, MN, and built a relationship with Pastor Thiem Baccam. Upon completing his studies, Kunthapanya returned to Laos, but the connection between the Robbinsdale congregation and the LEC continues. Pastor Baccam visits Lao congregations once a year and occasionally brings young adults from Laos to visit churches in the US.

4. Ascension Lutheran Church, Milwaukee, WI

After the 2011 ALIC in Pattaya on the east coast of the Gulf of Thailand, young adults from Ascension Lutheran Church and their pastor traveled to Chiang Mai in Northern Thailand to visit a Hmong village. A year later, the church pastor went back to preach at the 2012 Hmong Youth Retreat, with more than 200 youth attending. Additionally, this congregation supported a seminarian at the Bangkok Institute of Theology and hosted a Hmong student to Ascension in 2014.

5. Lutheran Church of the Resurrection, Huntington Beach, CA

This congregation has networked with the Japan Evangelical Lutheran Church (JELC) ever since the start of the Japan-America Cooperative Evangelism (JACE) program in 1986. The JACE was a joint effort of the JELC, the Lutheran Church in America, The American Lutheran Church, and now the ELCA. The relationship has provided mutual benefits and support. For example, the JELC sent some retired pastors to care for the Japanese community in Los Angeles, while the ELCA funded the bulk of the pastors' salary package. The JELC also supported the building of a multipurpose hall for this congregation.

Making Connections: Individuals

The Asian Lutheran International Conference is still the first and only networking forum that brings Asian Lutherans from both sides of the Pacific Rim together. It has provided opportunities for Asian Lutheran leadership, staff, and friends related to Asian ministries to meet and to discuss ministry, theology, culture, religions, identity, friendship, and more. The impact has been enormous, as these comments show.

Lutheran Church of the Resurrection, Huntington Beach, CA

Coming to ALIC helped me to reconnect with my Lutheran roots more than ever. I have spent most of my life in the Western world. Coming to Asia and learning how Lutherans live and do ministry together helped shape who I am as an Asian American.

Frederick E. N. Rajan, chair
ALIC Steering Committee

As an Asian living in the US, I have developed a hybrid identity. I am Indian, and I am American. It is a significant fact that 75% of Asians living in North America are immigrants. It is important for them to come home to the countries of their origins. ALIC is a valuable opportunity to reconnect with the church-at-large and family.

J. Paul Rajashekar,[7] professor and dean
Lutheran Theological Seminary at Philadelphia

The Asian Lutheran International Conference has provided me a time to learn and further enhance my leadership of the church, to know of Asian church struggles in North America, the global context, and especially in the Asian region. Thank God for Asian leaders who can come together and share our resources, to improve what each of us is doing in Asian community outreach!

Thomas Tsen, bishop
Basel Christian Church of Malaysia

I love to come to ALIC. First, to get to know friends and catch up on what's happening in their ministries, their lives, and the needs of their respective contexts. Second, through the presentations and sharing by church leaders from America and Asia, we gain a broader perspective on what God is doing around the world and especially among Asian people in America and Asia.

Terry Kee, bishop
Lutheran Church in Singapore

I was impressed by the gathering that was open to women and their gifts. It was my first experience being with people from other churches and countries. I have been blessed by the Lord in being able to use my gifts. I hope that ALIC will continue to grow in its broad perspective for the sake of unity of the church of Jesus Christ.

Uengfah Phoeichanthuek, seminarian
Luther Seminary in Thailand

The Asian Lutheran International Conference in Chiang Mai provided a spiritually dynamic experience for me: it was a venue of free-spirited worship and fellowship. The interaction with the local young Christians was such a lively experience. To this day, I am in contact with a few local Chiang Mai young Christians and church leaders.

Brigitte Van Le, lay person
Iowa City, IA

---

[7] For biography, see Yee and Rajashekar, pp. 357-361.

At the first conference in Hong Kong, I met several people who helped us do South Asian ministry in New York City, so that was practical and useful for me. I later attended the ALIC in Hong Kong again, and now this is my third. In directing Domestic Mission in the ELCA, I find this conference really helpful for networking and hearing theological voices from the Asian context. I am very grateful for the opportunity. It helps me to understand how big and broad God's love and grace are.

Steven Bouman, executive director
Domestic Mission, ELCA

I have been attending the gatherings since 2001. I hear good theological conversation and dialogue. I can understand more about the cultures of immigrant people who are coming to my synod. A few of our congregations are developing ministries among Asian people. I also made new friends and colleagues. We have shared our resources. We've even gained several mission pastors in our synod from our ALIC connections. I give thanks for ALIC and will continue to attend in the future!

Murray Finck, bishop
Pacifica Synod, ELCA

Today as we began our event with singing at the worship service and seeing the cross in the processional…it seemed to me more than ever before that singing songs of praise to Jesus is a witness in this culture. I am grateful for this because it teaches me—a person who lives in a culture that thinks it is Christian —to have an experience of feeling what it is like to witness to Jesus.

Judith Spindt, Domestic Mission, ELCA
and assistant to the bishop, Southwestern Texas Synod

This seventh Asian Lutheran International Conference has been a true blessing to me: a Christ-centered celebration of faith, family, and fellowship. A wonderful group of praise team leaders brought inspiration and festivity to the gathering. Sermons were deeply inspirational, focusing us on the life of Jesus Christ as incorporated into the community. We also celebrated the church family in Asia, hearing stories.

James Echols, director
Theological Education and Network, Office of the Presiding Bishop, ELCA

To come to the East, and realize that the Scripture is written in an Eastern context, has really helped to "reframe me theologically." It helps me to experience what Christianity is like in this context where it is a minority because that is something that we in America are going to be experiencing more and more.

Mark Cerniglia
European Descent Lutheran Association for Racial Justice, ELCA

Indeed, the Asian Lutheran International Conference has touched people's lives and benefited ministries East and West. It has also impacted the ELCA by contributing toward reaching churchwide goals — such as:

1. Multicultural Ministry. The Asian Lutheran International Conference stimulates awareness and learning in ethnically diverse church contexts, enhancing congregational and pastoral leadership skills, helping the ELCA affirm its commitment to becoming a diverse church.

2. Increase Youth and Young Adults Participation. Almost one out of every three persons attending the seventh ALIC gathering was a young adult, with another 60 young adults in a one-day Young Adult Program Track. We intentionally reached out so that more young persons would attend the gathering.

3. Continuing Education Opportunity. The Evangelical Lutheran Church in America churchwide staff, especially directors for evangelical mission, and synod staff who work with Asian ministries are among those who came to ALIC to learn. Through lectures, workshops, and field trips, they gained first-hand knowledge of Asian Lutheranism, churches, religions, cultures, politics, and economics.

Funding Sources, Amounts and Tensions

From 1999 to 2019, ALIC has received financial support from various sources.

Division for Global Mission, ELCA (1999)	$30,000.
Lutheran World Federation (1999)	$30,000.
The Evangelical Lutheran Church in Bavaria (1999)	$10,000.
Asian and Pacific Islander Ministry office, ELCA (1999)	$20,000.
Division for Global Mission, ELCA (2001)	$30,000.
Asian and Pacific Islander Ministry office, ELCA (2001)	$20,000.
Division for Outreach, ELCA (2001)	$7,000.
Division for Global Mission, ELCA (2003)	$5,000.

Commission for Multicultural Ministries, ELCA (2003)	$5,000.
Division for Outreach, ELCA (2004)	$4,000.
Worship Resource office, ELCA (2009)	$5,000.
Asian and Pacific Islander Ministry office, ELCA (2004-2013)	
$45,000/each conference x 5 conferences	$225,000.
Association of Asians and Pacific Islanders-ELCA (2013-2019)	
$5,000/each conference x 4 conferences	$20,000.
Young Adult Ministry, ELCA (2013)	$5,000.
Global Mission, ELCA (2015)	$25,000.
Asian and Pacific Islander Ministry office, ELCA (2015-2019)	
$40,000/each conference x 3 conferences	$120,000.
Global Mission, ELCA (2017 and 2019)	
$20,000/each year x 2 conferences	$40,000.
Asian Lutheran International Conference Young Adults (2019)	$12,000.
(Multipurpose hall project)	
Metropolitan New York Synod (2019)	$10,000.

Additional funding sources without specific amounts:

- Donations from the AAPI Asian caucuses, congregations, and individuals.
- Selling ads in the annual Asian community yearbook.
- Registration fee for other-than-Asian participants
- 15% over regular registration fee

Even though the LWF's promised support did not materialize for the second conference, the conference planning continued, led by Rajan and Limthongviratn. While they were in Bangkok in 2000 to work out the details, "a knotty problem surfaced in Chicago. At the center of the difficulty were issues of money and power."[8] Will Herzfeld, the associate executive director of the Division for Global Mission (DGM), argued that companion church relationships fell under the purview of DGM and reneged on a previous verbal commitment to fund ALIC. Herzfeld's action undermined the Asian Lutheran communities' efforts to determine the direction and shape of ALIC. Rajan's diplomatic efforts helped settle the issue of self-determination, but funding issues remained unresolved. This conflict signaled the first round of tension between CMM and DGM regarding ALIC.

The second round extended from 2006 until 2015. After Rajan resigned as CMM's executive director and DGM's Executive Director Bonnie Jensen retired, the new directors of

---

8 Yee, p. 190.

CMM and GM (Global Mission, no longer a division after 2005) did not share Limthongviratn's understanding of the nature and function of ALIC.

Limthongviratn was in a difficult position. On the one hand, his new supervisor, Sherman Hicks, saw ALIC as an ELCA event while the Asian community viewed it as a spiritual network. On the other hand, Raphael Malpica-Padilla, the executive director of GM, emphasized GM's mandate to accompany ELCA companion churches. He viewed ALIC as being outside of this mandate. Both Hicks and Malpica failed to grasp how the phenomenon of globalization demanded a more integrated vision of mission, one not limited by mid-twentieth-century categories of domestic and international. Moreover, Limthongviratn staked out the theological position that the "church is not a country, but a communion." The ELCA churchwide executive for administration convened several meetings to assuage the tension.

Meanwhile, Limthongviratn almost resigned. He did not want to oppose his former bishop, now serving as executive director of multicultural ministries. However, by the fall of 2006, Hicks began to understand ALIC in the same way as Asian Lutherans did. While the tensions soared between CMM and GM, ALIC continued. Conferences took place in Bangkok (2007), Hong Kong (2009), Pattaya (2011), and Chiang Mai (2013).

In 2015 Global Mission resumed financial support for ALIC, finally acknowledging its value as an arena for networking, leadership development, and intellectual exchange on both sides of the Pacific Ocean.

Positive Evaluation

After the 2013 Conference, Executive Director of Congregational and Synodical Mission of the ELCA, Bouman, told Limthongviratn that the Office of the Presiding Bishop wanted an extensive evaluation of ALIC done that summer. The treasurer of the ELCA instigated the review. Knowing that this evaluation resulted from ongoing tensions, Limthongviratn consulted with key Asian elders such as Rajan, Yee, and Rajashekar. They advised him to stay close to Bouman — who, as it turned out, became very supportive of Limthongviratn. Meanwhile, Limthongviratn prepared a report with testimonials from past participants of ALIC.

The outcome of the evaluation was positive. Limthongviratn also recognized the value of diplomacy. He convinced the ALIC Steering Committee to reinstate the GM director for Asia and the Pacific, whose participation on the committee had been interrupted by the ongoing tension between CMM and GM.

Conference Facts and Figures

Here is a panoramic view of ALIC conferences 1999 to 2019.

The First Asian Lutheran International Conference

Venue: Hong Kong, China
Date: January 22-26, 1999
Theme: Asian Lutheranism: Which Way?
Speakers: J. Paul Rajashekar
              Lam Tak Ho
              Frederick E. N. Rajan
              Edmond Yee

Demographics:
  Number in attendance: 110.
  Race/ethnicity:

Lutheran Theological Seminary, HK, venue of the 1st ALIC

   93% Asians, half from the US and Canada, and half from Asia. 7% other than Asian, representing ELCA staff and LWF's North American desk.

  Gender tally:
   70% male and 30% female

  Age distribution:
   90% adults and 10% young adults and youth.

The Second Asian Lutheran International Conference

Venue: Bangkok, Thailand
Date: March 30-April 3, 2001
Theme: Asian Ministry: Challenges and Opportunities
Speakers: Frederick E. N. Rajan
              J. Paul Rajashekar
              Jubil Raplan Hutauruk
              Hiroshi Suzuki

Demographics:
  Number in attendance: 110.
  Race/ethnicity:

Royal Princess Hotel, Bangkok, venue of the 2nd ALIC

   92% Asians, half from the US and Canada, and half from Asia. 8% other than Asian, representing ELCA staff and pastors.

  Gender tally:
   65% male and 35% female.

  Age distribution:
   90% adults and 10% young adults and youth.

The Third Asian Lutheran International Conference

Venue: Bangkok, Thailand
Date: February 13-17, 2004
Theme: Transforming Asian
                Ministries
Speakers: Edmond Yee
                Jubil Raplan Hutauruk
                Wi Jo Kang[9]

Demographics:
  Number in attendance: 100.
  Race/ethnicity:
      95% Asians, half from US and

Ambassador Hotel, Bangkok, venue of the 3rd ALIC

Canada, half from Asia. 5% other than Asian, representing ELCA staff and pastors.
  Gender tally:
      60% male and 40% female.
  Age distribution:
      90% adults and 10% young adults and youth.

The Fourth Asian Lutheran International Conference

Venue: Bangkok, Thailand
Date: February 8-12, 2007
Theme: Asian Ministries in Contemporary Context
Speakers: Maria Gracia Sijera-Grant
                Nelson Siregar
                Yutaka Kishino[10]
                Nicholas Tai

Demographics:
  Number in attendance: 180.
  Race/ethnicity:
      80% Asians, half from the US and Canada, and
      half from Asia. 20% other than Asian, representing
      ELCA staff, pastors, and laity, and J-Term students
      from Luther Seminary.
  Gender tally:
      65% male and 35% female.
  Age distribution:
      90% adults and 10% young adults and youth.

*The Church of Christ in Thailand Head Office,
venue of the 4th ALIC*

---

9 For biography, see Yee and Rajashekar, pp. 281-283.
10 For biography, see Yee and Rajashekar, pp. 286-287.

The Fifth Asian Lutheran International Conference

Venue: Hong Kong, China
Date: February 6-10, 2009
Theme: Asian Churches in Changing Societies
Speakers: J. Paul Rajashekar
              Robinson Radjagukguk
              Teresa Chow

Demographics:

Number in attendance: 120.

Race/ethnicity:

85% Asians, half from the US and Canada, and half from Asia. 15% other than Asian, representing ELCA staff and pastors.

Gender tally:

65% male and 35% female.

YWCA, Hong Kong, venue of the 5th ALIC

Age distribution:

93% adults and 7% young adults and youth.

Limthongviratn, a musician and composer, composed the following song for this Conference:

The Sixth Asian Lutheran International Conference

Venue: Pattaya, Thailand
Date: January 27-31, 2011
Theme: Reading the Bible
in Asian Contexts
Speakers: J. Paul Rajashekar
Martin Sinaga

Demographics:
Number in attendance: 110.
Race/ethnicity:

Town in Town Hotel, Pattaya, venue of the 6th ALIC

85% Asians, half from the US and half from Asia. 20% other than Asian, representing ELCA staff and J-Term students from Lutheran Theological Seminary at Philadelphia.
Gender tally:
65% male and 35% female.
Age distribution:
90% adults and 10% young adults and youth.

The Seventh Asian Lutheran International Conference

Venue: Chiang Mai, Thailand
Date: January 25-29, 2013
Theme: Being Asian, Being Christian
Speakers: Evangeline Anderson-Rajkumar
Hayley Bang
Thu En Yu
Monica Melanchthon [11]
William (Bill) E. Wong[12]

Demographics:
Number in attendance: 110

Lanna Palace Hotel, venue of the 7th ALIC

Race/ethnicity:
91% Asians, half from the US and half from Asia. 8% other than Asian, representing ELCA staff and pastors. 1% Asian staff from the Lutheran Church in Australia.
Gender tally:
55% male and 45% female.
Age distribution:
70% adults, 30% young adults and youth.

---

11 For biography, see Yee and Rajashekar, pp. 306-308.
12 For biography, see Yee and Rajashekar, pp. 406-409.

Limthongviratn composed the following song for this conference:

**Being Asian, Being Christian
The 7th ALIC Theme Song**

Words and Music: Pongsak Limthongviratn
© 2013

The First ALIC Young Adult Gathering

Date: January 26, 2013
Number of Participants: 60

This was the first one-day young adult gathering organized by ALIC in conjunction with its Conference.

The First ALIC Young Adult Gathering

191

The Eighth Asian Lutheran International Conference

Venue: Kuala Lumpur, Malaysia

Date: January 30-February 3, 2015

Theme: Understanding Jesus in Asia

Speakers: J. Paul Rajashekar

                Winfred John Sundaraj

Demographics:

Number in attendance: 118

Race/ethnicity:

90% Asians, with half from the US and half from Asia. 9% other than Asian, representing ELCA staff and pastors. 1% Asian staff from the Lutheran Church in Australia.

Armana Hotel, venue of the 8th ALIC

Gender tally:

57% male and 43% female.

Age distribution:

68% adults, 32% young adults and youth.

Participants of 2nd ALIC Young Adult Gathering

The Second ALIC Young Adult Gathering

Date: January 28-February 1, 2017

Number of Participants: 50

This is the second young adult gathering organized by ALIC. The gathering took place four days in a retreat center one hour away from Medan. Fifty young adults and university students spent time in fellowship and working at a local congregation.

The Ninth Asian Lutheran International Conference

Venue: Medan, Indonesia

Date: February 1-6, 2017

Theme: Re-Visioning Reformation in Asia

Speakers: J. Paul Rajashekar

                Man Hei Yip

                Rospita Siahaan

Demographics:

Number in Attendance: 145

Race/ethnicity:

93% Asians, half from the US and half from Asia. 6% other than Asian, representing ELCA staff and pastors. 1% Asian staff from the Lutheran Church in Australia.

Gender tally:

55% male and 45% female.

Participants of the 9th ALIC Gathering

Age distribution:

55% adults, 45% young adults and youth.

The Tenth Asian Lutheran International Conference

Venue: Udon Thani, Thailand
Date: January 24-29, 2019
Theme: Singing the Lord's Song:
               Migration and Mission
Speakers: Margrethe S. C. Kleiber[13]
               Rospita Siahaan
               Songram Basumatary

Demographics:

Number in attendance: 225

Race/ethnicity:

Participants of the 10th ALIC

84% Asians, with half from the US and half from Asia. 14% other than Asian, representing ELCA staff and pastors, and the ELCA Glocal Music Team. 2% Asian and Australian staff from the Lutheran Church in Australia.

Gender tally:

55% male and 45% female.

Age distribution:

53% adults, 47% young adults and youth.

3rd ALIC Young Adults Work Camp

The Third ALIC Young Adult Gathering

Date: January 19-22, 2019
Number of participants: 52

Fifty-two people attended the event four days before the tenth ALIC. Before going to their gathering site, young adults raised about $12,000 to build a multipurpose hall

---

13 For biography, see Yee and Rajashekar, pp. 289-292.

for a congregation located one and a half hours southeast of Udon Thani. Funds were channeled through a church to start the construction. Young adults finished the project by doing painting and landscaping work. Conference participants dedicated the multipurpose hall to the host congregation, which belongs to the Church of Christ in Thailand, an ELCA companion church.

The Asian Lutheran International Conference Steering Committee always considers both ELCA commitments and the needs of the Asian communities in the US and Asia. The committee will continue to:

1. Strengthen the young adults and youth emphasis. This aspect has become prominent. It has had the effect of increasing young adult and youth participation through a special track devoted to young people's needs and interests.

2. Support women's leadership. The ALIC steering committee supports women's leadership in the church and society. Over the years, the number of women participating in ALIC has increased.

3. Strengthen ALIC's partnership with ELCA units, especially Global Mission. For this reason, the GM director for Asia and the Pacific has a seat at ALIC planning meetings.

We cannot predict the future. Yet, upon reflecting on what ALIC has accomplished thus far, we believe it will continue to evolve in response to the churches needs in the US and Asia. We project that its influence on Lutheran ministries in the US and Asia will continue to increase. Moreover, it will continue to offer other than Asians an authentic window into Asia, Asian cultures, and an opportunity to engage with Asian Lutherans as valued partners in ministry.

Pongsak Limthongviratn, Edmond Yee, and Margrethe S. C. Kleiber

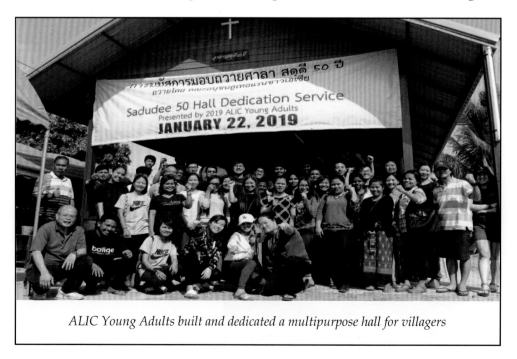

ALIC Young Adults built and dedicated a multipurpose hall for villagers

Look! Thy Servants Produced: Publications for Ministry

Your servants know that seeds will not germinate without being watered. Similarly, ministries may not grow without nurturing, including the support that written resources provide. Therefore in 1980 the Asian Lutheran community began urging the Lutheran Church in America (LCA) and The American Lutheran Church (TALC) to produce bilingually and culturally appropriate materials for Asian ministries. The mission executives "were sympathetic and decided to explore the possibility of producing bilingual materials for Sunday school."[1] Unfortunately this exploration only led to the LCA deciding "to translate a number of social statements into Chinese."[2]

By 1983 the officials of the two churches had discontinued their conversation on bilingual materials. But the Lutheran World Federation stepped in, offering $40,000 "as a one-time grant so that a Chinese staff [member] could be placed at Fortress Press to assist the publisher in obtaining materials from Taosheng Publishing House, a Lutheran press in Hong Kong and Taiwan, or to help to produce the much needed materials."[3] After much negotiation between the staffs of Division for Mission in North America (DMNA), LCA, and Fortress Press, the LCA rejected the offer.

But Fortress Press was not about to give up the idea of providing bilingual materials to congregations. It proposed to "Taosheng that it was willing to purchase and sell the Chinese materials on a consignment basis."[4] Taosheng rejected the proposal.

Two years before the merger of the Association of Evangelical Lutheran Churches, LCA and TALC, a group of people of color worked with the Division for Parish Services, LCA on a series called "Living Waters of Faith." Led by Lily R. Wu, Frederick E. N. Rajan and Edmond Yee, the Asian group produced a cultural resource with a separate Leader Guide called *Eternal River: An Asian Cultural Awareness Resource.* This work was dedicated to the late Eiichi Matsushita. It was the first curriculum produced in the US by and for Asian Lutherans.

It appeared that the pending merger of the three churches had derailed the much needed bilingually and culturally appropriate materials for Asian ministries. However, since 1988 the Asian and Pacific Islander Lutheran community together with the LCA[5] and the Evangelical Lutheran Church in America have produced the following resources. These books, booklets, hymnals and web curricula were primarily designed as ministry supports. Yet they also raised denominational awareness of the Asians present in the US and of their cultures. This list is classified into ten categories for ease of reference.

---

[1] Edmond Yee, *The Soaring Crane: Stories of Asian Lutherans in North America* (Minneapolis: Augsburg Fortres, 2002), p. 131. [Hereafter cited as Yee.]

[2] Yee, p. 131.

[3] Yee, p. 131-132.

[4] Yee, p. 132.

[5] The confirmation series was produced under the sponsorship of the LCA.

Catechism

Title: 路德小問答. *(Luther's Small Catechism (Translations available in Vietnamese and Laotian.)*

Translator: Unknown.

Publisher: Chicago: Commission for Multicultural Ministries, ELCA, n.d.

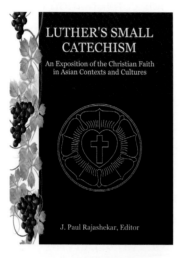

Title: *Luther's Small Catechism: An Exposition of the Christian Faith in Asian Contexts and Cultures.*

Editor: J. Paul Rajashekar.

Publisher: New Delhi: Christian World Imprints, 2019.

Confirmation

Title: 基督教会. *(Jidu Jiaohui.)*

Editor: Edmond Yee.

Publisher: Minneapolis: Augsburg Publishing House/ Fortress, 1989.

Title: 基督徒生活. *(Jidutu Shenghuo.)*

Editor: Edmond Yee.

Publisher: Minneapolis: Augsburg Publishing House/ Fortress, 1989

Title:	我信上帝. *(Wo Xin Shangdi.)*
Editor:	Edmond Yee.
Publisher:	Minneapolis: Augsburg Publishing House/ Fortress, 1989.

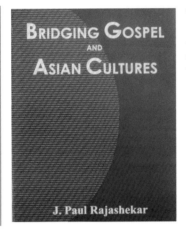

Title:	*Bridging Gospel and Asian Cultures.*
Author:	J. Paul Rajashekar.
Publisher:	Chicago: Association of Asians and Pacific Islanders-ELCA, 2006.

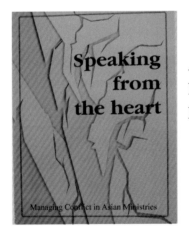

Title:	*Speaking from the heart: Managing Conflict in Asian Ministries.*
Author:	Lily R. Wu.
Editor:	Rosemary Dyson.
Publisher:	Chicago: Evangelical Lutheran Church in America, 2002.

Title:	*Eternal River: An Asian Cultural Awareness Resource (with a separate Leader Guide).*
Authors:	Lily R. Wu, Frederick E. N. Rajan, and Edmond Yee.
Editor:	Edmond Yee.
Publisher:	Minneapolis: Augsburg Publishing House/ Fortress Press, 1988.

Title: *Asian Spirit Journey: An Anthology of Devotions and Prayers.*

Editors: Lily R. Wu, Edmond Yee, and Pongsak Limthongviratn.

Publisher: Chicago: Association of Asians and Pacific Islanders-ELCA, 2003.

Title: *Sacred Sea: An Anthology of Devotions and Prayers.*

Editors: Lily Wu and Edmond Yee.

Publisher: Chicago: Association of Asians and Pacific Islanders-ELCA, 2003.

Title: *Asian Lutheranism: Which Way?*

Editors: Paul Rajashekar, Lily Wu, and Pongsak Limthongviratn.

Publisher: Chicago: Commission for Multicultural Ministries, ELCA, 2000.

Title: *Asian Lutheran Discipleship.*

Editor: Lily R. Wu.

Publisher: An online resource available in five tracks: High School Students; College Students; Young Adults/Professionals; Adults/Immigrants; and Older Adults. See AsianLutherans.com.

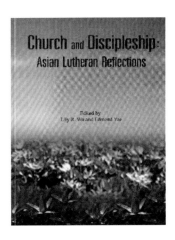

Title:	*Church and Discipleship: Asian Lutheran Reflections.*
Editors:	Lily R. Wu and Edmond Yee.
Publisher:	Chicago: Commission for Multicultural Ministries, ELCA, 2005.

Title:	*Asian and Pacific Islander Ministry Strategy.*
Contributors:	Asian Strategy Task Force Members.
Editor and Compiler:	Lily R. Wu.
Publisher:	Chicago: Commission for Multicultural Ministries, ELCA, 2001. (Available in English with a synopsis in eight Asian languages.)

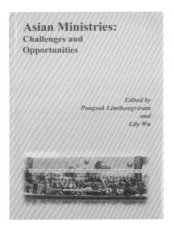

Title:	*Asian Ministries: Challenges and Opportunities.*
Editors:	Pongsak Limthongviratn and Lily Wu.
Publisher:	Chicago: Commission for Multicultural Ministries, ELCA, 2001.

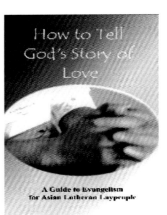

Title:	*How to Tell God's Story of Love: A Guide to Evangelism for Asian Lutheran Lay People.*
Author:	Lily Wu.
Publisher:	Chicago: Division for Congregational Ministries, Evangelical Lutheran Church in America, 2002. (Translations available in Cambodian, Hmong, Japanese, Korean, Laotian, Thai, and Vietnamese.)

Title: *Reaching Asians and Pacific Islanders.*
Contributors: Project Team.
Writer and Editor: Lily R. Wu.
Publisher: Chicago: Evangelical Lutheran Church in America, 2006.

Title: *Welcome, Welcome: A guide to ministry with Asian church members for English-speaking congregations.*
Author: Lily R. Wu.
Editor: Rosemary Dyson.
Publisher: Chicago: Evangelical Lutheran Church in America, 2001.

Title: *Lutheran Basics.*
Editor: Beth Ann Gaede.
Publisher: Chicago: Division for Congregational Ministries, Evangelical Lutheran Church in America, 2003. (Translations available in Cambodian, Chinese, Hmong, Japanese, Korean, Laotian, Thai, and Vietnamese.)

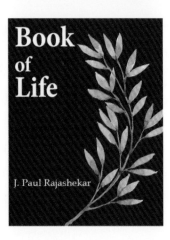

Title: *Book of Life.*
Author: J. Paul Rajashekar.
Publisher: New Delhi: Christian World Imprints, 2021.

History

Title: *The Soaring Crane: Stories of Asian Lutherans in North America.*

Author: Edmond Yee.

Publisher: Minneapolis: Augsburg Fortress, 2002.

Title: *Abundant Harvest: Stories of Asian Lutherans.*

Editors and Compilers: Edmond Yee and J. Paul Rajashekar.

Publisher: Minneapolis: Lutheran University Press, 2012.

Stewardship

Title: *Cheerful Giving: Asian Lutheran Stewardship.*

Author: Pongsak Limthongviratn.

Editor: Lily R. Wu.

Publisher: Chicago: Evangelical Lutheran Church in America, 2006. (Translations available in Chinese, English, Hmong, Indonesian, Japanese, Korean, Laotian, Thai, and Vietnamese.)

Worship

Title: *Chinese Book of Worship.*

Editors: Kevin Anderson and Chinese Worship Team

Publisher: Minneapolis: Augsburg Publishing House, 2006.

Title: *New Hymns of Praise.*
Editors: Chinese Songbook Team.
Publisher: Hong Kong: Taosheng Publishing House, 2011.

Title: *Jeevan Sangeeth Songs of Life: South Asian Worship Songs.*
Editor: Philip K. Mathai.
Publisher: Chicago: Association of Asians and Pacific Islanders, 2003.

PART V

Thus So

V | Gaze and Glimpse

Part I of this book told how Asian Lutheran ministry developed historically and why it did not move forward. We also described how and why the situation turned around and what later joys and challenges Asian leaders faced. Now let us gaze into that past with some critical thought to analyze and assess the ministry's initial stagnation, gradual progression, and sudden retrogression. Then, as the years to come cannot yet be seen, let us take a glimpse into the future of Asian Lutheran ministry in the Evangelical Lutheran Church in America (ELCA). We will divide our review into three periods.

Period of Experiment: 1941-1964

During this period, the churches' focus was on Japanese ministry. The aim was to minister with the *Nisei* (second generation) Japanese on the West Coast by integrating them into Caucasian congregations. A former missionary, L. S. G. Miller, assisted by a Hawaiian-born Japanese American, Paul T. Nakamura, led one initiative in the Los Angeles area.[1] In another case, Shigeru Samuel Ujiie, a Wyoming-born Japanese American, headed the mission in the San Francisco Bay area.[2] A former missionary to Japan and his wife staffed the ministry in the Fresno, CA area.[3] These people put in good efforts, yet the ministries went nowhere. Why?

Several factors impeded the development of Japanese ministry in the 1940s and 1950s. In Fresno, poor interpersonal relations between the missionary and the Board of Home Missions secretary were partly responsible. Other factors, both internal and external, affected Miller's and Nakamura's work in the Los Angeles area,[4] and Ujiie's ministry in the San Francisco Bay

---

[1] For details on Nakamura's ministry and biography, see Edmond Yee, *The Soaring Crane: Stories of Asian Lutherans in North America* (Minneapolis, Augsburg Fortress, 2002), pp.44-51; [Hereafter cited as Yee.] Also Edmond Yee and J. Paul Rajashekar (eds. and comps.), *Abundant Harvest: Stories of Asian Lutherans* (Minneapolis: Lutheran University Press, 2012), pp. 322-324; [Hereafter cited as Yee and Rajashekar.] Jonathan H. X. Lee, Fumitaka Matsuoka, Edmond Yee, and Ronald Y. Nakasone (eds), *Asian American Religious Cultures* (Santa Barbara: ABC- CLIO LLC, 2015), 676-677. [Hereafter cited as Lee, Matsuoka, Yee, and Nakasone.]

[2] For biography, see Yee, pp. 52-54.

[3] For details, see Yee, pp. 34-39.

[4] For details, see Yee, pp. 44-51.

Area.[5]

One factor was demographics. Before WWII, most US Japanese lived on the West Coast. By the 1940s, the total US Japanese population had dropped to 126,948, a decrease of 11,886 from 1930.[6] The *Nisei* population was a smaller subgroup of this total. Moreover, Japanese Americans' internment in concentration camps across the country during WWII also reduced the West Coast population. After the war, some Japanese Americans relocated to cities near their internment sites. Yet another factor was religious proclivities. Religiously, the majority of US and Japan-born Japanese were Buddhists and Shintoists.

American racism against Asians and racism within the ecclesiastical institutions also inhibited the growth of Asian Lutheran ministry. The well-known 1882 Chinese Exclusion Act targeting Chinese and the internment of Japanese speak volumes about American racism. And the Lutheran denominations' sin of racism, perhaps, is best illustrated by the Board of American Missions' (BAM) attitude toward Japanese ministry, and by the recommendation by the Committee on Boards and Committees of the United Lutheran Church in America (ULCA), an ancestor of the ELCA.

The Synod of California, sometime during the biennium of 1934-1936, submitted a request to BAM asking it to "consider the sad condition of the thousands of Japanese on the Pacific Coast."[7] What was BAM's reaction to the plea? "BAM gave 'unfavorable financial condition' as the reason for not honoring the synodical request."[8] If this was a reasonable refusal, the following memorandum from the Committee on Boards and Committees to the Executive Board of the ULCA on February 25, 1953, certainly had an undeniably racist overtone. We think it is significant enough to warrant quoting it in full.

> Under date of February 25, 1953, the Board of American Mission transmitted to Secretary Reinartz the following memorandum regarding evangelism among Orientals in reply to the request of the Executive Board at the January 1953 meeting 'for the Board of American Missions to state its views and present intentions regarding this subject': Complying with item (1) of the Executive Board's recommendation concerning evangelism among Orientals, the Board of American Missions has long felt a responsibility toward the Orientals on the Pacific Coast. In fact, at one time, it was sponsoring work among them until evacuation during the World War ended it. A quest for proper personnel to supervise the work has finally resulted in our employment of the Rev. L. S. G. Miller, D.D. to head it up. Our view for his task is primarily to ascertain the need for and response to Lutheran work among Orientals. Practically his primary purpose is to get pastors of

---

[5] For details, see Yee, pp. 51-54.

[6] According to "U.S. Army Western Defense Command (1940), p. 400."

[7] Minutes of the Tenth Biennial Convention of the United Lutheran Church in America, October 14-21, 1936, p. 167.

[8] Yee, p. 41.

existing churches interested in and to work among these people and correspondingly to help interest the Orientals in membership in existing churches. Whenever there is such a concentration of them as to make it embarrassing to existing congregations to have so many of the Orientals unite with them, the Board will consider supporting the organization of separate congregations. As to the part of the Board of Social Missions (BSM) should have in this task, we have no knowledge at present. It is our opinion on the facts at hand that the Orientals are self-sufficient citizens and need nothing in the field of social welfare work beyond that of any group of Americans.[9]

This memorandum is clear about how important it is to keep "the Orientals" separate, as any growing presence of Japanese would be "embarrassing" to the existing Lutheran congregation. The BSM soon noticed the racial overtone of the statement but decided that it "carries no element of racial prejudice but refers to practical problems of administration and organization within the congregation."[10]

However, the synod convention in 1954 also picked up the racial overtone and asked for clarification whether or not "the phrase, 'race prejudice' and 'practical problems of administration and organization within the congregation' were synonymous or contrasting."[11] "The conclusion," after consulting with executive secretaries of BAM and BSM, "was that the 'practical problems' referred to were *linguistic* and not *racial* and that the original phraseology 'carried no element of race prejudice.'"[12] "An incredible explanation," exclaimed Edmond Yee[13] in his book *The Soaring Crane: Stories of Asian Lutherans in North America*, "since the mission was supposed to integrate into existing congregations the English-speaking *Nisei* or those Japanese who would have no problem with English."[14]

Period of Growth: 1965-2009

Asian Lutheran ministry began to rise in the Lutheran Church in America (LCA) with the ordination of Wilson Wu in 1965 in Monterey Park, CA;[15] Herman Liu in 1974 in Vancouver, BC, Canada;[16] and Yee's dual appointments in 1978.[17] Later there was the emerging leadership of Joseph Wong and Benjamin Shum in The American Lutheran Church (TALC). Of course, the partnership between the Asians and their denominations was also a contributing factor.

---

[9] Minutes of the Nineteenth Biennial Convention of the United Lutheran Church in America. October 6-13, 1954, p. 310. [Hereafter cited as Minutes.]

[10] Minutes, p. 310.

[11] Minutes, p. 310.

[12] Minutes, p. 310.

[13] For biography, see Yee and Rajashekar, pp. 422-426.

[14] Yee, p. 47.

[15] For details, see Yee, pp. 55-57.

[16] For details, see Yee, pp. 73-74.

[17] For details, see Yee, pp. 105-118.

Let us examine four impacts during this period that fueled the growth of Asian ministries in the ELCA and its predecessor bodies.

Socio-political Context in the US and Asia

The decades of 1960 and 1970 significantly transformed US society. The assassinations of President John F. Kennedy, his brother Robert, and Martin Luther King, Jr. shook the nation to its foundation. With the death of Kennedy, Lyndon B. Johnson succeeded the presidency. Johnson initiated legislation resulting in the 1965 Celler-Hart Act, which widely opened the door to Asians who wanted to immigrate to the US. The Refugee Acts of 1975, 1980, and 1987 followed, all of which resulted from the war in Vietnam. With Saigon's fall on April 15, 1975, the US suddenly experienced an influx of refugees, who added more colors and textures to the fabric of society and the churches.

In the meantime, the wind of political change in Hong Kong was blowing. The United Kingdom's (UK) 99-year lease on the Kowloon peninsula would end in 1997, and the UK and China were negotiating the terms of Hong Kong's return to Chinese governance. The prospect of the colony's return to its rightful owner frightened some residents. Some decided to immigrate to the US and Canada, giving both nations a boost on the Asian population. Pastors were among those who left Hong Kong, benefiting Lutheran churches in North America by their presence.

Socio-technical Growth in the US

The rapid development of technology in the US continues to attract many well-educated immigrants from India. Likewise, the need for qualified tech workers provides Chinese students an opportunity to remain in the country after graduation from college. After receiving an offer of employment, individuals can apply for H-1B visas. Unlike other types of non-immigrant visas, this particular visa permits the recipients to apply for legal residency, thus giving them the option of remaining in the US.

The Civil Rights Movement and the Churches' Response

The US Lutheran churches of European and Scandinavian origins in the 19th and early 20th centuries were fragmented communities loosely connected by some common doctrines based on Reformation heritage. Nevertheless, "there were also complex theological differences among various Lutheran groups that partially accounted for their views on slavery and race."[18] Therefore, in the main, the Lutherans had no unified voice on slavery and race in the 19th century. In fact, "As far as the northern Lutheran church was concerned, slavery remained an invisible issue."[19] The Franckean Synod was the only one that was anti-slavery. But its small size and limited power and influence

---

[18] Forrest G. Wood, *The Arrogance of Faith: Christianity and Race in America from the Colonial Era to the Twentieth Century* (New York: Alfred A. Knopf, 1990), pp. 340. [Hereafter cited as Wood.]
[19] Wood, pp. 351-352.

did not enable the synod to gain any foothold in the broader Lutheran community.[20]

Despite the lack of early Lutheran traction on slavery and race issues, the Civil Rights Movement, as it hit a crescendo in the 1960s, did affect the predecessor bodies of the ELCA. At its second biennial convention, held on July 2-9, 1964, in Pittsburgh, PA, the LCA was the first to adopt a statement on "Race Relations." The preamble reads:

> The current racial revolution has thrust the church into a time of travail and perplexity but also of opportunity and hope. Injustice, which for a long time was either ignored, rationalized, or mutely borne, is now seen more clearly for what it actually is. Injurious discrimination based on race is a violation of God's created order, of the meaning of redemption in Christ, and of the nature of the church....Implicit in such discrimination are unbiblical views of God and of humanity....At the heart of life of the church is prayer.[21]

The statement ends with a series of prayers. The Lutherans at this convention also approved the "Resolution of Civil Rights Act," which was signed into law on July 2, 1964.

The American Lutheran Church, at its Seventh General Convention, also adopted a statement on "Racism in the Church," on October 14, 1974. This document consists of ten points. It begins with a general statement:

> Racism is one of the most destructive sins in today's world. It refuses to honor God's mighty acts in creation, redemption, and sanctification. Racism simply does not trust the gospel. It builds on human pride and prejudice, abusing power for self-advantage. Racism dishonors God, neighbor and self. It rejects the meaning in God's becoming incarnate in Jesus Christ, because in rejecting another person one rejects Jesus Christ.[22]

The statement goes on to say that racism is White racism. The people of color may not need TALC, but the church needs them. Further, it states that "The American Lutheran Church is aware that time for study and statements on racism is largely passed."[23] Then it issues a call to act:

> The time for action is at hand. It therefore requests the general president, as the spiritual leader of the church, the symbol of its hopes and unity, and its chief executive officer, to give his continuing personal endorsement, leadership, and commitment to the elimination of White racism in The American Lutheran Church.[24]

The document concludes, "Remembering our Lord's experience in the temple, after he read from the prophet Isaiah (Luke 4: 16-30), we have the answer of faith that dares the impossible possibility."[25]

---

[20] For detailed discussion on Lutherans attitudes on slavery and race, see Wood, pp. 346-353.

[21] "Race Relations," p. 1.

[22] "Racism in the Church," Point 1, p. 1. [Hereafter cited as "Racism."]

[23] "Racism," Point 7, p. 3.

[24] "Racism," Point 7, p. 3.

[25] "Racism," Point 10, p. 3.

Statements on race relations and racism and the call to act are different from action itself. Nonetheless, these are useful tools in the endeavor of opening the church to people of color. And the future ELCA was pushed into action after its birth in 1988. The initiative came from the Transcultural Seminars. These seminars were "deeply rooted in the African-American community. The initial focus was on the black church, but quickly developed into a gathering of five ethnic groups — Asian, African- American, Hispanic, Native American, and White from the AELC, The ALC and the LCA — under the auspices of LCUSA."[26]

The Lutheran Council of the United States of America (LCUSA) convened two seminars in 1981. The participants drafted and signed a document, "Our Word to Our Church for Our Church." This statement articulated the demand that the new church set a growth goal of becoming 10% people of color within ten years of its formation and that it ensures the representation of people of color and White women at all levels of the church. Furthermore, it recommended creating a Commission for Women and a Commission for Multicultural Ministries to assist the new church in meeting these demands. The seminars' participants authorized Will Herzfeld to transmit the document to the Commission for a New Lutheran Church (CNLC), which later requested Herzfeld and Yee to design the representational principles or the quota system, as it was called.

The Commission for a New Lutheran Church members received and accepted the recommendations of "Our Word to Our Church for Our Church." In its final report, the CNLC recommended that the new church incorporate the demands of the Transcultural Seminars into its constitution.

Through its constitution, the ELCA committed itself to the 10% goals. Ultimately, however, it was an underfunded mandate, as the leaders of Generation II and III bemoaned.[27] Nonetheless, Asian ministry made significant gains, growing from 31 congregations or ministries at the beginning of the ELCA to 125 in the mid-2000s.

Asian Leadership in the Church

A critical factor in the growth of Asian ministry during this era was the partnership between the Lutheran denominations and Asians. Among the early instances of this partnership was the LCA's appointment of Yee to a dual position in 1978.[28] Later examples were TALC's cooperation with Wong and Shum and the ELCA's appointment of William E. Wong to a full-time position as director of Asian ministries in 1988.

All of these factors, we believe, contributed to the growth of Asian ministries in the ELCA.

---

[26] Yee, p. 132; For details of the Transcultural Seminars, see Richard J. Perry, *Catching A Star: Transcultural Reflections on a Church for All People* (Minneapolis: Lutheran University Press, 2004). [The original manuscript was edited by Lily R. Wu.]

[27] For details, see *"See! Thy Servants Labor: Asian Lutheran Witness in the USA"* in Part I in this volume.

[28] For details, see *"See! Thy Servants Labor: Asian Lutheran Witness in the USA"* in Part I in this volume.

Period of Challenge: 2010-2020

The Lutheran Church in America and The America Lutheran Church began to decline in membership, starting in 1969. The decline coincided with the flourishing of Asian life in the US. In 1960, the Asian population stood at 980,337. By 1970 the number had grown to 1,526,401. Ten years later, the population more than doubled, and two years after the birth of the ELCA, it had reached the 7,273,662 million mark while continuing to grow. With such a phenomenal increase in population, Asian ministry in the ELCA should have had a promising future. But what turned this opportunity into a challenge for Asian ministries beginning in 2010? Contributing factors follow.

Membership Decrease and the Statement, "Human Sexuality: Gift and Trust"

The United States mainline denominations began to lose members in the 1960s, and Lutheran denominations were no exception. But such a decline did not affect the growth of Asian language-specific ministries at all. Instead, the decline forced church leaders to reckon with their failure to be receptive to Asians and other people of color. West Coast Lutheran leaders engaged in multiple activities to encourage White congregations to open their doors to people of color. On the national level, the LCA advocated "inclusive ministry" as a theme for mission. As a result, Asian ministries experienced growth, albeit with the usual ebb and flow of all ministry developments. We, too, had to disband 16 ministries under development and merged five others since 1997. Even so, Asian ministry development was not adversely affected until 2009. In that year, the total Asian membership of the ELCA was 20,770 (1% of all ELCA active participants), with an estimate that 65% of this number worshiped in White congregations.

However, by 2018 the church experienced a 7% decrease in Asian and Pacific Islander participation.[29] Furthermore, the Planning, Research, and Evaluation team also projected three scenarios for Asian membership in the church. First, if the decrease continues the way it has been, there will be 12,257 Asian members by 2040 compared to 19,279 in 2018. However, the team also forecast two other possibilities for the year 2040: an "Upper Confidence Bound" [a higher figure] of 14,537 Asian members and a "Lower Confidence Bound" [a lower figure] of 9,976.

What caused the sudden decrease? From the perspective of Asian congregations and ministries, it has mostly to do with the statement, "Human Sexuality: Gift and Trust," approved by the ELCA's Churchwide Assembly in 2009. Eventually, 18 Asian congregations and ministries left the church because they did not share the values of the ELCA. Today, 86 Asian congregations and ministries remain with the ELCA, down 31% from the peak number of 125.

Another challenge we face is the lack of second and third generation bilingual or multilingual leaders. Today out of the 86 congregations and ministries, only 11 provide English language ministry, and only a few are staffed by English-speaking Asians. Some congregations have contracted with White seminarians for their English language outreach.

---

[29] ELCA Office of Presiding Bishop, Planning, Research and Evaluation, January 2020.

Another possible contributor to the decrease of Asian membership may be the proliferation of Asian religions in America, ranging from Shamanism to Hinduism, with Buddhism being the fastest-growing tradition. Such availability offers Asians in the US a variety of familiar spiritual choices. And according to Tu Wei-ming, a retired Harvard University professor, "East Asians may profess themselves to be Shintoists, Taoists, Buddhists, Muslims, or Christians, but by announcing their religious affiliations seldom do they cease to be Confucians."[30]

Glimpse into the Future

The Asian American population of the US continues to grow. In 2018, it was 22.6 million. Such rapid growth could conceivably favor various religious traditions. Up to 2009, that was the case in Asian Lutheran ministries, with fresh waters flowing in like a gentle and steady stream. However, in 2002, Yee foresaw the potential of the stream diminishing in the Asian community. In his book, *The Soaring Crane: Stories of Asian Lutherans in North America,* he sounded a warning. Yee stated,

> If Asian Lutheran ministries are to flourish and soar like the supple, graceful and beautiful crane, gaining new angles of vision as it surges higher and higher, Asian Lutheran professionals must assume a greater responsibility. We must develop suitable hermeneutic tools so that a theology responsive and responsible to an Asian-American context might result and with which we may meet our own people's needs, spiritual and mundane.... [31]

He then offered a caveat, "In the course of developing a responsive and responsible theology, we must pay attention to the various traditions. They must not be indiscriminately discarded or retained. But first...' we must ask, what role could and/or should the traditions play in our ascending the mountaintop to view a new horizon.'"[32]

Yee's warning call, though limited in retrospect, and his caveat are still valid. However, our community, along with society, has changed since 18 years ago. Today we face twenty-first-century challenges within and beyond the church, enlarging our vision of reality. Because of these challenges in Asian ministries, we invited eight Asian theologians and community leaders on August 14, 2020, to discuss what it might take to advance Asian ministries in the church.[33] We asked them to provide insights on church, leadership, and community, with migration as a framework for starting the discussion. Their wisdom and concerns are summarized and italicized below to distinguish them from comments we added to invite broader community reflection and discussions.

1. *Theologies and Theological Education: We need suitable theologies and a relevant theological education system for our community.*

---

[30] Tu Wei-ming, *Confucianism in an Historical Perspective* (Singapore: The Institute of East Asian Philosophies, 1989), p. 3.

[31] Yee, p. 206.

[32] Yee, p. 206.

[33] Sarah Anderson-Rajarigam, Evangeline Anderson-Rajkumar, Surekha Nelavala, Moses Paul Peter Penumaka, J. Paul Rajashekar, Tuhina Verma Rasche, and Teresita Clemente Valeriano. Man Hei Yip was unable to attend.

Euro-American theologies and the present theological education model do not speak to Asian and Asian American realities in the US. When Luther and the confessions are read exclusively through a Euro-American lens, this does not address our community concerns. We need to read Luther and the confessions in light of our own experiences and realities. Asian America is as diverse ethnically, culturally, linguistically, religiously, and economically as the land from which our ancestors and some of us came. There is no single unified Asian culture among Asians in the US. We need to consider this reality when developing relevant theologies and new educational models.

Fully aware of this reality, Asian Lutheran leaders have begun to articulate appropriate theologies for our communities. For example, *Luther's Small Catechism: An Exposition of the Christian Faith in Asian Contexts and Cultures* edited by J. Paul Rajashekar, among others, points in this direction.[34] The themes of some Asian Lutheran International Conferences — such as "Asian Lutheranism, Which Way?" — likewise affirm the serious intentions of Asian leaders to address these issues.

In the area of theological education, Asian Lutherans have also made contributions to three different models.

1. The Theological Education for Emerging Ministries (initially called Alternate Route to Ordained Ministry) model can be traced to the presence of Albert Pero, Carlos Benito, George Tinker, and Yee at the Consultation on Theological Education for the New Church (CTENC).[35] The CTENC had been in progress before the four served from 1982-1985. They argued for a new model of theological training. Yee was the first to organize such a program in 1989 at Pacific Lutheran Theological Seminary in Berkeley, CA. Stephen Brookfield, distinguished university professor at the University of St. Thomas, lauded the program's effectiveness, stating, "In 40 years of teaching, I have never come across a program that has such a high level of relevance in the eyes of students."[36]

2. The Asian Theological Summer Institute directed by Rajashekar at United Lutheran Seminary is another example. This one-week summer program brings together Asian theology students at the doctoral level in North America to be mentored by Asian scholars. It "has sought to provide a venue for Asian/Asian American scholars to interact with one another, strengthen their Asian identity and foster a network of emerging Asian scholars and theologians for the church and the academy."[37]

---

[34] For publication details, see *"Look! Thy Servants Produced: Publications for Ministry"* in Part IV in this volume.

[35] The Transcultural Seminars sent the four of them to the Consultation on Theological Education for the New Church to represent the African American, Asian American, Hispanic, and Native American communities. The four of them served from 1982-1985.

[36] See, "Assessing the Effectiveness of the Theological Education for Emerging Ministry (TEEM) Program of the ELCA Western Mission Cluster: A Report by Stephen Brookfield, Distinguished University Professor, University of St. Thomas, Minneapolis-St. Paul. This research was funded under the Lilly Foundation Grant 'Creating a Culture of Call for the Twenty First Century' February 2009," p. 33.

[37] From private email exchanges between J. Paul Rajashekar and Edmond Yee, September 11, 2020.

3. The Asian Lay Evangelist project was constructed more recently by Pongsak Limthongviratn, Moses Penumaka, and Teresita Clemente Valeriano. This initiative is a one-year training program focusing on theological education, outreach, and pastoral ministry utilizing Asian and Asian-American experiences and perspectives. This program began in December 2020.

2. We need to develop ways to attract and provide support to young leaders and walk with pastors and leaders who are bi-vocational for lack of funding.

Despite the small numbers of Asians in the ELCA, Asian leaders' contributions to the church and related institutions and organizations are unquestionable. [38] The challenge is to attract and provide support to young leaders into the church for parish ministry and walk with bi-vocational pastors and leaders. Currently, thirty of the 86 Asian congregations and ministries are served by bi-vocational persons.

Retaining and incorporating second, third, and fourth generation Asian leaders, as well as Asian adoptees, biracial and multiracial Asians into the community is another pressing need. While second, third, and fourth generation Asians can be found in White congregations, they face unique dynamics in the call process and the leadership role. They may be the only Asian in their congregation or even in their conference or synod. Racist viewpoints about Asians shape the way the dominant culture views their leadership. It is necessary to strategize ways of reducing their isolation and providing them with the tools they need to address racism in their contexts.

3. Identities and Spiritualities and Interfaith Relations: We need to articulate an Asian and an Asian American and Asian American Lutheran identity and how to rediscover Asian spiritualities as well as interact with believers of other faiths.

Our leaders raised the question of identity on three levels: Asian, Asian American, and Asian American Lutheran. Perhaps we can add another layer to it: Asian American Lutheran Hindu or Buddhist or Confucian or animist or Asian American Hindu or Buddhist or Confucian or animist Lutheran? In our diverse community, achieving a single Asian identity is unthinkable, if not impossible. Therefore, when we speak of Asian identity, we must be mindful of our multiple identities. Identity is a critical issue that requires further conversation and articulation.

The matter of spirituality is another weighty issue for our community. According to Ronald Y. Nakasone," *'The Study of Spirituality'* traces the expression and notion of 'spirituality' to 15th and 16th century European Christian interest in mystical experiences that were believed to lead to an overarching supra-empirical reality."[39] Does this understanding of spirituality fit our understanding? Perhaps; perhaps not, depending on how we define the term. Certainly we cannot use the word "spirituality" in its singular when we address the issue. We suspect Asian Lutherans

---

[38] For details, see *"Lo! Thy Servants on the Move: Flowing Far and Wide,"* in Part III in this volume.
[39] Lee, Matsuoka, Yee, and Nakasone, p. 146.

knowingly or otherwise often possess multiple spiritualities because we are deeply rooted in the fertile soils of both shores.

Asian Christians in the 1960s and 1970s in Asia raised the question of how to interact with people of other faiths. Converting them to the Christian faith was the traditional aim. With a changing world and a more enlightened understanding of other religions, that no longer seemed to be an option. They concluded that now the question was how to live with our neighbors of other faiths.

As previously mentioned, all Asian religions and spiritual traditions are active in the US, so the question raised by our leaders was a valid one. How we answer it may well have implications for the future of Asian Lutheran ministries.

4. *Community and Anti-racist Commitments and Practices: We need to embody and provide accompaniment to second and third generations, deal with our internal diversity and diversity within the ELCA, and connect ourselves with being part of the institution. Moreover, we need to deal with patriarchy, walk with vulnerable communities, including Asian undocumented persons, and address justice issues for ourselves and others, including racism within our community.*

Our community is both unified and diversified. Unity is achieved through the pan-Asian association, whereas diversity lies with its caucus system. The beauty of this arrangement is that it affirms unity and diversity at the same time. The flip side is that it may hinder us from acting in unison to embody and provide accompaniment to second and third generations. Our comfort with the current arrangement could lull us into complacency in dealing with our diversity and the diversity within the ELCA.

Our community faced two major justice issues in the past: the Vincent Chin murder and redress for Japanese Americans. Concerning the Chin case, Yee in 2002 wrote,

> No case, however, galvanized Asian and other ethnic communities more than the Vincent Chin case. In 1982 on the night before his wedding, Chin, a Chinese-American, was killed by two white unemployed Detroit autoworkers…who mistook him for a Japanese. The judge sentenced the two killers to a three-year probation and a $3,000 fine each, which outraged not only Asians but persons of color from other communities as well.[40]

Some Asian Lutherans were alarmed. We submitted resolutions and recommendations to the Lutheran churches requesting them to advocate for justice and to educate the entire church about anti-Asian violence. However, "The churches took no particular action."[41]

---

[40] Yee, pp. 133-134.
[41] Yee, . 134.

The Asian Lutheran community was more or less unified in the Redress Movement about the internment of Japanese Americans during WWII. "The Asian Caucus meeting in 1981… endorsed the Redress Movement of Japanese Americans."[42] And yet, the Chinese pastors walked out of the room after the motion passed because they could not forget Japanese atrocities in China during the war.[43]

Today the community continues to wrestle with matters of justice internally and externally. Internally, how will we address patriarchy, views on undocumented persons, and attitudes toward the LGBTQ community? Externally, how will we confront racism, classism, and casteism in our communities to become an anti-racist coalition that walks in solidarity with other peoples of color?

Our leaders laid out a big agenda for the community to consider. Even if we implement the leaders' concerns and try to strengthen Asian ministries in these ways soon, the questions facing us remain: can we prevent the projected membership decrease? Can we learn new and authentic ways to attract persons who consider religious faith meaningless or irrelevant? Or, when there are many other spiritual paths to choose? The future glimpses offered here are by no means a prediction. However, we are confident that Asian leaders, members, and partners in the church and community will continue to serve as part of the ever-flowing stream.

Edmond Yee, Margrethe S. C. Kleiber, and Lily R. Wu

---

[42] Yee, p. 135.
[43] Yee, pp. 135-137.

PART VI

Appreciations

VI | Appreciations

Someone once stated,

> Pongsak has an intellectual and deeply visionary concept of the nature and function of ministry in Asian/Asian American settings, and he implements this concept with realistic approaches, unquestionable commitment and unparalleled passion.[1]

Indeed these qualities have enabled him to serve as program director for Asian and Pacific Islander Ministries for nearly a quarter of a century in the Evangelical Lutheran Church in Amerca. In celebrating his retirement, we selectively invited the following people, who know him on many levels, to write some words of thanks and appreciation to him.

Thiem Baccam (US)

On behalf of the Laotian caucus I extend my thanks for your leadership, wisdom and kind counseling in the church. We appreciate your energy, enthusiasm, resourcefulness and skill. You have provided a rich contribution to the ministry. We are enlightened and empowered through all the years that you demonstrated deep passion into our community. Through generosity, devotion and passion, you helped us spread the gospel of Jesus Christ to a multitude of people. We are humbled and blessed by your leadership. I am deeply and sincerely grateful. Rev. Dr. Pongsak Limthongviratn, thank you so much for all the gifts that you have shared with us.

---

[1] Tom Holmes, *Pongsak: Advocate for Asian Ministries* (Bangkok: Luther Seminary, 2015), p. 11.

Songram Basumatary (India)

My interactions with you were limited at Asian Lutheran International Conference (ALIC) Steering Committee meetings and conferences. Yet I found in you a dynamic and multi-talented personality. Your multi-dimensional leadership quality can only be compared with what St. Paul claimed in I Corinthians 9:22, "... I have become all things to all people so that by all possible means I might save some!"

What an amazing person you are, dear Pongsak! In ALIC, I could see you as a multi-purpose machine. Wonder of wonders, you were the youngest of all young ones in the young adult track of ALIC conference, but you were the oldest of all old ones in the entire ALIC conference! Truly you have run the race. God bless your years to come!

Chris Desina Sianturi (Indonesia)

Dr. Pongsak Limthongviratn has greatly contributed to the Lutheran theological journey in Asia. I remember a song he composed for the Asian Lutheran International Conference: "ALIC together we are, together we stand….Crossing the differences, crossing the races, crossing the barriers. Asians together, God bless our lands." You have provided opportunities for Asian adults and youth to share the joys of God's grace as Lutheran people together internationally. You are such an amazing pastor who crosses the ocean to do ministry in Asia. Thus we bless you and may you keep on shining.

David C. Chen (US)

In 1997, you and I were the final candidates interviewed for the position of director for Asian Ministries, Commission for Multicultural Ministries, Evangelical Lutheran Church in America (ELCA). Though I did not get the job, we became good friends and partners working closely for Asian ministries in the ELCA, particularly in establishing the Center of Chinese Ministry, where I served as the first Director. It has been a joy working with you. You are a faithful, compassionate, and determined man, with deep enthusiasm for the gospel. Your contributions to the Asian Lutheran community have been both domestic and international. Thank you deeply, Pongsak, for your friendship and your caring for Chinese ministry.

Terry Kee (Singapore)

I have yet to meet anyone as gifted and versatile as you. You are able to converse in Thai, Mandarin, Cantonese, English and several other languages. You are not only a piano and guitar player, but also a composer of songs at short notice. Your love for God and your commitment to connect Asian church leaders in America with their counterparts in Asia are evident in the way you have developed and run the Asian Lutheran International Conference program. Many lives have been touched and many churches blessed by you. May the Lord continue to bless you richly according to God's love and grace.

Margrethe S. C. Kleiber (US)

I once looked up the word peripatetic after the late Rev. Dr. Will Herzfeld called you the peripatetic Thai. Peripatetic means, "traveling from place to place, in particular working or based in various places for relatively short periods."

My dear friend, this single word sums up your life working for the gospel. Like St. Paul, you are always on the road meeting people, connecting people, imagining new ways to build the kingdom of God. I have watched and admired your unfailing dedication, clarity of vision, and seemingly ceaseless energy as you move between Asia and the United States, between board rooms and classrooms, laboring in multiple time zones and using every conceivable mode of transportation. Perhaps peripatetic is just another way of saying apostle.

Richard Lui (Hong Kong)

During your time at Hong Kong Lutheran Theological Seminary, we called you Paul Lin. And just like the Apostle Paul, you travel a lot; in your case, connecting people between the United States and Asia. You are a person with many talents, in language, music, theology and pastoral ministry. I always wonder how many hours are in your clock, as you fulfill so many responsibilities and connect people in different time zones. Thank you for letting me have a part in the Asian Lutheran International Conference. I know I gained much more than I could offer. Retirement means moving into another track of life, and I am sure you will bear more fruits by the gifts that the Lord has given to you.

Frederick E. N. Rajan (India)

I am profoundly grateful for Pastor Pongsak's life and ministry. He never forgets who he is and where he came from. He has given his life to witness for the gospel in the US and in Thailand. Pongsak has innate abilities and talents that he uses to glorify God. No matter what he puts his mind to, he always rises to the occasion and does it with love and compassion. He is a tough leader who never takes no for an answer. His determination, dedication, passion, and intellect break barriers and hurdles. Through innovation and scholarship, he always explores ways to accomplish what God calls him to do. Thank you, brother Pongsak. More than you realize, we are blessed by you.

J. Paul Rajashekar (US)

Having known you and worked with you for over 30 years, I could only think of one word that captures your gift and graces: "incredible". You are a man of deep faith and commitments, a genuine pastor, musician, humble leader with outstanding organizational ability, theological teacher, scholar, and a generous and caring person. Your dedication to furthering Asian/Pacific Islander ministry in the ELCA and your leadership in the theological formation of Asian pastors and leaders are commendable. Your contributions to the church include so many ministries, projects, publications, and the Asian Lutheran International Conference. I am proud of all your accomplishments and service in the Lord's vineyard. May God continue to bless you.

Rospita Siahaan (Indonesia)

I met you for the first time at the 9th Asian Lutheran International Conference in Medan. The year was 2017. I did not know many people at the conference because I was there only for a few hours to deliver my presentation. However, I felt you warmly welcomed me and was friendly to me over lunch as if we had known each for a long time. You are a global person who keeps your Asian personality friendly and humble. You are truly a dedicated pastor and theologian who can work with anyone, youth or adult, lay or clergy. You embody 1 Corinthians 9:20-22: "To the Jews I became as a Jew, in order to win Jews. To those under the law I became as one under the law…so that I might win those under the law….I have become all things to all people, that I might by all means save some."

Maria (Gigie) Gracia Sijera-Grant (US)

Picture a worship gathering in which a large number of people from different cultures are praying the "Lord's Prayer" in different languages – Hmong, Laotian, Tamil, Telugu, Tagalog, Korean, Thai, Mandarin, Cantonese, English, and more. This powerful image represents your leadership in Asian ministries. You have a gift for seeing the big picture and connecting all the dots. Your dedication, tireless energy, and creative ways of resolving challenges never cease to amaze me. You have mastered the art of "Asian economic strategy" – not only in ensuring that participants are fed well but also in producing prolific literature for Asian ministries. With your sense of humor, you have the ability to build relationships and invite others to actively participate in God's work. What a blessing to work with you!

Amnuay Tapingkae (Thailand)

Your work as the program director for Asian and Pacific Islander Ministries in the Evangelical Lutheran Church in America and as the lead pastor of St. Paul Thai Lutheran Church in Chicago has had a lasting and beneficial impact on ecclesial relations in Thailand. I believe it is fair to attribute the Lutheran contributions here to your energetic and insightful encouragement, which has strengthened partnership between the ELCA and the Church of Christ in Thailand. Beyond that, your personal relationships with people here in your homeland, including me and my family, have built bridges of friendship and understanding. I am glad your colleagues have dedicated this book to you to honor your ministry and to celebrate your retirement.

Josephine Tso (Hong Kong)

It is my privilege to congratulate you, my dear brother in Christ, on your retirement in 2021. I still remember our good old days at Hong Kong Lutheran Theological Seminary in the early 1980s. As a member of the Lutheran church in Asia, I thank you especially for the contributions you have made to Asian Lutherans in our region as well as for those in the Evangelical Lutheran Church in America. The biennial gatherings of the Asian Lutheran International Conference provide a very meaningful platform for church leaders to share, to learn, and to cooperate. These really enriched the understanding and connection among us. As you step into a new phase of your life, I wish God's continued blessings on you and your family.

William (Bill) E. Wong (US)

Asian Pacific Islander Lutheran ministry is demanding. People who respond to God's call to this ministry offer their hearts, hard work, a strong desire to be faithful to God, a passion for people, a vision for the future, and a desire to build up and develop the outreach, pastoral care, and the services needed to grow community, form relationships, and meet Jesus. Pongsak Limthongviratn exemplifies this call. For 24 years on the churchwide staff of the Evangelical Lutheran Church in America as the program director for Asian and Pacific Islander Ministries, he has labored faithfully in the Lord's vineyard, building up and growing ministries across the land and with partners across the seas. To this good and faithful servant, I say well done and offer praise and thanksgiving to God for him and his ministry.

Lily R. Wu (US)

Pongsak is like the dynamic conductor of a very large symphony orchestra. AAPI members are like the musicians called to the work. The conductor sees from the musical score how the parts fit together. He guides the orchestra so that we learn to listen, blend and harmonize. Our role is to focus with the group to produce our best quality results. His role is to present the vision, then coordinate how we all contribute to the greater whole. Pongsak has brought our diversities into collaborations again and again for deeper, stronger ministry. Thank you, Pongsak! Your passionate faith has inspired and brought out the best in so many of us as Asian Lutheran "musicians in concert" for God!

PART VII

Appendixes

VII| Appendixes

Our view of the stream has not yet touched upon two elemental subjects: first, the Bible, which is the foundation of our faith, and second, migration, which brought our ancestors across many seas and countless bridges to come here. We have inherited two rich legacies that inform both our faith and our daily lives.

What does this mean for how we read and understand the Bible in our unique, diverse contexts? To guide us, we asked theologian J. Paul Rajashekar for permission to reprint his keynote address on this topic, delivered at an Asian Lutheran International Conference (ALIC). And how might we find deeper meanings and connections between our own family stories of migration and our Christian faith? For insights on this subject, we asked Margrethe S. C. Kleiber, a scholarly thinker and a daughter of immigrant parents, for permission to reprint her keynote address from another ALIC conference.

Come, sit by the stream with us and reflect.

Appendix I
Perspectives on Reading the Bible in Asian Contexts and Cultures

The Bible, like any scripture or ancient text, needs interpretation for it to come alive for contemporary readers. Any interpretation also calls for evaluation. How then should Asians and Asian Americans read this text? It was written in ancient Hebrew and *koine* Greek and then translated into different languages before being read in Asia and Asian America. For guidance through the maze, here is "Perspectives on Reading the Bible in Asian Contexts and Cultures" by J. Paul Rajashekar. This essay is an adaptation of his keynote address at the Sixth Asian Lutheran International Conference, Pattaya, Thailand, January 27-31, 2011.

Perspectives on Reading the Bible in Asian Contexts and Cultures
Introductory Questions and Issues

The Bible is the sacred scripture and source and norm of the Christian faith. It has been read, interpreted, understood, preached, and appropriated in the life of Christian communities in diverse contexts and cultures for more than two millennia. It has been revered as a story of God's engagement in history and a testimony to God's revelation in Jesus Christ. The Bible has been a source of comfort and consolation, a moral guide, the foundation of Christian beliefs, teaching and worship and a powerful vehicle for transforming the lives of people and cultures. Asian Christians use their Bible in daily devotions and family prayers. They dutifully carry their Bibles to church on Sundays in some cultures, as I did when I was young. Undoubtedly, the Bible is the most important source of life for practicing Christians in Asia.

Given the significance of the Bible in human history and its influence upon cultures, our topic can be explored in many different directions with a wide range of questions to consider. In this essay, it will not be possible to enumerate them all or address the range of questions implied. Let me mention a few by way of introduction.

First, how do we approach the authority, interpretation and inspiration of the Bible as the Word of God? The authority of the Bible and its use and abuse in relation to specific issues have been a subject of debate among Christians and often of division in many societies, especially in the

West, for over two centuries. How one understands biblical authority has implications as to how one understands and interprets the Bible. There is no reading of the Bible without interpretation. All translations are from the original languages of Hebrew and Greek are interpretations. For this reason, Christians have sometimes disagreed among themselves when interpreting the Bible in relation to social issues of the day. It seems that there is a growing divide between Christians who read the Bible literally and those who read it figuratively by using modern historical-critical tools in their interpretation.

It is to be expected that there is no one, singular, univocal interpretation of a scriptural passage because we read scripture from our own cultural and contextual vantage point. Our cultural assumptions of what words and concepts mean often lead to different and divergent understandings, nuances and their appropriations in specific contexts. For this reason, even the story of Jesus comes to us in four gospels, written for different communities or audiences, suggesting different understandings and portrayals of Jesus. So, the important question is not which interpretation is correct or accurate but, rather, "What kind of interpretation is valid or relevant for us today?"

Second, what is the place of the Bible in Asian histories and societies, both past and present? This issue involves the role and place of the Bible in the expansion of Christianity in Asia, especially during the modern missionary era. How has the Bible been received as a sacred book in the context of Asian cultures where it is one sacred book among many Asian sacred classics and scriptures? How should we read the Bible *in relation to* or *over against other* Asian sacred texts and scriptures?

This essay will not explore the important issue of whether Christian Scriptures supplement or supplant other Asian sacred texts. However, Asian Christians should be cautious in making judgments about scriptures of other religious traditions, their validity and authority, without properly understanding the role of scripture in different religions and cultures. It is a futile exercise to quote the Bible over against the claims of other sacred texts of Asia, for others could in return quote their texts, some of which are older than the Bible. Which scripture represents an authentic revelation is impossible to determine in multi-scriptural societies!

Third, are there distinctive ways of reading and understanding the Bible different from other readings from other contexts? Contextual interpretation of the Bible amidst the plurality of cultures lends itself to divergent views and understandings. We do not read the Bible from a neutral place or standpoint. We read it as people of a particular race, ethnicity, gender, age, culture and education, living in a particular corner of the world. Our readings of the Bible are often influenced by our socio-political context and often in relation to social issues that affect our society. Are there distinctive Asian ways, strategies, methods and tools that help us understand the Bible differently from the dominant European and Western interpretations?

Furthermore, it is important to remember that Asian Christians read the Bible in the vernacular (their native tongue). Therefore, their interpretation is heavily influenced by the idioms, concepts, syntax and cultural assumptions of the language they use. This leads us to ask:

"Does the Bible preach differently in Asia, India, China, Thailand, Japan or the US?" If so, which preaching or reading is legitimate or appropriate? Thus, interpreting the Bible amidst a plurality of cultures does not diminish the meaning of scriptural passages. Instead, it enriches our collective understanding since it exposes the values and biases of our own reading and that of others. Divergent readings of the Bible enhance the depth and riches of scriptures.

As I have said, these questions can be multiplied in many directions, depending on where you are coming from and what questions you bring with you. Some of you are reading this from Asia, and others from the US. You are pastors, theologians, or laypersons, with concerns related to your specific contexts. Some of you are theological students from other-than-Asian backgrounds, wanting to learn how Asian readings of the Bible differ from your own. Then there are those of us of Asian background living in the US and straddling two different settings in two different continents. We are neither here nor there, yet seeking to build bridges while challenging and questioning some of our cherished assumptions in both contexts.

I also want to clarify that my reference to "Asia" is not restricted to geography or a territorial understanding of it. Asia, in my view, refers to a collective worldview drawn from diverse values, traditions, cultures, ethnicities, and practices of the Asian continent. Asia is more than a geographical territory. It is a *concept,* a way of thinking, a way of life and a view of life that encompasses the values of Asian people collectively. Though our particular location, culture, and context may differ from one another, it is with a sense of a collective identity as Asian Christians that I frame this presentation.

The Bible is an Asian Scripture

At first sight, Christianity, as it is packaged and presented, appears alien to the Asian mind. There is a common misconception that the Bible is a "White man's book" brought to Asia by Western missionaries. As a matter of fact, the Bible is an Asian book. Few realize that Christianity was born in Asia. For various political reasons in the modern era, the region where Christianity was born was named "the Middle East." Palestine is not in the Middle East (a geographically absurd designation) but the western part of Asia when seen as a continent.

Another misconception is that Western missionaries introduced Christianity to Asia. Nothing could be further from the truth. Long before Europe or the Western world became Christian, Christianity flourished in Asia. Soon after its birth, already in the time of St. Paul, Christianity spread eastward before it did westward. It is an often-overlooked fact that out of the 27 books of the New Testament, nearly half of those were either written in Asia minor or written as letters to the Christian communities there. Historian Samuel Moffett has observed that the church began in Asia.

> Its first centers were Asian. Asia produced the first known church building, the first New Testament translation, perhaps the first Christian king, the first Christian poets, and even arguably the first Christian State. Asian Christians

endured the greatest persecutions. They mounted global ventures in missionary expansion the West could not match until after the thirteenth century.[1]

Some of the first Christian churches were built in Asia. Christian presence in Asia goes back to the first century if you consider the arrival of St. Thomas to India in 54 CE. It was the Nestorian Christians (known as the Church of the East) who spread the faith in Asia. The Nestorians, named after Bishop Nestorius of Constantinople (now known as Istanbul in Turkey), were one of those early Christian groups that believed that Jesus Christ had two natures, human and divine. The Bishop's opponents in Alexandria in Egypt believed that Jesus had only one nature, divine and human, fused together. So, the Nestorians were condemned to be heretics and pushed out of the church.

The Nestorians, however, were great evangelists. They spread their faith from Syria to India to China and all the way to Mongolia by the eighth century.[2] The first Old and New Testament (NT) translations from Hebrew and Greek were not to Latin but Syriac, popularly known as *"Peshitta"* (meaning 'simple') translation. Syrian versions of the Old Testament date back to the 2nd century CE. The Syrian Orthodox Christians use the *Peshitta* translation to this day as their scripture.

The Syriac translation of the Bible was carried to China and Mongolia in the seventh century CE. From a monument erected in 781 CE (the Alopon tablet),[3] we gather that the Nestorian Christians translated portions of the Syriac NT to Mongolian. Another example of Nestorian activity is the Jesus-Messiah Sutra, 206 verses, indicating an attempt to communicate the gospel in Buddhist style and terminology.[4] The first Chinese translation of the NT and Psalms appeared in the late 13th and early 14th century, translated by a Roman Catholic missionary, John Montecorvino. It took another 600 years before the entire Bible was translated into Chinese. Interestingly it was done in India by Joshua Marshman and published in 1822. An independent translation by Robert Morrison appeared a year later.[5]

We need not spend more time on the early history of the Bible translations or the history of Christianity in Asia. What is important to note is that the early Syriac version of the Bible attained a venerable status as an icon rather than a text to be read. Only summaries of the gospels were shared with the common people. As Syriac was not a familiar language to local cultures, the Bible was hardly read and used except in liturgical settings. It is only in the 19th and early 20th centuries that vernacular translations made the Bible accessible to people in Asia.[6]

---

[1] Samuel H. Moffett, *A History of Christianity in Asia*, Vol. 1 (New York, Orbis Books, 1998), p. xiii.

[2] Moffett, p. 291-292.

[3] This tablet known in Chinese as 大秦景教流行中国碑 (daqin jingjiao liuxing zhongguo bei) is housed in the Xi'an Stele Museum in China today. [Editors.]

[4] R.S. Sugirtharajah, *The Bible and the Third World* (London: Cambridge University Press, 2001), p. 22.

[5] Samuel H. Moffett, *A History of Christianity in Asia, Vol. II* (New York, Orbis Books, 2005), pp. 286-288.

[6] Sugirtharajah, pp. 18-21.

The Bible in the Modern Missionary Era

The fortunes of Christianity declined in Asia for a variety of reasons after the eighth century. By the 15th century, Christianity almost disappeared from the continent. Among the many plausible explanations for its disappearance is geographical isolation, numerical weakness, persecution, formidable challenge from Asian religions, ethnic introversion and internal conflicts and divisions.[7] The revival of Christianity in Asia had to wait for the arrival of Roman Catholic missionaries in the 16th century and the first Protestant missionaries in the early 18th century. Both traveled first to India and then to the rest of Asia.

While Christianity declined in Asia, it emerged as a dominant religion and influence as it spread northward to Europe. However, the Bible in Europe was read primarily by the clergy and confined to Catholic monasteries in the Holy Roman Empire. As in the East, the Bible was available only in Latin and inaccessible to common people until the Reformation in the 16th century. It was Martin Luther's German translation of the Bible that made it more accessible to the common people. In response to the Reformation, the Catholic Church at the Council of Trent discouraged vernacular translations lest the common people rebel against the church by using the Bible.

The Reformation of the church also coincided with European territorial expansion and the birth of colonialism. Naturally, the Bible accompanied colonial rulers to Asia, Africa, and Latin America. The formation of the British and Foreign Bible Society in 1804 made possible the diffusion of the Bible worldwide.

The Bible Society made it a priority to translate the Bible into vernacular languages in Asia and Africa. Knowingly or unknowingly, these translations became power tools to support and maintain colonial power. For example, in the first ten centuries of Christian history, the Bible was translated into fewer than ten languages (Greek, Syriac, Coptic, Ethiopic, Armenian, Slavonic, Gothic, Arabic and Anglo Saxon). However, by the first part of the 19th century, the Bible was translated into 165 different languages and dialects, thanks to the efforts of the Bible Society.[8]

The Bible Society tried to produce cheap Bibles in local languages for distribution, but the process of translation was not easy. Some languages lacked comparable words, categories and concepts to convey biblical words and meanings in native languages. This resulted in different names for God (in Chinese, for example) among Protestants and Catholics.[9] Consequently, in parts of Asia, Roman Catholicism and Protestantism are officially considered two different religions to this day.

The translation process also contributed to the alphabetization of certain languages and cultures. The Bible played an important role in literacy and education, a practice common even now in Asia. And portions of the gospel are still used to teach the English language in China, Thailand,

---

[7] Moffett, Vol. I, p. 333

[8] Sugirtharajah, pp. 140-172.

[9] Julia Ching, *Confucianism & Christianity: A Comparative Study* (Tokyo, New York & San Francisco: Kodansha International, 1977), pp. 19-24. [Editors.]

and other parts of Asia.

Obviously, the Bible has been the primary tool in the evangelization of Asia. Asian churches distributed portions of the gospel freely. Native Christians, book peddlers, and the so-called "Bible Women" were the primary distributors and evangelists, then and now. While it served as a civilizing instrument, the Bible, as interpreted during the missionary period, tended to support colonial rule and denigrate Asian cultures and Asian sacred texts and traditions. It was often thought that reading the Bible would dispel the darkness and enlighten the natives in Asia. The higher ranking given to the Bible in missionary interpretations undermined Asian sacred literatures and alienated native converts from their cultural heritage. This also resulted in a loss of cultural memory.

It must be said that the interpretations of the Bible offered during the missionary era were not entirely negative. It is true that the Bible was used to maintain the colonial powers and their authority and to Europeanize Asian society. We all know that evangelization of the world is inextricably tied to Western colonization of Asia, Africa, and Latin America. Nonetheless, the translation of the Bible also served to empower the marginalized or oppressed groups and provided native intellectuals with a potent tool for resistance against colonial occupation. The ethical dimensions of the Christian gospel served to liberate oppressed communities in Asia, empowering them to challenge some of the cultural evils such as the caste system, widow burning, tribalism, and the traditional hierarchical structures. The Bible played a significant role in the resurgence of traditional Asian cultures as well.

Asian Appropriations of Scriptures

How Asian Christians received and read the Bible varies among Asian cultures depending upon their traditions and attitudes toward sacred texts in general.

- In Indian and Chinese cultures, sacred or classical literature was accessible only to the privileged elite, such as scholars, philosophers, monks and other religious functionaries. In the Hindu culture, scriptures were rarely written down.
- They were transmitted orally by memorization, controlled by and limited to those who were high caste Brahmins. Common people had no access to Hindu scriptures, nor were they allowed to touch them.
- In the Chinese cultures, the classical Confucian literature was read and interpreted by scholars and civil servants in Imperial courts. It was used to educate, inculcate values and train administrators and rulers. In contrast to the Indian culture, where writing down scripture was considered a form of idolatry, the Chinese culture emphasized texts and textual interpretation of the writings of great masters, sages and philosophers.
- Buddhist cultures developed a textual tradition as well. As Buddhism spread from India to the rest of Asia, new scriptures were created to make

the sayings of Buddha relevant to new contexts.[10]
So, for the most part, reading and meditating on scriptures was limited to the elite, religious scholars, priests and gurus. Common people received scriptural wisdom through hearing it through oral culture. This often took the form of stories, parables, epics, enactment of religious stories, dramas, mythologies, proverbs, and sayings of great teachers. Given this background, it was revolutionary to have free and easy access to the Bible to the common people in their native tongues. Hearing the Bible read aloud, expounded in preaching, sung in hymns and lyrics, performed in dramas, and, more importantly, owning a copy for one's own reading and memorization made the Bible a unique object of reverence and the foundation of Christian religious experience in Asia. Therefore, unlike in the West, the Bible in Asia plays a decisive role in shaping and transforming the lives of Asian Christians.

Asian Christians tend to read for the plain meaning of a passage, or "literally," believing this is important because they believe the Bible is the word of God. Critical readings of scriptures are practiced in Asian seminaries, too but reading in the plain sense is the common practice. Generally, the tendency to read literally is because Asian Christians seldom question the authority of the Bible as a guide for daily living.

It is significant to realize, too, that the biblical world is not so distant from Asian and African cultures. The world of Jesus may appear distant and disconnected to Western societies, but not so in Asia and Africa. The stories of the Bible, whether from the Old Testament or the parables of Jesus, seem very real and credible in these societies. Pressing issues of the rich and the poor, social and political inequality, debt and credit, oppression and exile, corruption and conflict, persecution and martyrdom, famine and plague, disease and demon possession, idols and animal sacrifices, sowing and harvesting, are all everyday experiences to most Asian Christians. In Asia's agrarian cultures, the parables of the sower and the seed, the absentee landlord, unjust steward, reaping a bountiful harvest, the poor widow with her mite, the lost sheep and the lost coin, etc., are contemporary imageries. The biblical narratives, in their wholeness, seldom appear alien to Asians. As an Asian scripture, the Bible reflects the realities of Asia more than it does of the West.

For this reason, Asian readers of the Bible do not spend energy in excavating biblical texts nor waste time in studying issues of authorship, source, form, structure and editing of biblical books. The Bible opens multiple worlds of understanding life in Asian societies and therefore finds a significant place in the life of practicing Christians. The obsession with finding the true or singular meaning of scripture or biblical writers' intentions that has occupied much of Western biblical scholarship has not been a priority to Asian interpreters of the Bible.

Asian Christians, therefore, have not written very many commentaries. Asian pastors tend to rely on translated Western commentaries, interpretations or readily available sermons on the web. Access to internet resources has made it even easier to adopt Western interpretations

---

[10] William A Graham, *Beyond the Written Word* (New York: Cambridge University Press, 1987), p. 86.

of scriptures that are ubiquitous. Until relatively recently, it was rare to find much Asian biblical literature in English or vernacular languages.

To discover the vitality of Asian appropriations of the Bible, one must look to the literature in the vernacular or commentaries in native languages not easily accessible to outsiders. Few are translated into English. The fluidity with which biblical narratives come alive in vernacular preaching and writings is an important source for understanding the Bible in Asia. Unfortunately, Asian scholars have a tendency to rely on Western commentaries and interpretations, and this dependency has stifled indigenous readings of the scripture. Many theological books are translations of Western productions.

In this regard, it is worth noting that in Asian cultures, especially those influenced by Hindu and Buddhist cultures, religious texts are not viewed as an end unto themselves. To use a Buddhist analogy, scriptures are like a raft or a boat to cross the river. After crossing the river, you leave the raft behind and keep going to your destination. Similarly, scriptures are instruments or vehicles for facilitating and engendering religious experience or the experience of the divine reality. This instrumental value is often lost when the Bible becomes an end unto itself or when we become too preoccupied with the world of the text and ignore the context to which it speaks. This Asian insight into the "instrumentality" of the scripture is not alien to the Christian faith. As a matter of fact, the Church Father Augustine saw the Bible for its instrumental value as a vehicle for the beatific vision of God.

Re-reading the Bible with Asian Eyes and Ears

The first point to remember is that no one reads the Bible in a vacuum. We understand that interpretation is something inherited, that we have been taught to read and understand in particular ways. From Sunday school to confirmation classes to Sunday sermons, we have been taught. How we read the Bible, of course, is significantly influenced by the tradition of interpretations in Christian history.

We in Asia, for example, still use the catechisms of Luther. Many of these traditions of interpretation developed in Europe or in Western societies. Whether in Luther's time or later in history, the issues, questions, presuppositions and patterns of thinking in Western cultures have indeed influenced the way the Bible has been read in Asia. This being the case, Asian appropriations of scripture must recognize the limitations of these inherited interpretations. They may not always speak to Asian realities or address questions posed by Asian cultures and religions. This is true of Luther's catechisms in Asia.[11]

If we are to read the Bible in relation to Asian realities, then we must read it with Asian eyes and hear it with Asian ears and not through the eyes and ears of others. It is one thing to

---

[11] J. Paul Rajashekar, *Luther's Small Catechism: An Exposition of the Christian Faith in Asian Contexts and Cultures* (New Delhi: Christian World Imprints, 2019). [Editors.]

read Western interpretations of the Bible or translate Western commentaries and books into our languages. It is another thing to re-read the Bible immersed in Asian ways of thinking. However helpful and illuminating other readings may have been, they are not Asian readings. They do not consider the distinctive issues and challenges of our contexts, our cultural codes, our reality of religious pluralism, the existence of other religious scriptures in our midst, our traditions, values, and our understanding of life and what it means to live in community.

Reading the Bible in our native tongues sheds light on a world of meanings in relation to our cultural heritage. This is not a rejection of other interpretations from other cultures. Different interpretations can certainly enrich our understanding. But we also need to be consciously critical of our received traditions and their interpretations of scriptures.

Our critical reading may expose assumptions and bias found in other readings as well as our own. Some Asian churches are still captive to missionary understandings of the Bible and have taken them as standard, once for all interpretations of the Christian faith. Such a view hinders Asian appropriations or adaptations of the Bible. We must reclaim the Bible as an Asian scripture.

My second point pertains to persuasive "biblical fundamentalism" among Asian churches. As I pointed out earlier, Asian readings of the Bible have generally tended to be literal, taking the plain sense of the text in the context of its original readers. But in recent decades, there is a growing tendency among Asian Christians to adopt biblical fundamentalism, that is, to directly apply biblical passages to today's contexts without regard to the original context of those passages. Citing texts out of context or proof-texting can often distort the original meaning and intent of those scriptural texts and can easily lead to the abuse of scriptures. The growth of sectarian Christian groups or the proliferation of Christian denominations in Asia is partly attributable to distorted readings of the Bible and partly due to the influence of Western sectarian groups seeking to establish their own mission outposts in Asia.

Fundamentalism tends to make one meaning of the text absolute, while a critical reading may offer multiple meanings. There is a big difference between reading the Bible as a whole and reading it from the standpoint of one isolated verse with one meaning ascribed to it. Often such interpretations are influenced by social and political ideologies of the time. To reduce the meaning of the Bible to one viewpoint or a singular meaning is to distort the wholeness of the Bible. Such readings tend to make the gospel one-dimensional, thus violating the integrity of the scripture.

The overwhelming preoccupation of these televangelists and sectarian groups is the salvation of the souls, a responsibility that they have usurped from God. We need to be careful not to undermine the depth and riches of the Christian gospel in Asia. The Bible is not one-dimensional, and where we stand in our social context offers different meanings. So, we must resist and counter imported interpretations of Christianity that have sowed the seeds of discord and conflict and fragmented the church in many Asian societies. A recovery of Asian narrative approaches to scriptures is therefore essential, for it opens imaginative and culturally relevant readings of the Bible.

I want to make a third point that is sometimes ignored. Reading the Bible in Asia also means recognizing that the writings of the Bible have their contexts too. It is often problematic to apply scriptural texts directly to 21st century contexts. God did not write the Bible. It was written down by inspired humans as a narration of God's intervention in the history of a particular people. The perspectives, biases and contexts of those who wrote down the Bible are clearly evident.

Old Testament readers may find it astounding that God rescues one oppressed people by oppressing and destroying other people. The Old Testament is full of stories of violence, deceit, war, murder, injustice, debauchery, polygamy, conquest, colonization, and the forceful occupation of other people's lands. All these stories do not portray a positive image of God of the Old Testament.

Furthermore, the Bible has supported slavery, subjugation of women, patriarchy and the destruction of our ecology. In reading the Bible, we tend to ignore these stories or fail to question the human motives and hidden agendas behind such stories. Reading the Bible in Asian contexts will involve critical study of these stories. Not all biblical stories are spiritually edifying! The Bible can be abused to legitimize injustices in our society, or it can be an instrument for liberating people in society. The Bible can be used to support authoritarianism or promote human freedom and liberation. As Luther put it eloquently, the Bible has a wax nose that can be twisted anyway one wants!

Reading from the Perspective of Grace

The primary contribution of Martin Luther and the Lutheran Reformation is that Jesus Christ is the key to scripture. Luther's fundamental insight in interpreting scripture is that if you do not understand a scriptural text, throw it on the rock of Christ. It is God's grace as revealed in Jesus Christ that makes the biblical witness relevant and meaningful to all of us, regardless of who you are, where you come from and what culture you represent. In hearing the testimony to God's grace active in human history, we are drawn to faith. As St. Paul said, "So faith comes from what is heard, and what is heard comes through the word of Christ" (Rom. 10:17). Therefore, we must strive to understand the scripture from the perspective of grace.

It is a temptation to read the Bible as if it were a book of laws containing rules for our behavior. But what supersedes all the legal codes, prohibitions, the dos and don'ts or the commandments in the Bible is the offer of Divine Grace. Surely God's commandments and laws are valid. They point to our sinfulness and inability to fulfill the laws of God. Obedience to the law, despite our best efforts, drives us to condemnation and enslavement. God's laws are intended to drive us to Christ Jesus and the offer of grace in Him. God's grace, therefore, transcends all laws and prohibitions.

Similarly, the Bible is not a textbook on science, physics or a manual on the natural world. The Bible says a lot about the created world so that we may cherish the world and the created order as God's gift to us. More importantly, the Bible, through its many narratives of God's acts in history, stories, and sayings, helps us to understand this overarching fact: that God is the creator of the world and is in control of everything in it. The Scripture testifies that God loves and cares for us and the created world, as demonstrated in the words and deeds of Jesus Christ.

Lutherans, therefore, distinguish the "Word of God" and the "words of God." The "Word of God" refers to "the incarnate Word" in the person of Jesus Christ, and the "words" of God" refer to the written scriptures, both the Old and New Testaments. The written scriptures, especially the books of the NT, are testimonies to the Word of God as manifest in Jesus Christ. Martin Luther described it well when he wrote that the Bible is the "manger in which Jesus lays."

The Bible is indeed a powerful book not because it binds us to particular ways of living and practicing the faith. Rather it frees us to live in faithfulness by mediating God's grace in the stories it narrates and the witness it offers. The Bible is authoritative not because it contains divine laws valuable to life, but because it communicates the grace of God in Jesus Christ. *Asian readings of the Bible, therefore, cannot but be gracious and grace-filled.* It is to be read in its totality, that is, in terms of overall teaching, not focusing on isolated verses in a piecemeal fashion. When the Bible is read in an isolated way, we not only misunderstand but also do injustice to the Bible itself.

If scripture mediates God's grace, then it must be interpreted anew for each day! This is because we receive God's grace every day in new ways. Therefore, we cannot rest content with past interpretations, even yesterday's interpretations, however valuable and insightful they may be. What makes the books of the Bible so dynamic is that they become scripture for us every day in our relation to it. Through scriptures, God engages us with promise, forgiveness, and hope, setting us free to love and serve. Through the Bible, God draws us to the grace offered in Christ and we receive it in faith and trust. So when we read the scripture, we must always be attentive to how God's liberating grace is mediated to us in our day, how that grace transforms our lives and our relationships with others, and how it sheds light on specific issues confronting our world. We read the Bible so that we may become bearers of God's grace in our world. So, in applying scripture to contemporary issues, we should err on the side of grace rather than law!

Reclaiming the Bible in Asia

The Bible, as I have noted earlier, is an Asian scripture. It has now been translated into nearly 2,500 languages and dialects. No other book has ever attained such a status. This worldwide diffusion of the Bible has made it the perennial bestseller. Without the translatability of the Bible, the fortunes of Christianity would have been different. In the English language, believe it or not, the Bible is now available in over 450 different versions! Unfortunately, in the modern West, the Bible has become a commodity, commercialized and marketed as a product by the publishing industry by offering denominational focused Bibles (like Catholic Bible, Lutheran Bible, Believers Bible, etc.). The term "Bible" has been loosely employed in our culture to refer to all sorts of things, like "Golfer's bible," "Chocolate bible," "Hindu bible" (referring to *Bhagavadgita*), etc. This practice may have contributed to the erosion of biblical authority in our societies. Despite the proliferation of the English translations and the availability of free Bibles online, biblical illiteracy is pervasive in English-speaking countries.

The Bible is now freely available in almost all Asian countries in vernacular languages. Fortunately, Asian Christians do not have to contend with multiple translations, although there are nearly a dozen Chinese translations available because of various dialects. World Bible Translation Center based in Texas now offers downloadable translations in Asian languages on the Internet. These technological developments will undoubtedly change our perceptions and uses of the scripture in the future. Nonetheless, there is a real danger that the Bible may become another commodity in Asian societies as well.

The free accessibility of the Bible in Asian languages could be a blessing as well as a curse. On the one hand, the Bible becomes available to all, whether Christian or not. On the other hand, it encourages privatized reading of scripture without reference to the broader framework of the Christian community or one's social, cultural and religious contexts. Private and solitary reading of the Bible without communal engagement may lead to sectarianism. Christian sectarianism, often supported by Western evangelistic groups, has fragmented Christian communities in Asia and distorted their witness.

As a minority community amid other faiths or cultures, it is essential that Asian Christians reclaim the Bible as an Asian sacred text and read it collectively in the context of the Church and the ministries of the Christian community. The Bible becomes authentic and revelatory as the Word of God when read, understood and interpreted in the presence of the community that accepts it in faith and trust. The Bible becomes scripture only in a dynamic relationship with the community. Otherwise, it is just another book!

J. Paul Rajashekar

Select Bibliography of Works Consulted

David, Immanuel S. (1987). *The Bible and the Believer.* Madras: Gurukul Lutheran Theological College.

England, John C. (1996). *The Hidden History of Christianity in Asia: Churches of the East Before 1500.* New Delhi: SPCK.

Graham, William A. (1987). *Beyond the Written Word.* New York: Cambridge University Press.

"How Lutherans Read the Bible" (2006). *Dialog: A Journal of Theology,* Vol 45:1.

Jacobson, Diane L. and Stanley N. Olson, et al. (2008). *Opening the Book of Faith: Lutheran Insights for Bible Study.* Minneapolis: Augsburg Fortress.

The Lutheran World Federation (2016). *The Bible in the Life of the Lutheran Communion: A Study Document on Lutheran Hermeneutics.* Geneva, Switzerland.

Moffett, Samuel H. (1998). *A History of Christianity in Asia: Beginnings to 1500.* Second revised edition. Maryknoll, New York: Orbis Books.

Moffett, Samuel H. (2005). *A History of Christianity in Asia, Vol. II: 1500-1900.* Maryknoll, New York: Orbis Books.

Pui-Lan, Kwok (2003). *Discovering the Bible in the Non-Biblical World.* Eugene, Oregon: Wipf and Stock Publishers.

Rajashekar, J. Paul (ed.) (2019). *Luther's Small Catechism: An Exposition of the Christian Faith in Asian Contexts and Cultures.* New Delhi: Christian World Imprints.

Sugirtharajah, R. S. (2001). *The Bible and the Third World.* London: Cambridge University Press.

Appendix II
Migration as Metaphor for the Christian Faith

Ever since ancient times, people have been on the move. Migration is a given reality in human life. Like the people in the Bible, our ancestors also have been on the move. Some of us have migrated from our homelands to strange lands where we may have asked, "How shall we sing the Lord's song in a strange land?"[1] Others may be migrants within their own lands for political, professional, or other reasons. We are on the move. Margrethe S. C. Kleiber[2] shares here what she has discovered about the close relationship between migration and our faith. This essay is an adaptation of her keynote address at the Tenth Asian Lutheran International Conference, January 24–29, 2019, at Udon Thani, Thailand.

Migration as Metaphor for the Christian Faith
Introduction

I am intrigued by our topic, migration and mission. I am particularly intrigued with migration as a critical metaphor for understanding the Christian faith. The implications are fascinating because migration is about movement and displacement. It is about crossing over into new territory and possibly even breaking down barriers in the process. Since that is the case, then the call to mission is a call to be a migrant. It is a call to be on the move, to be boldly crossing borders literally and figuratively. The church is God's people on the move.[3]

I will talk about migration in general and highlight how political and economic forces drive migration. I will emphasize that migration wears a human face. Some of my father's story, which I will share, suggests that migration adds more layers to our already complicated identities. Then, I will ask us to consider intersectionality, a way of thinking and seeing with a bias for justice, as a

---

[1] Psalms 137:4, (NRSV).
[2] For biography, see Edmond Yee and J. Paul Rajashekar (eds. and comps.), *Abunant Harvest: Stories of Asian Lutherans* (Minneapolis: Lutheran University Press, 2012), pp. 289-292.
[3] I have unabashedly borrowed the phrase from the title of *God's People on the Move: Biblical and Global Perspectives on Migration and Mission* edited by vanThahn Nguyen and John M. Prior, Kindle Version (Eugene, OR: Pickwick Publications, 2014).

helpful tool as we consider the migrant experience.

Next, I will consider how migration is missional. Biblically, God has always worked through the movement of peoples to further God's purposes. Last, I will explore migration as a metaphor for the Christian faith. I will suggest that intersectional theologies may be a tool for the migrant church, for God's people on the move.

Flexible Citizens

Anthropologist Aihwa Ong opens her book *Flexible Citizenship* with this story.

> On the eve of the return of Hong Kong from British to mainland-Chinese rule, the city was abuzz with passport stories. A favorite one concerned mainland official Lu Ping, who presided over the transition. At a talk to Hong Kong business leaders, he fished a number of passports from his pockets to indicate he was fully aware that the Hong Kong elite has a weakness for foreign passports. Indeed, more than half the members of the transition preparatory committee carried foreign passports. These politicians were no different from six hundred thousand other Hong Kongers (about 10 percent of the total population) who held foreign passports as insurance against mainland- Chinese rule.

Ong describes this approach to national identity as "flexible citizenship."[4]

Last fall, I learned that one of my husband's brothers, who moved to Australia, plans to apply for Australian citizenship. He will keep his US passport, but there are some economic advantages to being an Australian. He, too, is a flexible citizen.

The practice of holding multiple passports raises fascinating questions about the relationship between nationality and identity. In many instances, the multiple passport holder views nationality as a matter, not of the heart, but pragmatic self-interest. It is a migration strategy of the elites in response to shifting political and economic conditions.

While not everyone has multiple passports, people of all economic stations are on the move. Migration is at unprecedented levels. In an increasingly globalized world, we need to be aware of how migration adds to the complexity of identities. Likewise, we need to be mindful of how power structures reward and privilege some migrant identities and punish and constrain others.

What is Migration?

Simply put, migration is "the movement of people to a new area or country to find work or better living conditions."[5] Migration can involve crossing international borders, or it can be internal to a country. Migration can be voluntary. Migration can be forced, as when people are fleeing war and violence; or when people are trafficked.

---

[4] Aihwa Ong, *Flexible Citizenship: The Cultural Logics of Transnationality*, Kindle Version, (Durham, NC: Duke University Press, 1999), p. 1.
[5] "Migration," English Oxford Living Dictionary, https://en.oxforddictionaries.com/definition/migration.

Migration is Political and Economic

Political forces frequently drive involuntary migration. Who can forget the 1947 partition of India, which displaced more than 15 million people?[6] Or the wars in Southeast Asia that created more than 3 million refugees? In our own time, the Syrian war has created 6.6 million internally displaced persons and 5.6 million refugees.[7] Since August of 2017, violence against the Rohingya has caused 723,000 people to flee their native Myanmar for Bangladesh.[8] Thailand, where we are gathered today, continues to be a destination for people fleeing persecution. The United Nations High Commissioner for Refugees manages nine refugee camps in Thailand for the estimated 100,000 refugees. Most are ethnic Karen from Myanmar,[9] 50% of whom are Christians who bring their faith with them.

Economic incentives often spur voluntary migration. Annually, 10 million overseas Filipino workers send 31 billion dollars in remittances to the Philippines.[10] Around the world, migration from rural areas to urban centers has fueled the growth of megacities, defined as cities with a population of over 10 million.[11] It is noteworthy that nine of the top ten megacities are here in Asia.[12]

Economic incentives also drive human trafficking, which, like other forms of migration, can be a transnational process or a domestic phenomenon.[13] In 2016, the International Labor Organization estimated that 40 million people, on any given day, are held under conditions of modern-day slavery.[14] The motive for this crime is greed. In 2014, human traffickers generated profits of approximately 150 billion dollars.[15]

Migration is a controversial subject in the 21st century. While migration is frequently a response to political and economic forces, the movement of peoples across borders also prompts political and economic reactions. Currently, the US government is in a partial shutdown because of President Donald Trump's desire for a border wall with Mexico. His desire for a wall is a

---

[6] William Dalrymple, "The Great Divide: the violent legacy of Indian partition," *The New Yorker,* June 29, 2015, https://www.newyorker.com/magazine/2015/06/29/the-great-divide-books-dalrymple.

[7] UNHCR https://www.unhcr.org/syria-emergency.html.

[8] UNHCR https://www.unhcr.org/en-us/rohingya-emergency.html?query=rohingya.

[9] UN-HCR.https://www.unhcr.or.th/sites/default/files/u11/Thailand_Myanmar%20Border_Refugee%20Population%20Overview_%20Dec%202018.pdf.

[10] Aurora Almendral, "Why 10 Million Filipinos Endure Hardship Abroad as Overseas Workers, *National Geographic Magazine,* December2018,https://www.nationalgeographic.com/magazine/2018/12/filipino-workers-return-from-overseas-philippines-celebrates/.

[11] Johnny Wood, "Here's what you need to know about the megacities of the future," *World Economic Forum,* October 10, 2018, https://www.weforum.org/agenda/2018/10/these-are-the-megacities-of-the-future/.

[12] "Top 20 Megacities by Population," *Allianz,* March 2016, https://www.allianz.com/en/press/extra/knowledge/demography/150316-top-20-megacities-by-population.html.

[13] Human Rights First, Human Trafficking by the Numbers: Fact Sheet September 2017, https://www.humanrightsfirst.org/resource/human-trafficking-numbers.

[14] International Labor Organization, *40 Million in Modern Slavery and 152 Million in Child Labour Around the World,* September 19, 2017, https://www.ilo.org/global/about-the-ilo/newsroom/news/WCMS_574717/lang--en/index.htm.

[15] Human Rights First, Human Trafficking by the Numbers: Fact Sheet September 2017, https://www.humanrightsfirst.org/resource/human-trafficking-numbers.

reactionary move to an imagined threat. Along similar lines, high anxiety about immigration was undoubtedly a factor in the United Kingdom's vote to leave the European Union. Brexit was a rejection of the European Union's stance on the free movement of people within the European bloc.

Migration is Personal

Politics and economics are the macro forces that drive the movements of people. Yet, migration wears a human face. Migration is a human experience that shapes the stories of our lives.

I am the daughter and the granddaughter of immigrants. Driven by economic incentives, my paternal grandparents immigrated to Hawaii from Okinawa to work on the sugar plantations. This makes my Hawaii-born father and his siblings Nisei or second generation immigrants. Theirs was the generation who lived through WWII. My dad watched the bombs drop on Pearl Harbor, and my Uncle Harold served in the 442nd Infantry Regiment, the all-*Nisei* unit that fought in Europe.

My mother was the first generation immigrant in our family. Born on a small farm in Denmark and coming to the US in her late 20s, she spoke with a distinct accent all her life. English was her second language. After marrying my father and moving to Hawaii, she was the only *haole,* which is what White people are called in Hawaii, at our family gatherings. Except for my Auntie Kiyoko, she was the only one who was not a native English speaker.

My father married a second time. My stepmother was a first generation immigrant from Japan. She originally came to Hawaii as a war bride with her first husband, who was a Hawaii Nisei serving with the US forces in Japan after WWII.

Migration Exposes the Complicated Reality of Identity

Although most White Americans saw my father and stepmother as Japanese, my father's Okinawan family believed that he had married foreigners — people outside his race — not only once, but twice. When he went to Japan with my stepmother, my dad became an American from Hawaii. Depending on the context, my father carried a different label. However, none of these labels adequately described the complexity of his lived experience or how he used ambiguity to maneuver within oppressive structures.

He tells a story about riding a bus with my mother in the segregated South of the United States of the 1950s. They get on the bus and sit in the front seat — in the White section of the bus. My dad can tell that the bus driver doesn't know what to do with them. My mom is White. My dad is not White, but he is not Black. The bus driver's either-or thinking did not equip him for this situation. Which rules apply?

My dad, a charming, outgoing, extroverted rascal, finesses the situation by talking the driver up and telling him stories about Hawaii. My parents ride the bus and arrive at the destination. Of course, the tragic irony of this is that my dad certainly could not have done this successfully had he been a dark-skinned native Hawaiian. Race, gender, marital status, and ethnicity all intersected in such a way that enabled him to pull this stunt.

Identity is too complicated to be construed along a single-axis or pole. In my father, multiple identities intersect, and these identities interact in complex ways with his cultural and social environments. This dynamic became especially evident whenever he crossed borders. As he moved between countries, between the US and Japan, or as he moved inside the US, he had to negotiate differing norms and power structures that sought to define him. His experiences highlight the limitations and absurdities of single-axis thinking or either-or thinking.

There may be stories in your own families that illustrate these realities as well. Perhaps there was no crossing of international borders, but there may be other kinds of border crossings, some physical and some emotional and psychological. It might be a story of relocation from a rural area to an urban center. It may be a change in socioeconomic status as a result of education, marriage, or misfortune. It may be a story of someone in your family who came out as gay or transgender. It may be a story of a religious conversion. These border crossings, literal and figurative, complicate identity, reminding us that our identities cannot be defined along a single-axis.

Intersectionality

Let's pause and reflect on a way of thinking and seeing called intersectionality. I believe this can be a useful tool as we consider how border crossing complicates identity. Later I will look at how it can be a tool for the church, for God's people on the move.

I am wading into dangerous territory here because I am no expert on the subject. However, I am fascinated by the capacity of intersectionality to embrace complexity in ways that hold potential for coalition building and doing justice.

Intersectionality has been described as "matrix thinking in a single-axis world."[16] Matrix thinking sees connections. It is networked rather than linear. It recognizes linkages. It is "both-and" thinking in a world of "either-or." Intersectionality offers a tool for analyzing the nuances and complications of identities as they overlap or intersect.

A US law professor, Kimberlé Crenshaw, coined the term "intersectionality" in 1989. She argued that Black women experienced the double bind of race and gender oppression at the intersection of these two identities. This is not a new insight. Women of color have long articulated the ways multiple identities can constrain or enable individuals. Crenshaw, however, was the first person to use this particular terminology.[17]

Because the roots of intersectionality lie in justice work, specifically Black women's theorizing around justice, it displays a bias for action.[18] Because it exposes how seemingly unrelated

---

[16] Vivian May, *Pursuing intersectionality, Unsettling Dominant Imagery*, Kindle Version, (New York & London: Routledge, 2015), p. 18.

[17] Grace Ji-Sun Kim and Susan M. Shaw, *Intersectional Theology: An Introductory Guide*, Kindle Version (Minneapolis, MN: Augsburg Fortress Press, 2018), location 228 of 2892.

[18] May, op.cit., p.2.

oppressions interact and reinforce each other, it encourages coalition-building among people who seek to resist inequality.[19]

Intersectional analysis considers how ethnicity, gender, sexual orientation, national origin, religious affiliation, and class, caste, or social location, converge and shape our lives. Intersectionality pays attention to power. It analyzes the cultural norms and power structures within which we live and which regulate our behavior. It exposes how these structures reward and privilege certain individuals and how these structures punish or constrain others. As an example, we need only consider the immigration systems of most countries. Contrast the privilege of multiple passport holders with the restrictions placed on asylum seekers and refugees.

Intersectional analysis understands that institutions reward or privilege those who conform to a particular mythical norm. In the US, this norm has been described as "male, white, heterosexual, financially stable, young-middle adult, able-bodied, Christian."[20] In other contexts, other countries, other cultures, the mythical norm would be very different.

Those who approximate the mythical norm encounter fewer obstacles as they maneuver within institutions and structures. Those who exist outside of this mythical norm, whatever it may be, are often labeled "deviant, difficult, inferior, or just plain 'wrong.'"[21] Intersectional analysis helps us see more clearly how structures oppress those who do not conform to the norm and how they privilege those who do. Importantly, it "calls us to be aware of …our identities," both dominant and subordinate, within these power structures.[22]

Consider how subordinate and dominant identities interact in the opening scene of the movie Crazy Rich Asians. When Eleanor Young and Felicity Leong arrive at the Calthorpe Hotel in London with their children, they face outright racism. The general manager refuses to honor their reservation. He sees people of subordinate identities: women, children, and Chinese. And he uses his dominant identity as male, White and British, to put them in their place. What he doesn't know is that Eleanor and Felicity are crazy rich Asians, women married to very powerful business-men. Felicity contacts her husband, Harry, who plays golf with the owner of the hotel. Harry calls him up and purchases the Calthorpe Hotel for his wife. She then returns to the hotel and fires the manager.[23] Felicity's wealth and class intersect with her identities as female and Chinese in unexpected ways.

The Migrant Experience and Intersectionality

Intersectionality is relevant to the migrant experience because migrants live in the intersection of multiple identities. Migrants navigate within and between different contexts, and these contexts have differing norms and power structures that seek to define and regulate people. As a result, the

---

[19] Ibid., p. 48.

[20] Kim & Shaw, op.cit., location 2618.

[21] Audre Lorde, quoted by Kim and Shaw in *Intersectional Theology*, location 290 of 2892.

[22] Ibid., location 2529 of 2892.

[23] Kevin Kwan, *Crazy Rich Asians*, Kindle Version, (New York: First Anchor Books, 2013), pp. 3-14. Note that the screenplay differs from the book in certain details. In the movie, it is Eleanor's husband who buys the Calthrope.

migrant experience exposes the limitations and absurdities of single-axis thinking and reveals the mechanisms of power.

For example, when my dad is on the mainland US, White Americans see my father as a minority "Japanese." In Japan, he becomes "Hawaiian" or "American." Whether in Japan or the mainland US, single-axis thinking is incapable of describing the complexity of my father's lived reality. The migrant experience serves to expose the norms of single-axis thinking for what they are: myths.

This suggests another reason migration has become such a controversial subject. National identities[24] are imagined identities symbolized by a single passport. Outsiders or newcomers to a nation who fall outside the boundaries of that imagined identity, who hold two passports if you allow me the metaphor, challenge the myth. They remind us that personal, national, cultural identities are fluid. Identities shift, overlap, and change with time. Newcomers are emblematic of the changing nature of reality.

Donald Trump's wall is a symbolic attempt to shore up the norms and power structures of a mythical America; the imagined "male, white, heterosexual, financially stable, young-middle adult, able-bodied, Christian."[25] In Trump's wall, this mythic identity is pitted against the reality of a globalized world where people are on the move.[26]

Migration is Missional

Migration is a story about the political and economic forces driving the movements of people. Migration is also the personal stories of individuals and families caught up in these movements. And, because migration is about people, God is at work in their journeys and struggles. Migrants are missionaries, and missionaries are migrants. The church is God's people on the move.

Biblical People Move

Migration has always been part of the biblical narrative. The book of Genesis is filled with stories of displacement and movement, echoing our contemporary headlines of migration. At the same time, Genesis puts a human face on migration.[27] Adam and Eve are exiled from the Garden of Eden. Cain kills his brother Abel, and so must flee and make his home in Nod. Noah and his family become boat people and have to rebuild their lives from nothing when they reach dry land.

Significantly, the story of Israel begins with migration. God tells Abraham: "Go from your country and your kindred and your father's house to the land that I will show you."[28] Three

---

[24] Benedict Anderson, *Imagined Communities*, Kindle Version, (New York & London: Verso Books, 2016).

[25] Kim and Shaw, *op.cit.*, location 2618.

[26] Jorge Ramos, "Trump is the Wall," *The New York Times*, January 9, 2019, https://www.nytimes.com/2019/01/09/opinion/jorge-ramos-trump-wall.html?action=click&module=Opinion&pgtype=Homepage.

[27] Nguyen and Prior, op. cit., loc. 78. Please also note that much of this section has been inspired by the different essays. See chapter 1 by Sarita Gallagher on Abraham.

[28] Genesis 12:1, NRSV.

generations later, Joseph is trafficked to Egypt as a slave. Later, Jacob and his sons migrate to Egypt to escape famine. The next four books of the Bible, Exodus to Deuteronomy, describe Israel's migration from Egypt to Canaan.

Even after the Hebrew people settle in Canaan, migration complicates their history in unexpected ways. In the book of Ruth, the family of Elimelech moves to Moab when there is a famine in Judah. Despite the prohibition on marrying foreigners, Elimelech's sons marry Moabite women. Later, one of these women, the widowed Ruth, accompanies her mother-in-law to Bethlehem, where she again marries an Israelite. A foreigner thus becomes the great-grandmother of King David, busting the myth of pure bloodlines.

As in today's world, war also precipitates the movement of people in the Bible. The destruction of Jerusalem and its temple marks the beginning of the Jewish diaspora, an event that has significant implications for the Christian story. Much of Acts is about mission in and with the diaspora, with migrants as missionaries and missionaries as migrants. Acts describes the church as God's people on the move.

The First Century

In our 20th and now 21st centuries, various technologies, including and perhaps especially digital technologies, have led to the increasing integration of the world economy, facilitating the flow of goods and services, capital, information, and peoples.

In the first century, the setting of the book of Acts, the not-so-new technology that connected peoples and integrated economies was roads. Wherever the Romans went, they built roads. Roman roads extended from Britain to what is present-day Iraq, from the Danube River over to Spain, and down into North Africa.[29] At the height of Rome's power, "29 great military highways radiated from the city."[30][31] Roads were critical to Roman military success.[32] Roads were an intentional strategy to assure Roman's military dominance, facilitate commerce and communications, and maintain control over the sprawling empire. Roads also expedited travel for ordinary people, including a man called Saul of Tarsus.

Saul of Tarsus

Saul was a diaspora Jew. He was born not in Palestine but Tarsus, a city in present-day southeast Turkey. He was likely educated at Greco-Roman schools until the age of twelve or thirteen and then sent to study in Jerusalem. He was a Pharisee,[33] signifying that his family had enough wealth to allow their son to devote himself to the study of the Torah. Lastly, we know that he was born a

---

[29] Encyclopedia Britannica, "Roman Roads," from britannica.com, https://www.britannica.com/technology/Roman-road-system, last accessed January 2019.

[30] "Roads in Ancient Rome," http://www.crystalinks.com/romeroads.html, last accessed January 2019.

[31] Roman Roads, Wikipedia, https://en.wikipedia.org/wiki/Roman_roads, last accessed January 2019.

[32] Evan Andrews, "Eight Ways Roads Helped Rome Rule the Ancient World," History.com https://bewh.history.com/news/8-ways-roads-helped-rome-rule-the-ancient-world, last accessed Janu-ary 2019.

[33] Philippians 3:4a-6, NRSV.

Roman citizen,[34] which afforded him certain privileges. When we encounter Saul in the book of Acts, we are meeting a man from a migrant family and who himself had the experience of migrating to Jerusalem for his education. Migration shaped his complex identity, or rather his complex and multiple identities.

After his conversion, concerns about his safety prompted Saul's return to Tarsus. He remains in Tarsus for thirteen years until another diaspora Jew seeks him out: Barnabas, born on the island of Cyprus.

Antioch

Before he sought out Saul, Barnabas had been visiting the church in Antioch. Acts 11:19-26 describes this church's vibrancy, which began when persecuted believers fled Jerusalem after the martyrdom of Stephen. Followers of Jesus flee Jerusalem and scatter "as far as Phoenicia, Cyprus, and Antioch."[35] Most of these migrants speak "the word to no one except Jews."[36] In Antioch, however, it's different. Here we learn: "men of Cyprus and Cyrene…spoke to the Greeks also, proclaiming the Lord Jesus." [37] This detail makes Antioch unique. It's a congregation that has crossed into new territory, metaphorically speaking, by breaking down barriers between Jew and Gentile. The Antioch congregation was a messy place, full of complicated identities and complicated power dynamics.

The Holy Spirit blesses their efforts, and a vibrant church is established. It needs leadership, and Barnabas remembers and recruits Saul from Tarsus. The two of them work teaching people and building the church in Antioch.

Spiritual formation is a two-way street. I have pastored several congregations in my career. To the best of my ability, I have preached, taught, and encouraged faithful living and service to Jesus. The congregations I have served, however, have formed me as well. Yet the assembly that has most shaped my vision of community in Christ, as "a great multitude … from all tribes and peoples and languages,"[38] was a diaspora church. There is little doubt in my mind that the congregation in Antioch, a migrant church that included both diaspora Jews and Gentile Greeks, inspired Saul's vision of community. He eloquently describes this ideal in Galatians, where he declares, "there is no longer Jew or Greek, there is no longer slave or free, there is no longer male and female; for all of you are one in Christ Jesus."[39]

It is also significant that Antioch instigates the first intentional mission journey. Before Antioch, mission was the accidental by-product of persecution. In Antioch, the Holy Spirit speaks to a receptive congregation and directs the community to set aside their best leaders, Saul and

---

[34] Acts 22:28, NRSV.
[35] Acts: 11:19, NRSV.
[36] Acts: 11:19, NRSV.
[37] Gary Gilbert, notes to Acts 11:19–30, *The Jewish Annotated New Testament*, (New York: Oxford University Press, 2011), p. 221.
[38] Revelation 7:9, NRSV.
[39] Galatians 3:28, NRSV.

Barnabas, for mission.[40] The community lays hands on them and sends them out.[41] Antioch, a diaspora migrant congregation, is the first mission congregation.

It is equally striking that those receptive to the gospel are migrants. Lydia, who opens her home in Philippi to Paul and Silas, is a gentile migrant from Thyatira.[42] Aquila and Priscilla, diaspora Jews whom Paul meets in Corinth, are in that city because they had been expelled from Rome.[43] They accompany him to Ephesus, where the two are instrumental in instructing Apollos of Alexandria, another diaspora Jew, in "the Way of God."

The depiction of mission in the book of Acts is not a top-down, centralized, managerial exercise. It is a grassroots movement spurred by the Holy Spirit. It is a story of migrants as missionaries and missionaries as migrants. The church is God's people on the move.

Jesus as a Migrant

This depiction of the church should not surprise us. After all, Jesus was always on the move. His public ministry was that of an itinerant rabbi. In the gospels, he is always on the road, traveling throughout Galilee and beyond, into the Decapolis and down into Samaria, through cities and villages, healing the sick and proclaiming the good news of God's favor. In his ministry, he moved across cultural and social boundaries, speaking with a Samaritan woman, healing a Syro-Phoenician's daughter, and curing the servant of a Roman centurion.

His most significant migratory move was the incarnation. The Evangelist John describes the Word becoming flesh and living among us, pitching his tent with us, as it were.[44] In Philippians, Paul quotes an early Christian hymn that depicts Christ as emptying himself to take the form of a slave and be born in human likeness.[45]

Migration as Metaphor for the Christian Faith

If Jesus was a migrant who said, "Foxes have holes, and birds of the air have nests; but the Son of Man has nowhere to lay his head,"[46] then his followers need to see themselves as migrants. If we understand the church to be Christ's body in the world, we will want to reimagine the church as a migrant church, more like Antioch than Jerusalem. If Jesus was always on the way, then the church must be God's people on the move.

New Testament writers describe Christians as strangers, exiles, foreigners, and aliens.[47] In the first century world, that was *literally* true of many Christians. Priscilla and Aquila, Lydia, Paul,

---

[40] Samuel Escobar, *The New Global Mission: The Gospel from Everywhere to Everyone,* Kindle Version, (Downers Grove, IL: InterVarsity Press, 2003), p. 93, p. 124.

[41] Acts 13:1–3, NRSV.

[42] Acts 16:14–15, NRSV.

[43] Acts 18:2–3, NRSV.

[44] Adele Reinhartz, Notes to John 1:14, *The Jewish Annotated New Testament,* (New York: Oxford University Press, 2010), p. 158.

[45] Philippians 2:7, NRSV.

[46] Matthew 8:20, NRSV.

[47] Ephesians 2:19, Hebrews 11:13, 1 Peter 2:11, NRSV.

Barnabas—they were all migrants with complicated identities. They knew what it was like to be in the minority. They knew just how hard it is to move across cultural and linguistic borders. As outsiders, they challenged cultural norms, such as the requirement of circumcision, and the power structures that enforced this mythical norm, including the church in Jerusalem, that posed obstacles to the gospel.

For many of us in this room, the experience of migration is a lived experience. We may have left our homelands voluntarily for political, economic, or even religious reasons. Or, we may have left involuntarily, as refugees or as exiles. We have experienced learning a new language, negotiating the subtleties of a new culture, or even the frustration of being lost in a strange city without even the ability to read the street signs. We know that sense of displacement that comes from trying to sing the Lord's song in a strange land.

For some of us, migration may lie several generations back in our family history. Or, our family stories may be stories of forced displacement and exile in our places of origin, such as that of the native Hawaiians and other aboriginal peoples. For others among us, the immense human trafficking enterprises of the transatlantic slave trade, or the British transplantation of Indian indentured labor throughout their colonies, have shaped our diaspora experience. For a few of us, our family stories may be stories of rootedness in a single place with thousands of years of history.

However, all of us are challenged by the New Testament description of the Christian life as that of being "strangers and foreigners on the earth"[48] and the example of the first Christian migrant missionaries. The early Christians embodied the humility and vulnerability of the newcomer and the stranger. The Holy Spirit gave them, at their best, the courage to break down barriers and create diverse communities of faith.

Imperfect Strangers and Exiles

These early Christians were by no means perfect. We may wish to critique Paul for his admonition that "women should be silent in the churches"[49] and his tacit acceptance of slavery.[50] We may also want to question the household codes and their legitimation of the patriarchal family.[51] Early on, the church began to articulate a hierarchal view of social relationships. When the migrant church of Acts became the settled church of the Roman Empire, the church became even more hierarchal, modeling itself on the structures of empire and patriarchy.

Here lies the danger. It is not easy being a migrant people. It is not easy being God's people on the move. As strangers, exiles, aliens, and foreigners, it is natural for us to want to be settled, to seek a homeland.

The temptations of empire and settlement are real. Some of the most chilling moments in

---

[48] Hebrews 11:13-14, NRSV.
[49] I Corinthians 14:34, NRSV.
[50] 1 Corinthians 7:21, Philemon, NRSV.
[51] Colossians 3:18–4:1, Ephesians 5:21–6:9, 1 Peter 2:18–3:7, NRSV.

the Bible are in the book of Joshua, as the wanderers in search of the Promised Land become conquering settlers who put to the edge of the sword, "men and women, young and old, oxen, sheep, and donkeys."[52]   Equally disturbing are the accounts in Ezra and Nehemiah of the exiles' return and resettlement of Jerusalem. They build walls and demand that all Jews who had married foreign women repudiate their wives and disown their children in a vain attempt to restore a mythical past that never was.

How do we resist the temptation to become settlers? How do we continue to embrace the experience of being strangers, exiles, aliens, and foreigners? How do we learn to be at home in the diaspora, which is a messy place, full of complicated identities and complicated power dynamics? How do we muster up the courage to challenge the multiple oppressions that are an obstacle to the gospel?

Intersectional Theology — a Tool for the Migrant Church

Earlier, we saw that intersectionality was applicable to the migrant experience. It is also relevant as a tool for the church. Because intersectionality is a way of thinking and seeing, with a bias toward justice, it can be a tool for us as we reimagine the church as God's people on the move, as a migrant church. Because intersectionality aims to reveal uncomfortable truths, it shows us our sin. Because it is a call to action, it is a call to conversion and repentance and, ultimately, freedom. As Jesus reminds us, "You shall know the truth, and the truth shall set you free."[53]

This kind of seeing can help us wrestle with oppressive texts in the Bible that get in the way of the good news. It can expose the invisibility of power, privilege, and the ways in which we collude with empire and settlement. It can help us deal honestly with our identities, both subordinate and dominant, in a way that allows us to embrace the messiness of being a people on the move, a people at home in the diaspora.

As a lens for biblical interpretation, intersectional analysis can help "us unpack the context [and] culture…to get a deeper understanding of the multiple layers of identities and issues" within the Bible that lead either to oppression or freedom.[54]

Applying matrix thinking that sees connections, both/and thinking, we can look at Saul/Paul, for example, in all his complexity, including his subordinate and dominant identities. We can interrogate Paul's status as a male, as a minority Jew, as a Roman citizen, as a Greek-speaker, and as a well-educated Pharisee. Intersectional analysis will call our attention to the power structures he had to negotiate and how they served to reward and constrain him. This approach to Paul will complicate and enrich our reading of his writings and his theology. An intersectional lens with its bias towards justice will help us see how Paul's writings have enabled both oppression and liberation.

Likewise, an intersectional lens will also ask these same questions of past interpreters of

---

[52] Joshua 6:21, NRSV.
[53] John 8:32.
[54] Kim and Shaw, op. cit., location 1790.

scripture and the theologies that accompany them. How did past readers' identities, their class and caste, gender and sexual orientation, race and ethnicities, affect the way they interpreted scripture and did theology? How do these theologies oppress, and how do these theologies liberate?

Equally, if not more important, how do our identities, our class and caste, our gender and sexual orientation, our race and ethnicities affect the way we interpret scripture and do theology? And how do we read scripture and do theology in new ways that work towards God's justice? How do we reimagine the church, not as a settled community but as God's people on the move?

Conclusion

These are critical questions for us to keep before us if we take migration as a metaphor for the Christian faith. As we consider mission with and among migrants, we need to remember that we, too, are strangers and exiles. Therefore, our stance must be one of solidarity. And if we are to reflect the humility and vulnerability of the migrant in our mission and ministry, we must remember that God chooses to work, not through strength, but through "what is foolish…what is weak… what is low and despised in the world."[55] As did the church in Antioch, we need to realize that to be a people on the move in response to the Holy Spirit is to embrace messiness and conflict. An intersectional lens can help us recognize that our lives intersect and intertwine, moving us toward "embrace rather than suspicion of one another."   Rather than hide behind walls, we will be God's people on the move, crossing borders and breaking down barriers, building bridges, not walls.

We need to be flexible citizens at home in the diaspora.

Saul/Paul of Tarsus comes to mind. If people had held passports in the first century, he would have been a multiple passport holder. Both a diaspora Jew and a Roman citizen, he embodied all kinds of complications and contradictions as he sought to proclaim Christ. He described his approach in 1 Corinthians like this:

> 19 For though I am free with respect to all, I have made myself a slave to all, so that I might win more of them. 20 To the Jews I became as a Jew, in order to win Jews. To those under the law I became as one under the law (though I myself am not under the law) so that I might win those under the law. 21 To those outside the law I became as one outside the law (though I am not free from God's law but am under Christ's law) so that I might win those outside the law. 22 To the weak I became weak, so that I might win the weak. I have become all things to all people, so that I might by any means save some. 23 I do it all for the sake of the gospel, so that I may share in its blessings.[56]

Like the multiple passport holders of the 21st century, Saul/Paul of Tarsus held his identities lightly. For him, however, this was not a matter of pragmatic self-interest but a matter of the heart.

---

[55] 1 Corinthians 1:26-31.
[56] 1 Corinthians 9:19-23, NRSV

He knew himself to be a stranger and an alien in this world. He was part of the migrant church, a church sent by the Spirit to share the gospel's blessings, always crossing into new territory and breaking down barriers. The church is God's people on the move. If migration is a key metaphor for understanding the Christian faith, perhaps we, too, need to see ourselves as flexible citizens.

Margrethe S. C. Kleiber

BIBLIOGRAPHY

Almendral, Aurora. "Why 10 Million Filipinos Endure Hardship Abroad as Overseas Workers." *National Geographic Magazine.* December 2108. https://www.nationalgeographic.com/magazine/2018/12/filipino-workers-return-from-overseas-philippines-celebrates/.

Anderson, Benedict. *Imagined Communities. Kindle Version.* New York & London: Verso Books, 2016.

Dalrymple, William. "The Great Divide: The Violent Legacy of Indian partition." *The New Yorker,* June 29, 2015. https://www.newyorker.com/magazine/2015/06/29/-dalrymple.

Escobar, Samuel. *The New Global Mission: The Gospel from Everywhere to Everyone.* Kindle Version. Downers Grove, IL: InterVarsity Press, 2003.

Levine, Amy-Jill, and Marc Zvi Brettler (eds). *Jewish Annotated New Testament: The New Revised Standard Version.* New York: Oxford University Press, 2010.

Kim, Grace Ji-Sun, and Susan M. Shaw. *Intersectional Theology: An Introductory Guide.* Kindle Version. Minneapolis, MN: Fortress Press, 2018.

Kwan, Kevin. *Crazy Rich Asians.* Kindle Version. New York: First Anchor Books, 2013.

May, Vivian. *Pursuing Intersectionality, Unsettling Dominant Imagery.* Kindle Version. New York: Routledge, 2015.

New Interpreter's Study Bible: New Revised Standard Version with the Apocrypha. Nashville, TN: Abingdon Press, 2003.

Nguyen, vanThahn, and John M. Prior. *God's People on the Move: Biblical and Global Perspectives on Migration and Mission.* Kindle Version. Eugene, OR: Pickwick Publications, 2014.

Ong, Aihwa. *Flexible Citizenship: The Cultural Logics of Transnationality.* Kindle Version. Durham & London: Duke University Press, 1999.

Ramos, Jorge. "Trump is the Wall." *The New York Times.* January 9, 2019. https://www.nytimes.com/2019/01/09/opinion/jorge-ramos-trump-wall.html?action=click&module=Opinion&pgtype=Homepage.

Wood, Johnny. "Here's what you need to know about the megacities of the future," *World Economic Forum.* October 10, 2018. https://www.weforum.org/agenda/2018/10/these-are-the-megacities-of-the-future/.

Yee, Edmond. *The Soaring Crane: Stories of Asian Lutherans in North America.* Minneapolis, MN: Augsburg Fortress Press, 2002.